ESSAYS IN
IMPERIAL GOVERNMENT

Presented to Margery Perham

Essays in
Imperial Government

Presented to
MARGERY PERHAM

by
KENNETH ROBINSON
*Professor of Commonwealth Affairs, Director of the
Institute of Commonwealth Studies, London*

and
FREDERICK MADDEN
*Reader in Commonwealth Government, Fellow of
Nuffield College, and Director of the Institute
of Commonwealth Studies, Oxford*

OXFORD
BASIL BLACKWELL
1963

PRINTED IN GREAT BRITAIN
BY A. T. BROOME AND SON, 18 ST. CLEMENT'S, OXFORD
AND BOUND BY THE KEMP HALL BINDERY, OXFORD

CONTENTS

PREFACE

It is not for us, who followed her in the Readership that Oxford created for her, to attempt an account, still less an evaluation, of Margery Perham's contribution to African studies. But for British scholars, administrators, and politicians, for more than a quarter of a century, the academic study of the problems of government in Africa has been, it is hardly too much to say, identified with her name. To the study of Africa she brought many qualities but three most notably: first, the historical scholarship which set the contemporary problems of African government in the wider context of the history of British imperialism throughout the world; second, the imaginative insight of a woman whose first book about Africa was a novel and who has so often brought her theme to life by the vivid handling of words; lastly, and perhaps predominantly, a profound and continued preoccupation with the moral issues in the exercise of imperial rule, sharpened by her own Christian conviction no less than her familiarity with the great debates of nineteenth century humanitarianism in Britain. She has been a pioneer, not merely in her choice of the central theme of her life's work or in the conviction that academic study could contribute to the solution of practical problems of administration and government in a continent whose features remained, for most of her earlier career, unknown outside the small circle of those who worked there, but hardly less so in tackling the delicate issues of the empirical study of governments at work.

Because of the central position which she has so long occupied it would have been possible to conceive many different books which might have been offered to her by those to whom she has taught so much. Contributions might have been sought from university teachers scattered across the world who have been, in one way or another, her students; from colonial administrators whose work has always been close to her interests and to whose training in the academic disciplines relevant to their tasks so much of her life has been devoted in the development of the Overseas Service Courses in Oxford and the creation of the Institute of Commonwealth Studies there; from political leaders not only in Britain but in many African countries who have sought her

counsel and with many of whom she has maintained close friend-
ships through the years; from the Africans who have been her
students or friends in Oxford, many of whom now carry heavy
responsibilities in the United Nations and in the political leadership of their countries. To have attempted to represent all these
interests within the compass of a book of reasonable size would
have entailed a large number of very brief contributions and a
highly eclectic selection of topics and approaches.

Ours must, we concluded, be a much more restricted tribute;
indeed, in a sense, a domestic one. For if Margery Perham's name
spells Africa, it is also especially connected with Oxford in which,
except for a few years in the University of Sheffield, she has spent
her entire working life. This book has been written by a number
of those associated with her, as students or colleagues in Nuffield
College or in the Institute of Commonwealth Studies, two Oxford
institutions in each of which she has been a major figure from their
earliest beginnings. Much criticism has been directed to volumes
of this kind because it is seldom, if ever, possible to construct them
so that the various contributions are clearly related to a precisely
defined central theme. It would hardly have been possible to do
justice even to Margery Perham's more strictly academic interests
on such a basis, and it would certainly not have been possible for
such a volume to have been produced by the small group which
has been concerned in making this book. Yet, we have sought to
illustrate in our contributions most, though not all, of the aspects
of African studies which have been exemplified in her own
writings. We begin with two papers which are concerned with the
wider historical context of British colonialism; there follow four
papers devoted to the recent history of the two countries in Africa
that have taken the lion's share of her own work, Nigeria and Kenya
(we regret that there is nothing in this volume which reflects her
earlier interest in the South African High Commission Territories, her sustained yet judicious support of the Ethiopian cause,
or her long-continued association with the Sudan, but it was to
Nigeria and Kenya as it seems to us that her interests most
constantly returned); we end with a group of essays concerned, as
Margery Perham has been for so many years, with various aspects
of the transfer of power in Africa.

As is inevitable in such an enterprise, several of those whom
we should have wished to join us in this tribute were in the event

unable to do so. One of them cannot be left unmentioned. Professor Vincent Harlow, who had promised us a suitable and characteristic essay on the late eighteenth century imperial themes he had done so much to illuminate, died before he had been able to do more than make a few preliminary notes for his contribution.

We are grateful to many people who have helped us in the preparation of this volume but we wish to record our special indebtedness to Miss Jean Swann formerly of the Institute of Commonwealth Studies, London who has done so much to lighten the burdens of editorial work, and to Mrs. Audrey Martin, formerly one of Miss Perham's research assistants, for her help with the bibliography.

K.E.R.
A.F.McC.M.

FREDERICK MADDEN

SOME ORIGINS AND PURPOSES IN THE FORMATION OF BRITISH COLONIAL GOVERNMENT[1]

The possession of an empire has posed perennial and complex problems of constitutional engineering for the metropolitan authority: the need to establish law and order and to secure control over (and even subordination of) distant territories has taxed its powers of invention and adaption to the utmost. The suitability of the forms it has provided must, therefore, be an essential, even crucial part of any ' colonial reckoning '. What is clear is that the imperial government in Britain tackled these new-found responsibilities in their earliest formative period with few conceptions about the ends, and little new thinking on the means, of control.

It has been widely assumed that two opposed forces—one central, the other peripheral—have conditioned the evolution of colonial government: that the imperial power has sought to impose a mould upon colonies so that they should be governed under a constitution as much like that of Britain as possible, and that the colonists asserted their liberty to devise an appropriate form of self government for themselves. In one direction would lie the *assimilated* constitution made in Whitehall and conditioned by a period of *direct* rule under expatriate officials; in the other the *autochthonous* constitution made at home and fashioned in a period of *indirect* rule by local men according to local usage. It has, of course, been recognised that the degrees of assimilation or devolution have varied in practice, as between London and Paris, for example, or between European and non-European colonies. But whether of British or French policy, or of imperial or colonial attitudes, these labels are neither exclusive nor consistent. For example, in many British possessions it has been the colonists who have demanded nothing less than the British model and the imperial government which has pleaded for a consideration of

---

[1] This essay was stimulated by the introductory pages of Martin Wight's *Development of the Legislative Council* (London, 1946), edited by Margery Perham.

alternatives.[1] In any period distance and economy have inevitably provided that the product finally delivered at the frontier is different from the blueprint devised in the department. Distance has blurred the exactness of the copy, has aided the normal erosion of convention upon law and has permitted variants unsuspected at the centre or unknown in the prototype[2]; economy has deprived the experiment of detailed supervision from the centre and has allowed local hands to improve upon metropolitan intention and practice. So the necessity of establishing government on the frontiers of empire—to erect a rule of law and a system of control on settlements, conquests and trading stations—has provided the opportunity for a rich harvest of variations on a common theme, even in periods when the general purpose of empire has seemed to be clear. In new environment overseas traditional forms and expedients have evolved with fresh emphasis and invention. The institutions communicated have carried within themselves the germs of growth; and no more than their prototypes in Great Britain might they be moulded from without, for the instincts for self-government and liberty were a necessary inheritance from the common impulses of a shared history. Local convenience and habit soon hardened into a new constitutionality. Even by the middle of the seventeenth century it could already be said that ' the little limbs of the Commonwealth were erecting themselves into free states '.[3] Rare, indeed, were the occasions when English statesmen sought to impose uniform rule on the dominions of the Crown, irrespective of their differences or of the political dictates in the colony or in Westminster; and without exception such attempts have been disastrous.

The desire to foster a brood of Westminster models as a legacy of British rule has been a comparatively recent, even brief and passing, phenomenon in British policy. Exact identity with the British model was neither desired nor demanded: it was repudiated as inconvenient or inhibiting by both rulers and ruled. Imperial and colonial politicians quoted British example or precedent only where it was useful to their case. At times the claim to ' the right

---

[1] See, for example, the doubts about the appropriateness of parliamentary system expressed in the Simon and Donoughmore reports for India and Ceylon respectively.

[2] As Burke said, ' No contrivance can prevent the effect of this distance in weakening government. Seas roll and months pass between the order and the execution '.

[3] Cal. State Papers (Col.), 1574–1660, p. 408.

and privileges of free born Englishmen '[1] might be noisily demanded by Englishmen overseas, but it was imprecise. It had been intended perhaps as no more than an assertion, grandiloquent indeed, that settlers, though exiled in a mere dependency, were still Englishmen. At most it implied no more than a standard of judgment which would retain for the Crown its discretion and supervision. Though it might prove the basis for a claim of right to English law, the formula was not intended, nor was it interpreted, as introducing *all* English laws as an inalienable and comprehensive heritage in the settlers' baggage. Both parties—at home and overseas—were carefully selective. The Crown's ministers were concerned with identity in those matters in which the prerogative was involved: they sought to keep the prerogative intact from encroachments, whether or not these were made in imitation of English constitutional changes. On the other hand, the settlers were most concerned where the privileges of the subject were threatened or their advancement curtailed. English Common Law came to be respected in the colonies as a weapon, already proved, against an arbitrary prerogative and as a useful adjunct to local law when that proved unequal in the same struggle. For the British constitution was itself evolving simultaneously, and the internal balance between prerogative and privilege was being slowly adjusted. But new conventions had to harden and crystallise before they could be exported overseas: meanwhile in their embryonic stage they were largely unknown and misunderstood overseas where local variants were developing divergently to meet colonial needs. The respectful lip service paid to English law overseas was matched only, in the absence of printed reports and professional lawyers, by the colonists' ignorance of it. So while it could be stated by the Board of Trade in 1730 that

' it certainly was at all times the intention of the Crown that the several constitutions abroad immediately under His Majesty's government should resemble as much as might be the constitution of their mother country to whose laws and customs the said colonies are directed to conform themselves as far as may be applicable to their circumstances ',[2]

such a statement must be considered cautiously—as cautiously as

---

[1] e.g. in the patent for the Caribbees, 2 July, 1627: C.O. 29/1, pp. 1ff.
[2] Dominique, Bladen and Brudenell to Lt.-Gen. Matthew, 22 October, 1730: C.O. 154/15.

it was written. For, vague and general as this intention may have been, it was hedged about by a realistic recognition of local differences and respect for local usage which, in fact, made identity impossible. The grant of representative legislatures argued that laws would be made locally and assumed that there would be differences to tolerate[1]: to hold otherwise would be to nullify the legislative powers given: the charter to Penn, for example, expressly included a right to *alter* the law.[2] Colonies could not depend entirely on the laws of England, many of which would be inappropriate overseas. Statute and common law were scrambled together, and English law lacked that simple portable quality which a code like that of Moses, Justinian or Mahomet possessed. Moreover the Crown disallowed attempts by colonial assemblies to introduce English law wholesale and resisted their attempts to adopt the status and privileges of the House of Commons. Furthermore there was a tradition of toleration for reasonable local custom: this had been shown in the principality of Wales after 1284 and more especially for Denbighshire even after 1543 (34 and 35 Henry VIII cap. 26); Norman custom was followed by the Privy Council in cases from Jersey; and so too later indigenous non-English law was recognised in Quebec, Cape Colony, Mauritius and elsewhere. Local usage was accepted by the law officers of the Crown as binding, and, indeed, as a necessary part of the law of a colony: for example, in 1755 they declared themselves

'not . . . sufficiently informed to give an opinion upon the question so generally stated, because it depends upon the constitution of the Assembly of Jamaica and its usage. What the Assembly claims seems analogous to the law and practice here, but it does not from thence necessarily follow that it is or ought to be the law there. That must depend upon their own constitution and usage.'[3]

Difference was therefore accepted provided there was no limitation of ' the authority and just prerogatives of the Crown ', and (as we shall see later) no repugnancy to natural justice and to English

---

[1] See Rev. B. Coleman commenting on *Philips v. Savage* (1735–8) ' If every difference be esteemed a repugnancy . . . it were in effect to say we make no law at all but refer ourselves entirely to the laws of the realm from whence we derive '. ' If they had carried such laws with them ', argued Benjamin Franklin later, ' they might as well have stayed at home '. 12 Nov., 1735, quoted J. H. Smith, *Appeals to the Privy Council* (London, 1950), p. 530.
[2] See W. Macdonald (ed.) *Select charters* (1899), p. 187.
[3] Murray-Lloyd opinion, 29 April, 1755: C.O. 137/29.

law. So any instinct to export the Westminster model *in toto*, laws and institutions, was curbed. It was restricted by a liberal recognition of differing local circumstance, by a cautious (if vain) desire to prevent sowing the plantations with political discords and tensions which had torn the parent body, and by a developing sense of responsibility, even of trusteeship, for excluded or politically inarticulate sections of colonial society. Of course it was often true that repugnancy to natural justice was construed as repugnancy to principles of English law which therefore invaded and supplemented the sphere of natural law; but the degree to which the rights of Englishmen, or the laws and institutions of England were appropriate to non-British, let alone non-European, peoples was for long an unresolved question about which the imperial government showed itself at least tentative, at worst undecided and procrastinating.

But rationalisation was not a concern of those who took the first steps towards devising forms of colonial government in that period at the turn of the sixteenth century when the realms of England and Scotland found themselves drawn into the expansion of Europe. Monarchs were not noticeably interested in the extension of governmental responsibilities, but were ready, with some circumspection, to share in the possible profit of increased trade: they therefore preferred to work through unofficial instruments, individuals or groups, rather than to conduct colonial enterprise as a matter of state policy or planning. To provide for the detail of government on the far side of the Atlantic was a considerable task, best left to enthusiasts, yet authority must ultimately stem from the Crown; since the only conceivable laws of empire were those of personal land-holding from the sovereign on the analogy of ancient demesne and of delegated use of the Crown's powers within permissive and regulated limits. Ties deriving from feudal property law involved a personal link with the sovereign, rather than with the realm. So it became a rule of thumb to devolve on individual adventurers and on corporations those responsibilities properly belonging to the sovereign, while the Crown retained ultimate sanction and supervision. America was not regarded as posing a problem new in kind: ' New England ' was a projection of Old England, its business requiring no distinct department of state, and was entered up therefore by clerks in the same routine ledgers as that of the realm itself. Those faced with this task had no new blueprint and no new political ideas. The national instinct to make do seemed good enough. Such precedents as seemed to exist were naturally pressed into service, when men came to consider if there were indeed earlier parallels which might be applied or earlier lessons which might be useful.[1] The English for their part had in some sense experience of imperial governance already, even if it were largely unconscious; and the Scots, with not dissimilar experience of feudal law, found English expedients were logical deductions. It was natural that officials should look back to earlier centuries for models of extended, even extra-territorial, control.

England had become, by reason of the regular presence of the sovereign and his Council, the predominant dominion of earlier Norman and Angevin empires, the relics of which were still a reminder of a significant part of English conditional heritage. One of the legacies of feudalism was a sturdy tradition of local autonomy: substantial independence had to be tolerated at the perimeter. Local assemblies shared government with the representative of the King, whether he was Seneschal of Gascony, Warden of Jersey, Captain of Calais or Justiciar in Ireland,[2] and even when termination of the permitted subroyalties of fief or palatinate within the realm had rendered superfluous such representative government in the palatinate of Durham or the principality of Wales, similar assemblies continued to function in the outlying dominions of Ireland, Jersey or Man with an often jealous assertion of right.[3] On the other hand there was the demand for greater centralisation represented by the King whose authority, if footloose, gave some personal cohesion to a form of government which, while it permitted considerable latitude to local diversity, tended to follow similar forms in London, Bordeaux or St. Peter Port. Inevitably the centre would sometimes supersede the local authority, in the style of a Duke (of

[1] There was for example, an interesting discussion between Queen Elizabeth I and Sir Herbert Sidney on the relative merits of *direct* and *indirect* rule in Ireland, in R. Dunlop, ' Sixteenth Century Schemes for the Plantation of Ulster ', Scottish H.R. XXII (Nos. 1, 2 and 3), pp. 51–60; 115–126; 199–212.

[2] E. Lodge, *Gascony under the English rule* (1926), J. H. Le Patourel, *The medieval administration of the Channel Islands* (1937), G. A. C. Sandeman, *Calais under English rule* (1908), H. Wood, 'The office of chief governor of Ireland'. Proc. Roy. Irish Acad. XXXVI (No. 12), pp. 206–238.

[3] G. T. Lapsley, *The county palatine of Durham* (1900), W. R. Williams, *The parliamentary history of the principality of Wales* (1895), G. H. Orpen, *Ireland under the Normans* (1911), A. W. Moore, *A History of the Isle of Man* (1900).

Normandy) maybe, but with the prestige of a King. It was English blood and treasure which kept the empire together even before Normandy or Anjou were lost. In turn Gascony, Ireland and Wales had been subordinated to the English crown, and Wales indeed had been further incorporated in the English realm (27 Henry VIII cap. 26). Bannockburn alone saved Scotland from a similar fate.[1] Perhaps the failure of the efficient government of the Tudors to achieve uniformity in the British Isles by subordinating the Scottish kingdom facilitated a diversity which became a distinguishing failure of the British empire. However that may be, it is doubtful whether the distinction made between dominions of the *Crown* and those of the *realm* could be interpreted legally as a difference between lands subject to King in Council and those subject to King in Parliament; for the pre-Stuart body politic was governed by a mixed constitution of King, Council and Parliament. It only added to the uncertainty that the first great period of colonial expansion should have taken place just when in the early seventeenth century this synthesis was split, temporarily at least, and the balance permanently altered, by the king's claim to Divine Right and by Parliament's claim to supremacy, imperial as well as domestic.

Where belief in fundamental law and distrust of innovation combined to constitute orthodoxy, it was natural for administrative conservatism to persist. So those who had witnessed the closing of the English frontiers in the Celtic West,[2] the English declaration of independence by the rejection of external overlordship at the Reformation,[3] and the loss of the open door to ' continental destiny ' in Calais, tackled the problems created by the ensuing and newly released enthusiasms for expansion in the New World with traditional devices. Even as Rome had extended the law of a city to the outlying provinces of a wide empire, so the Normans had governed Ireland and Gascony by planting municipalities. It is evident that many Elizabethans regarded both Henry VIII's policy in Ireland (where a tribal was converted into a feudal society) and the Elizabethan plantations (where further anglicisation was attempted by direct colonisation) as being relevant to the American problems. The Gilbert and Raleigh schemes were,

[1] H. G. Richardson and G. O. Sayles 'The Scottish parliaments of Edward I', Scottish H.R. XXV, No. 4, pp. 300–317.
[2] A. L. Rowse, *The Expansion of Elizabethan England* (1955).
[3] See the preamble to 24 Henry VIII, cap. 12.

indeed, a trial run, from which few clear lessons were learnt.[1] So
Elizabethan and Jacobean officials were left to strain the law of the
fief, the guild and the borough to fit colonial circumstance. The
haphazard precedents, however inappropriate and ambiguous, (and
they were to prove more adaptable than they might seem) became
an integral part of the heritage of colonial government.

Medieval expedients must therefore still claim our attention.
This is partly so because the charters granted to individuals or
companies quite consciously refer back to earlier devices. Sometimes the model was identified by name: ' the county palatine of
Durham ' in the proprietary grant of the Caribbees (1627), or
' our manor of East Greenwich ' in the New England patent
(1620),[2] or the attempt, for example, to impose a bill ' like
Poynings' Law in Ireland' upon Jamaica in 1677. In other
cases, though no less derivative, the model might be less specific.
Clearly the patent to Sir Humphrey Gilbert in 1578 sought in
fact to make him a vassal of the Queen with all ' rites, royalties and
jurisdiction' in territories which would be a royal fief, in the same
way as the Black Prince had been in Pembroke or the Stanleys
were in the Isle of Man; or, indeed, as Alexander was under the
Scottish crown in Nova Scotia in 1622. But the homage expected
of Gilbert could hardly be appropriately expected from a company
and the provision for knight service *in capite*, though not finally
discarded,[3] was omitted from the Virginia patent and later from
that for London Derry. Moreover, the charters to embryonic
joint stock companies in the East Indies (1600) and Virginia
(1609)[4] were imitations of those to the Merchant Adventurers and
(more especially) to the Merchants of the Staple: the normal
methods of guild regulation developed for small self-governing
communities overseas in Muscovy (1555) or the Levant (1583).[5]
The government of the corporations was shared by ' committees '
(or assistants) in a court of directors and by freemen (share-

---

[1] S. Gwynne, *The History of Ireland* (1923), C. Falls, *The birth of Ulster*
(1936).
[2] C. T. Carr, ' Our Manor of East Greenwich '; J. Hurstfield, ' The Greenwich Tenures of Edward VI ': Law Q.R. XXIX, pp. 349–353, LXV, pp. 72–81;
E. P. Cheyney, ' The Manor of E. Greenwich in the County of Kent ', Amer.
H.R. XI, pp. 29–35.
[3] It reappeared for example, in the Avalon (1623) and the Caribbee (1628)
grants.
[4] Similarly the interloping Scottish East India Company of 1617.
[5] C. P. Lucas, *The beginnings of English overseas enterprise* (1917).

holders) in a general court. Such companies were indeed nurseries of imperial government: to these expatriate English traders substantial powers to experiment in local government were delegated by the Crown which still retained ultimate rights of supervision, control and revocation but granted what was not merely a trade monopoly but (since order was a prerequisite for fair commerce) a constitution. Furthermore, pre-seventeenth century examples might be employed to solve some problem of *machinery*, as for example, on the analogy of the Channel Islands, the appellate system of the Privy Council was considered as remaining part of the ' ordinary course of law ' overseas after the abolition of prerogative jurisdiction in the realm (16 Car. 1, cap. 10, sect. 5); or even some problem of *policy* whether respect shown for ' new subjects ' as in Wales in 1284 or Quebec in 1774, or their expulsion as from Calais in 1347 or from Nova Scotia in 1755. For precedents could be contradictory: the legislative subordination of the Irish kingdom to the English, for example, was balanced by the twin Kingdoms of England and Scotland, in personal but non-parliamentary union under Edward I and more notably under James VI and I.

Amid these confusions and contradictions the trial of *Calvin's case* in 1608 provided the occasion for lawyers to attempt to weave some new pattern out of the tattered shreds of medieval experience. For it provided the opportunity to determine not only the nature of the personal unions of the two Crowns and the rights of *post nati* Scots to English subjecthood and English law, but also to throw light on the clash between older feudal theories of personal *ligeance* with newer ideas of common law as the source of obedience and subjecthood; on the extent of the Crown's rights in conquered, inherited or settled dominions; and on the distinction between the *realm* and the *dominions* and the related problem of the legislative competence of the English parliament outside the realm. It was of course a preliminary skirmish between King and Commons and it was natural that, in a period of constitutional crisis, which coincided with territorial expansion, imperial policy should become an issue between the protagonists. Although they were fitful and unpredictable in their intervention and even criminally negligent in the confusions of their grants, the early Stuarts were jealous of their imperial powers and showed even less disposition than their predecessors to share them with Parliament. In the first Virginian

B

charter, regarded largely as James I's 'owne work',[1] the new
territories were claimed as ' appertaining to us '; and in 1621 the
Crown's spokesman in the fishing debate told the Commons that
it was ' not fit to make laws here for those countries which are not
as yet annexed to this Crown '. The opposition might indeed
claim that as an extension of the realm or as guilds of the realm
like other corporations, the new colonies were subject to Parliament, and might be deemed represented in it through the burgesses
of East Greenwich, of which manor their lands in certain charters
were held; but until the necessity was thrust upon it in the interregnum, Parliament might threaten, but did not take any action.
Even then in Ireland, the West Indies and Massachusetts,
colonists seemed to prefer the weaker and more manageable
Crown to the potential strength of parliamentary control and
attempted to assert a premature independence. ' The laws of the
parliament of England reach no further ' than England, they said.[2]
It was unfortunate that the first great period of colonial expansion
should have taken place just when this internal conflict of King
and Commons destroyed the old order. In 1606 this was undecided
and it is not surprising that even Coke (CJ) in *Calvin's Case* took
refuge in that contemporary dualism which, while it helped to
ease the ultimate settlement, bedevilled the immediate dilemma.
He found for the King (and for Calvin) without awarding defeat
to the Commons.

But the *dicta*, have an eventual significance greater than the
decision itself. The case brought to the cradle of a new Empire the
archives of the old, and it provided the opportunity for a consideration of what was still the relevant law of empire. The
interest of many of the Virginian adventurers in it showed that
this was realised at the time. Coke was able to distinguish, for
example, between *conquest* from a Christian prince and conquest
from an infidel, with whom (on Wycliffe's dogma) Christendom
was regarded as being in perpetual enmity. In the first case the
existing law remained until altered by the conqueror, though it was
subject to the will of the King alone, but once English laws had
been introduced by the King, as in Ireland, the law could not then
be changed without recourse to Parliament. If on the other hand

---

[1] A. Brown, *The first republic*, p. 7, 74–6.
[2] J. K. Hosmer (ed.), J. Winthrop, *History of New England* (1908), II, pp.
294. 297–303.

the territory were conquered from infidels, existing laws were abrogated and the King could govern absolutely, though with respect for natural justice. If, however, the King acquired a dominion not by conquest, but by *descent*, he could not alter the laws there without invoking parliamentary aid.[1] Coke considered acquisition only by conquest or by descent. Perhaps it might be deduced therefrom that, if dominion were not by descent, it must be implicitly by conquest, whether of Christian or of infidel: in either event the Crown's initial authority would thus be legally unimpeachable. But it could also be argued from Coke's reasoning on another point that English settlers took with them an inalienable right to be governed by ' the laws of England ': a right and a phrase which, we have seen, was difficult of interpretation. A natural axiom from this reading of Coke's argument would be the assumption that for a settled colony legislation could only be enacted by King in Parliament—or of course by a local assembly; but it was evident from the grant of ' the rights of free born Englishmen ' without provision for such a representative body in the Carlisle patent of 1627, for example, that the formula did not necessarily imply in practice the immediate grant of such a local institution.[2] However, it was not till the case of *Craw v. Ramsey* (1670) that the Crown's acquisition of ' dominion by plantation ' or *settlement* seems to have been specifically mentioned; and thereafter for many years the Wycliffite doctrine that dominion in lands previously owned by infidel ' indians ' must be by ' conquest ' persisted to diminish the force of the arguments from plantation and the extension thereto of English law as a part of settlers' rights.

On the question of parliament's rights to legislate for the dominions, Calvin's case provided later disputants with equivocal ammunition. This was partly due to Coke's cautious dualism and partly to the inadequate reports of the submissions and judgment. These oracles were used and misused with considerable plausibility by later Irish nationalists and American patriots who sought to deny extra-territorial powers to parliamentary legislation. Moreover by reference to the recorded judgment of Coke, both Professor McIlwain and Professor Schuyler found it possible to substantiate two wholly opposed theses on the imperial compe-

---

[1] 2 State Trials 638.
[2] V. T. Harlow, *A history of Barbados* (1926), p. 10.

tence of the English medieval parliament.[1] The statement made by Coke,[2] that the English parliament had legislated for Ireland could be dismissed by McIlwain as *dicta* while it was accepted by Schuyler as *ratio decidendi*. It is not necessary here to rehearse the contrary arguments in this great debate. Sufficient to say that while neither side doubted that there was a substantial amount of legislation made for export in the middle ages, McIlwain claimed that the effective part in the law making body was the King in Council, and Schuyler demonstrated that King in Parliament was only an enlarged session of that body and thereby heir to all its powers. The medieval legislature was not only a parliament for all England (including the outlying marches and palatinates) but also for Gascony, Wales, Man and Ireland. The frontiers might protest against metropolitan assumption of authority, as Cornwall did against the levy for the Scots war in 1497, but officials and lawyers at the centre did not doubt the validity of parliamentary enactment and Gascons, Irishmen and Jerseymen had petitioned parliament for redress. Schuyler showed that parliament had legislated for Ireland from as early as 1275, a grant of a duty on wool and hides; that statutes had applied to Wales before the Act of Union (1536) and even before the conquest, as, for example, the same grant of 1275; and that legislation had been passed to affect Calais as in 1413 or 1536, to Man in 1542 and to the Channel Islands in 1547. In the case of the *Merchants of Waterford* (1484) the rights of the English parliament to legislate for Ireland in a Staple Act had been upheld in the Courts. Tudor parliaments had taxed the dominions in 1536, interfered with their commerce in 1566, and regulated their navigation in 1571. In 1534 and 1536 the imperial parliament at Westminster had prescribed the King's title for all, whether in realm or in dominions; and in 1554 it had claimed to represent ' the whole body of the realm of England and the dominions of the same '.[3] Even under the Stuarts who were more jealous of their prerogatives, certain legislation applied to the dominions, such as the acts for celebrating Guy Fawkes' day (1605), for Sabbath observance

---

[1] C. H. McIlwain, *The High Court of Parliament and its supremacy* (1910) and *The American revolution* (1923). R. L. Schuyler, *Parliament and the British Empire* (1929).

[2] Coke seemed to revoke this in the debate of 1620–21 on free fishing in Virginia: see *Proceedings and debate in House of Commons* (1766), I, p. 328.

[3] 1 and 2 Phil. and Mary cap. 8 sect. 1.

(1625) and for Tonnage and Poundage (1605 and 1641). No doubt some statutes were not enforced, but that did not mean that they were invalid. As for MacIlwain's arguments based on the invalidity of statutes if repugnant to fundamental law, *Streater's* counsel in 1653 was forbidden to plead that the law was above Parliament. This was indeed at a time when (both MacIlwain and Schuyler are agreed) Parliament was asserting its imperial functions in a revolutionary manner: it had had to do so or renounce empire altogether. But in his *Institutes* a generation earlier the equivocal Coke had declared that statutes applied to the dominions if they were named in them[1]; while at a similar interval later the charter given to Penn provided specifically for the subjection of his colony to commercial legislation by Parliament.

It would seem that Professor Schuyler's evidence may scarcely be controverted; yet a faint doubt may linger. A recurrent problem of English constitutional history is whether what appear to be precedents really are precedents—or relevant precedents: did the men who made Magna Carta, for example, mean by their *liber homo* what Coke meant four centuries later? Many things might be done in parliament which were not done by parliament; but ordinances of the King, like the so-called Statute of Wales (1284), would seem in time to have had less weight than statutes of parliament and less and less could the King provide without parliament that protection in which the dominions claimed to be. But even when it can be proven that Parliament in the fourteenth century had legislated for subjects in the dominions who were unrepresented in its counsels, have we found an answer? If the parliament of Edward I or of Henry VIII had legislative authority over ' the dominions ', did that necessarily imply that that of George III had similar powers? Great constitutional changes lay between. On the one side of the gulf lay royal dictatorship and fundamental law; on the other an embryonic cabinet system and parliamentary omnicompetence. This was, so to speak, the ' *colonial period* ' of the English constitution itself, the advance from autocratic to representative, then to responsible government. In this process the growing power of the realm and the increasing authority of parliament in England upset what balance there may once have been and this tended of necessity to make the dominions subordin-

[1] E. Coke, *Fourth Institute*, pp. 350–1.

ate.[1] Can arguments from one side of the great divide be solved by reference to precedents from the other? There had been valid legislation, and even taxation, without representation, but where constitutionality is as much a matter of convention and opinion as of law, what is accepted as the constitution is what, in the evolving *ethos* of a nation state, seems conveniently constitutional to the generation of colonial leaders involved in working it. Further, as in Ireland, national sentiment may be stronger than constitutional law. Despite the absence of substantiating evidence, despite implicit evidence to the contrary, despite Poynings' Laws (1495), Declaratory Act (1719) or Union Act (1800), the Irish fostered the folk myth of Henry II's grant to John of an *independent* kingdom in Ireland.

At first glance it might seem strange that the precedent of Poynings' Law (10 Henry VII cap. 4, Irish Statutes) was not adopted in the new empire: it would certainly have obviated the long struggle over suspending clauses in America. But even in the medieval empire it was a unique arrangement for securing the dependence of a legislature upon the English government in respect both to sessions and to measures.[2] Yet, until Thomas Wentworth became Lord Deputy in 1633, this Law, made in the Irish parliament, was regarded as its safeguard (in alliance with the Crown) against a self seeking family compact of the Anglo-Irish executive: it had since proved a useful weapon of obstruction, and threats to suspend its operation had produced protests, as in 1569, from the Irish parliament.[3] But the Act had placed Irish parliamentary government in a straitjacket. It had frozen the Irish parliament in a permanent posture of subservience to the Crown: in 1495 indeed, this was admittedly little different from the relative position of its English contemporary, but in the intervening century that sister legislature, its initiative untrammelled, had grown in stature so that it was prepared to challenge the prero-

[1] Cf. the equality of ' this your realm and other your Highness ' dominions and countries' in 1 Elizabeth I cap. 1, and the subordination of ' the dominions and territories thereunto belonging ' to England in the Act establishing the Commonwealth (1649).

[2] J. G. S. MacNeil, *The Constitutional and Parliamentary History of Ireland* (1917); A. Conway, *Henry VIII's Relations with Scotland and Ireland* (1932); D. B. Quinn, ' The Early Interpretation of Poynings' Law ', Irish H. Studies 11 (No. 7), pp. 241 ff.; R. D. Edwards and T. W. Moody, ' The History of Poynings' Law ', *ibid.*, II (No. 8), pp. 415 ff.

[3] James I argued similarly in 1613 that this law was a protection of the legislature against the Irish executive.

gative itself at the very moment when its Irish counterpart, still no more than a registry office for Crown measures, was only just becoming conscious of its chains.

Nor was the precedent of another of Poynings' laws followed; for 10 Henry VII cap. 22 (Irish Statutes) had applied to Ireland all statutes recently passed in England. Since statute and common law were so closely woven together, such an extension of the laws of England was difficult. Statutes presumed a basis of existing common law which might be affirmed or modified. If that base were wanting, statutes made in reference to that common law in England would be inapplicable for a law without base must be, it would seem, a law without meaning. So it was that medieval courts had required express reference in Acts or specific extension subsequently if legislation were to be extra territorial. In Ireland the extension of the ' pale' of conquest and of settlement had facilitated the gradual replacement, over many centuries, of native custom (*brehon*) by English law, and therefore the base existed for the implementation of 10 Henry VII cap. 39. In the immediate context of America such a solution was less reasonable. The most that could be determined at the moment of expansion across the Atlantic was that law in the colonies should be ' agreeable and not repugnant upon reason nor against it, but as convenient and agreeable as may be to the laws, statutes, customs and rights of our kingdom of England '.[1] This restrictive admonition was derived by analogy from the need for the by-laws of corporation to conform with common law: a Plantagenet rule which had been given statutory effect under Henry VI (15 Henry VI, cap. 6) and subsequently. The rule of repugnancy, thus established, was rough, vague and confused and remained so for two centuries and a half with no consistency of interpretation in relation to common law, statutes or royal instructions, nor of consequent penalty of nullity or avoidance.[2] On the rare occasion when, as over primogeniture, colonial law was repugnant to English common law, unexpected difficulties developed, as in *Winthrop v. Lechmere* (1724–32); and in *Dutton v. Howell* (1694) it was held that the English law of

[1] Compare the similar phrases from the Virginia (1606), the Massachusetts (1629), the Maryland (1632), and the Pennsylvania (1681) charters.

[2] A limited definition in one particular was made in 7 and 8 William III cap. 22, and draft Colonial Laws Validity bills were considered in 1744 and in 1752, but never introduced into parliament.

tort did not apply in ' settled ' Barbados, although in the year previous in *Blankard v. Galdy* Holt (C. J.) had affirmed that English common law would be carried to such ' settled ' colonies by the first immigrants. As for statutes, even those expressly mentioning the dominions were sometimes considered as not applying,[1] and in practice colonial courts picked and chose which they felt convenient. The attempts to distinguish between declaratory and innovating legislation first made by Darcy and Molyneux in Ireland and later imitated in America by Adams and Wilson were no more than rationalisations. It is true that in 1720 and in 1724 departmental legal opinion attempted to formulate some rules about the rights of settlement and the extension of statute and common law, by fixing the legacy at the very moment of the first settlement of the colony.[2] This itself was awkward and did not prevent the Privy Council seeking to obtain greater uniformity in law. The facts were so diverse that they eluded a logical pattern. If settled Virginia might be considered *conquered* (from the infidels), so Jamaica, conquered from Spain in 1655, might be regarded as *settled* by virtue of the proclamation of 1661 which guaranteed the colonists ' the same privileges . . . as our own free born subjects in England.[3] Indeed in no two colonies were procedures, precedents or decisions identical. The birthright of English law, in effect, was reduced to a few general principles (like trial by jury) and to similar methods of reasoning in public law.[4] Despite imperial exhortation, the colonists created their own amalgam of law as seemed to them best suited to their condition.

Just as they were making their own laws, they were also developing their own constitutions. No subject could legally acquire dominion for himself; but where there was no royal commission or grant, expatriate-settlers were not inhibited from

---

[1] A. M. Whitson, *The constitutional development of Jamaica* (1929), pp. 102–3. See *Carpenter v. Potter*, 1748: J. H. Smith, *op. cit.*, p. 486. In Maryland in 1732 it was declared ' where the acts and usages of the province are silent, the rule of adjudicature is to be according to the laws and statutes and reasonable custom of England as used and practised within the province ': S. G. L. Sioussat, ' The English Statutes in Maryland ', Johns Hopkins Univ. Stud. XXI (1903), p. 111.

[2] For West's opinion (1720) and Yorke-Wearg opinion (1724) see G. Chalmers, *Opinions of eminent lawyers* (1814 ed.) I, p. 195, 220.

[3] See *R. v. Vaughan* (1769) for Jamaica and *Smith v. Brown* (1705) for Virginia. A. M. Whitson, *op. cit.*, pp. 15–19.

[4] P. S. Reinsch, *English common law in the early American colonies* (1899).

establishing government for themselves. Occasionally, as in Warner's commission of 1625 for St. Kitts, retrospective authority might be given to govern lands previously annexed; a community of settlers (like the Pilgrim Fathers first of the Virginia Company and then of the New England Council) might seek recognition for their rights as sub-let tenants first of one company and then of another; or, again, an association of fellow believers, or a cluster of townships, or a group of fishermen or logcutters, might establish their own forms of ' social contract ' government apart from any grant, if these free states later found it convenient to recognise the sovereignty of the King and seek the legalisation of their position by a royal charter, as the ' commonwealths ' of Connecticut and Rhode Island[1] did at the Restoration, to become in effect the first republics in the Empire. The Mayflower Compact of 1620, indeed, symbolised that instinct for autonomous self-government present in the very beginnings of English settlement overseas. Desiring law and order, the Pilgrims were self-reliant enough to provide their own government by a common will ' to submit to such government and governors as they should, by common consent, agree to make and choose '. Even where legitimate authority had been acquired from the Crown, an old device might develop unexpectedly into something quite new: the pattern of the guild, for example, in its joint stock form. The forfeiture by *quo warranto* of the Virginian Company charter and the establishment of the first royal province, the old Dominion, in 1624, gave warnings of control which the Massachusetts Bay Company sought to avoid. Shedding its joint stock form of directors and shareholders within eighteen months of its incorporation in March 1629, the whole government was by resolution transferred to New England as a corporate colony, and alongside the close theocratic oligarchy, elementary forms of representative government began to develop in what became a *de facto* self governing colony, ruled by the agents of its voters with scant respect for rival authorities in the realm. The second Massachusetts charter in 1691, a new beginning with (for the first time) a colonial constitution in a single document, was the compromise result of a century's experience of government overseas.

[1] A Board of Trade comment in 1740 declared of Rhode Island ' This government is a sort of republic. They acknowledge the King of Great Britain for sovereign but are not accountable to the Crown for any acts of government, legislative or administrative '.

Nor was the general pattern which developed in royal, corporate or proprietary colonies—the old representative system—an exact replica of the English constitution. The Governor was no substitute king; his prerogative was limited, his patronage trifling and his status undermined by his regular acquaintance with the brink of insolvency at the hands of his paymaster, the Assembly, and by the futile and irritating exhortations from the ministers of his royal master, the King, who could not support him adequately in his task. The Council, allegedly a buttress to the Governor and the prerogative, was no House of Lords rooted in local society and lacked the family influence over the lower house which its English counterpart enjoyed. As W. W. Grenville said later, both in the weight of the ' monarchical ' and ' aristocratical ' parts these were not copies of the English constitution, indeed American secession could not be caused by ' the communication of the British constitution, which in fact they never enjoyed.'[1] As for the ' democratic element ', the Assembly, developing from the meeting of freemen of a corporation (as in Virginia) or the freeholders of a marcher palatinate (as in Maryland) imitated from the first the example of the mother-of-parliaments in its struggle with the prerogative, not least in the control of finance; but, in the absence of any opportunity to forge some cabinet link between distant executive and local legislature, it was frustrated in developing towards responsible government on British lines and therefore developed techniques of its own to control executive policy. Annual bargaining with the Governor was a natural alternative to ministerial responsibility and proved an even more effective means of purchasing liberty in America than it was in Britain; but regular and widespread use of committees of the House to formulate policy and to supervise, account and audit its administration meant that Assemblymen took a path of executive involvement repudiated by the Commons at home who saw their task not as one of governing so much as one of criticism and law making. Suspicion and isolation of the officials meant at the same time that American colonies served an apprenticeship in the separation of powers. Furthermore, by disregarding instructions, by passing temporary legislation operative till disallowed, or then by re-enacting the same measures, they were establishing a virtual

---

[1] October 1789. V. Harlow and F. Madden, *British colonial developments* (1953), pp. 205–6.

autonomy in government which the Privy Council or the Board of Trade were powerless to prevent. The demonstrable impossibility of devising an administrative machine capable of securing a firm control half a world away permitted the divergent evolution of realm and plantation.

The British executive bumbled and bungled, reluctant to assume direct government itself, learning slowly perhaps but too late. Parliament was doubtful of its powers and, even after asserting them in the interregnum, was not notably interested. Still suspicious of the prerogative, it did not rush in to the aid of the Crown in its difficulties. The truth is that the Empire was cradled in a period of uncertain authority and was shaped in conflict, diversity, and rebellion. Each turn of fortune in old England peopled the new world with groups of those critical of or discontened with, what they had left behind: New England was from its birth a secession from Old England. Colonists were seeking a new life of their own, not a new lease of an old one: indeed there were those, like Francis Bacon or John Harrington, standing on the threshold of this new empire, who had no difficulty in foreseeing that plantations would develop into ' new kingdoms ' and ' wean ' themselves from the mother country. The sense of oneness as Englishmen was a wasting quality. Particularism will develop and a single nationalism soon seem too inelastic to stretch so far in space or in comprehension. In the meantime, because King and Parliament were both preoccupied elsewhere, being locked in a great struggle, neither had opportunity to enforce central authority, to establish in Charles I's words ' one uniform course of government in and through all our whole monarchy ', or to deal with incipient truculence, until the capricious and the erratic had become sanctified as a new orthodoxy and colonial self government was a sturdy self-made fact. Practice begot any necessary theory; old means became ends, and old techniques values; even charters, the badges of dependence, might be claimed as the warrants of self government. On the other hand, in the realm itself the constitutional conflict was permanently changing the balance in the parent model and liberating new ideas alien to those which were a mutual heritage of Englishmen and colonists at the turn of the seventeenth century. A belief in fundamental law for example, had been a common sheet-anchor, but it soon became evident that such dogma was loosening its hold on English jurists. Her confidence growing in the greater security of a flexible, parliamentary supremacy, England was slipping her cables from their joint anchorage yet leaving her American colonists tied up at that old rejected orthodoxy. When, at the Restoration, continuity of intercourse was interrupted by the drying-up of the great migrations, the communities of Englishmen at home and overseas grew slowly out of touch, in want of sympathy and growing in misunderstanding. The England of Samuel Pepys was very different from that of John Pym: it was a mother country for which the colonial-born sons of the Pilgrim Fathers could find little affection or respect.

The superficial acceptance of the notion of the common form of government which developed in royal, proprietary and corporate colonies is therefore misleading if it prompts the conclusion that this derived from any desire to export the Westminster model. The instruments of government which were devised by the Crown and its advisers were based on feudal or mercantile origins in palatinate or corporation. Perhaps it has relevance to the experience of parliamentary democracy among non-British people later to emphasise that it was the political *ethos* of Britons in exile which moulded the makeshift institutions they received into a likeness to the British. But there was no exact identity, for the needs and circumstances of America were different from those in Britain: the image of the alleged model was itself dated as well as blurred and distorted in transit across the Atlantic, and the institutions evolved in conformity to the spirit of the New World. That ' perfect image and transcript of the British constitution ' so dear to the sentimental made no consistent appeal to the pragmatic multitude of politicians, imperial or colonial: the discontents, the radicals, the nationalists, the ' little imperialists ' and ' little colonists ' were selective of those basic principles best suited to their circumstance, opportunity and purpose and developed their own do-it-yourself variant of a remote and distorted memory.

Among those responsible for imperial policy in Britain opinion remained uncertain and divided. In opposition to those who advocated assimilation, whether Grenville, Durham or Milner (and this very list surprises by its revelation of differences in meaning, emphasis and inspiration), there were those who argued its impracticability like Thurlow, Russell or Donoughmore. In the dependencies too there was no single view. While there were those like Lafontaine, Smuts or Nehru, who saw merit in a constitution on a British model, there were those who did not: Samuel Adams, Papineau or Nkrumah. It is, therefore, oversimplification to allege, in the context of hurried transfers of power in the mid-twentieth century, that the British have sought consistently to spawn a brood of little Westminsters. They have wavered. They have temporised, hoping for a stable form of government to evolve locally. It is true, of course, that by education and example colonial peoples were conditioned to view a British constitution as desirable, not least because its possession might reasonably create in Britain that confidence which might speed self government and independence. In the present reaction against the British legacy it is unhistorical to impute an imperialistic design to yoke independent nations with a clumsy alien system of government; but it is also natural that some Ghanaians should assert this in national self respect just as some Afrikaners impeached the agreement of 1909 as a British imposition. The British interest as an imperial power was in keeping colonies ' godly and quietly governed ': to secure that tranquil stability which would favour prosperity and development. It is not without significance that the first conscious attempt at assimilation should be made at a moment when new thinking was vital: an empire in America had been lost, and some working relationship between Britain and her remaining possessions on that continent must be devised. Assimilation to the British model would, it was argued, make the colonial status more acceptable; it would also, in the identity of those checks not present in the previous export models, make imperial authority more effective. Assimilation was a device to secure not only Canadian goodwill but British supervision: to solve anew the perennial dilemma of how to combine the aspiration towards colonial autonomy with the need for continuing imperial unity.

We should not therefore state that a British model has been *exported*. The identity of the transported variety, whether in Australasia or in Asia, is never exact. The most that we can say is that seeds of the concept of constitutionality from the parent model were *transplanted* to grow differently (and the more vigorously) as they became naturalised to their new environment. Unless the plant were to wilt overseas, assimilation to British forms might only be one recognising (as the early charters had it) that it must be ' as convenient and agreeable as may be ', or (as Grenville said in 1789 even when inaugurating the new policy of closer assimilation[1]) that it must note ' the differences arising from the manner of the people and from the present situation of the Province '. Within these reasonable limits the degree of assimilation can indeed be balanced by the degree of autochthony.

[1] W. P. M. Kennedy, *Statutes, Treaties and Documents of the Canadian constitution* (1930), p. 185.

DAVID FIELDHOUSE

BRITISH IMPERIALISM IN THE LATE EIGHTEENTH CENTURY: DEFENCE OR OPULENCE?

' Imperialism,' like ' empire,' has had many connotations:[1] here it is taken to indicate an attitude of mind to the possession and use of dependent territories by the metropolitan power. Attempts have been made to show that there has been a common basis to imperialist thinking at all times in history;[2] but most historians would agree that there have been differences both in degree and in kind, not only between different empires, but also at various times in the history of a single empire. This essay is an attempt to select some of the features of British imperialism which appear to have been of special importance in the late eighteenth century. It makes no claim to consider the whole range of British thought or practice in this period, and such important factors as the motives for British expansion in the east, the growth of humanitarian standards of judgement in dealing with dependent peoples, and experiments in methods of colonial government have had to be excluded. The aim is simply to pin-point one aspect of the imperial *zeitgeist* for the years after about 1750, which may be used as a basis for interpreting some of the more important aspects of British imperial policy in this period.

I

' The old British colonial system was essentially commercial,' wrote R. L. Schuyler;[3] but, he added later, ' it had to take cogniz-ance of other matters than trade.'[4] It is the central argument of this essay that, in the second half of the eighteenth century, this order of priorities was to some extent reversed: that defence rather

---

[1] See R. Koebner, *Empire* (Cambridge, 1961) and ' The Concept of Economic Imperialism ', *Economic History Review*, Second Series, Vol. II, no. 1 (1949), 1–29.

[2] *E.g.* by J. Strachey, *The End of Empire* (London, 1959).

[3] R. L. Schuyler, *The Fall of the Old Colonial System* (New York, 1945), p. 3.

[4] *Ibid.*, p. 30.

than the interests of commerce came, for the time being, to dominate British imperial thinking: that, although the British never
seriously doubted that the empire had a vital economic function,
whatever radicals like Adam Smith might say, they began to look
to it also for more immediate advantages in support of their naval
and military power, with results that were startling and profound.

There is, of course, a danger in trying to point contrasts of
emphasis too strongly: and it will be well to emphasize at the
start the underlying element of continuity in British imperial
thinking. Belief in the navigation laws scarcely wavered. Britain
continued to hold her monopoly of colonial markets, and still
insisted on colonial staples being sent direct to her alone. The
colonial trade continued, as Adam Smith complained, to take a
disproportionate place in British trade as a whole[1]: and re-exports,
largely of colonial ' groceries ', remained at about a third of total
British exports.[2] Bounties and preferences on colonial products,
and on British fisheries, continued, and were extended as time
went on, partly at least in the interests of economic self-sufficiency.
The legal ban on the emigration of artisans to foreign countries
continued until the 1820s. And even the development of free
ports in the Caribbean and elsewhere was designed to strengthen
rather than dissolve the monopolistic system of imperial trade. To
this extent it would be accurate to say that British commercial
policy remained ' mercantilist ' throughout the late eighteenth
century and into the early years of the nineteenth.

What, then, was new? What are the grounds for thinking that
British imperialism may have been changing its order of priorities
or developing along new lines in these years? A brief statement of
some of the more obvious trends away from the doctrine that
empire meant maritime commerce will serve as a basis for closer
examination.

First, there was a new preoccupation with continental America,
shown in the concern with the land defences of the thirteen colonies
in 1754, in the size of the military effort to capture Canada during

[1] See E. B. Schumpeter, *English Overseas Trade Statistics*, 1697–1808.
(Oxford, 1960) The relative share of Europe in British imports dropped from
53 per cent to 31 per cent in the eighteenth century: of British exports from
70 per cent to 45 per cent. Introduction, pp. 10 f.
[2] In 1700 re-exports were £2,132,000 out of total exports of £6,469,000. In
1770 they amounted to £4,764,000 out of £14,268,000. *Ibid.*, p. 15.

the war, and in the post-war interest in the organization of the western lands. The novelty lay in the fact that the British had never before shown interest in acquiring large land masses, as distinct from maritime settlements. They were conscious, even in the 1760s when they were already deeply committed to a continental policy, that colonies in the interior were unlikely to be of much commercial advantage, and might ' from their inability to find returns to pay for the manufactures of Great Britain, be probably led to manufacture for themselves. . . .'[1] Yet, despite this threat to mercantile principles, Canada had been kept rather than Guadaloupe—a limited fur-trade against a lucrative sugar supply.[2] The whole continental bent of British imperialism clearly showed deviationist tendencies from orthodox ' mercantilism '.

Second, there was the imposition of taxes on the Americans in the 1760s, and this was heresy on two counts. It was contrary to the usage that the British parliament did not tax her colonies for the sake of raising revenue, and that colonial autonomy should be respected as far as possible. Again, resistance to taxation endangered the trade with America; and, on commercial grounds, the policy of taxation should finally have been dropped once this danger became apparent. Yet it was persisted in to the point of forcing a colonial rebellion.

Third, there was the attempt after 1782 to induce the Irish to pay a perpetual contribution to imperial defence costs, even at the price of dropping British protective tariffs against Irish products of all kinds. And finally there was the peculiarly warped application of the principles of the old navigation acts to the West Indies after 1783 under the new conditions created by the independence of the United States. The refusal by Britain to allow American ships to trade with the islands, and the avowed aim of excluding American products also, were nominally consistent with mercantile principles. But the policy was directly contrary to the interests of the sugar producers in the islands, and ultimately to those of Britain. The motive behind it was in fact not commer-

---

[1] Report of the Board of Trade . . ., 7 March, 1768, in S. E. Morison, *Sources and Documents illustrating the American Revolution* . . . (Oxford, 1951, 2nd ed.), p. 72.

[2] The strategic arguments of Pitt were reinforced by the resistance of the British West Indian interest to retaining Guadaloupe as a rival to their own sugar production within the empire.

C

cial but political. The aim was to preserve at all costs an artificially large British merchant fleet by maintaining its monopoly in the Caribbean trade, and so to safeguard the supply of trained seamen for the navy in time of war.

Each of these examples of British policy shows a deviation from the principle that the colonial system was primarily commercial. They may reasonably be said to constitute an *a priori* case for thinking that there were new elements in British imperialism in the late eighteenth century.

II

The years between 1748 and 1763 were a watershed in British imperial history and the starting point of the new imperialism. The struggle with France in North America, the Caribbean and India was the climax of a century of colonial expansion by both nations, the first major war fought for the redivision of colonial empires. The wars arose in the first instance from local struggles at the periphery. But, in deciding to give strong support to their nationals, both Britain and France were led into making new assumptions and taking on new commitments. In the 1750s the British ceased to think of territorial conflicts in North America in terms of the individual colonies, and gradually developed a continental strategy which made necessary not only the conquest of Canada but also, for the first time, a coherent policy towards the Indian tribes. Such broad thinking inevitably involved military and naval expenditure on an unparalleled scale, and this in turn made necessary a redefinition of the relationship between individual colonies and Great Britain. By 1763 there could be no return to the casual attitude hitherto adopted by the British towards their American possessions. Victory over the French had eliminated old dangers, but it had also created many new problems.

Paradoxically the British did not face the challenge offered by the new conditions in a spirit of confidence arising out of their sweeping victories. On the contrary, their attitude was defensive and pessimistic. The peace led not to British confidence that the inter-imperial struggle was finally over, but to a nagging fear that it would shortly be renewed, and that the next round might be less successful for Britain. The French were now out of Canada, but they remained in New Orleans and in the Caribbean; and no-one really supposed that they would accept the loss of Canada as final.[1] Moreover, apart from Canada, it was generally assumed that the French would want to get their revenge for the loss of India, and would seek to rehabilitate themselves as the dominant power in Europe. Thus, in 1763, Britain found herself for the first time in her history a satiated power, forced to defend her vastly extended empire against powerful and jealous rivals.

Everything, therefore, would now depend on Britain's ability to maintain adequate naval and military forces throughout the empire: and this in turn raised the question of costs. By 1763 the national debt had risen to about £130 millions, with an annual interest of £4¾ million.[2] On top of this would have to come the cost of defending the expanded empire: and even if it proved politically possible to raise the necessary taxation in Britain, the danger remained that the burden would be too great for the economy to bear. If domestic taxation was too high, the British manufacturer might be unable to compete with his more lightly taxed foreign competitor, and might be priced out of valuable markets. This in turn might lead to the decline of industry and the emigration of skilled workers to set up rival industries abroad. The fate of Spain in the seventeenth century seemed an object lesson of a country being pulled down by the weight of international commitments: and it was the determination that they should not go the same way that induced the British in the 1760s to look for means of spreading their new burdens.

Taxation of the colonists had not, of course, been the original British solution to the problem, This had been the attempt to get effective American military help in the campaigns in North America which had led to the Board of Trade's plan in 1754 to organize the thirteen colonies into a quasi-federation for their own defence.[3] When this plan fell through after the Albany Congress in that year, the Board had turned to the system of requisitioning troops from each colony to serve, at colonial expense (part of which was recouped by Britain), under a British General Officer.

[1] See in particular the despatches of Carleton as Governor of Quebec, 25 November, 1767, and 20 November, 1768, printed in Shortt and Doughty, *Documents* . . . (Ottawa, 1907), pp. 196 f. and 227 f.

[2] J. Steven Watson, *The Reign of George III*, 1760–1815. (Oxford, 1960), p. 20.

[3] The best treatment of this question is still in G. L. Beer, *British Colonial Policy*, 1754–1765, (New York, 1907).

It was only because this system proved unsatisfactory during the war that it was decided not to continue it after 1763: and the idea of fiscal contributions from the colonies was in origin simply a commutation of the alleged obligation of the colonists to supply men and materials on demand for their own defence. In the place of the colonial militias, there would now be a standing British army both to police the western lands and to defend the continent against possible French invasion, and part of its costs would be met from colonial contributions to the imperial exchequer. The transition of ideas was natural, no new principle seemed involved, yet the British could hope that by this means they would shift onto the colonists some of the burdens resulting from too large a wartime investment in North American real estate.

Where, then, lay the novelty in imperial thinking after 1763? Substantially it lay in the fact that, impelled by their new sense of heavy imperial responsibilities, the British were acting on a new conception of the nature of the colonies. On the criteria of a commercial empire, the colonies were mere plantations. Since their trade was a source of continuous profit to the metropolitan power, it was the duty and interest of the British to defend them against external dangers. As British subjects, the colonists were obliged to give reasonable assistance to the British forces in time of actual war in their own territories, and to maintain a militia for their internal security at all times. But this was a limited liability. It certainly had not been thought to extend to the strategic defence of the empire as a whole. And if, as a result of their international commitments, the British now insisted on maintaining a strategic force in North America in time of peace, it was difficult to see on what grounds the Americans could be asked to contribute towards its costs.

This, at least, was the view taken by most colonists in the 1760s, and was ably expounded by Benjamin Franklin in giving evidence on the results of the Stamp Act before the House of Commons in 1766. In his eyes the war itself had been ' really a British war ', in which the colonists had been incidentally involved by British policy outside their control, and, by this standard, colonial contributions to the war effort had been generous.[1] This, however, was not the standard the British were now applying: and one of the questions put to Franklin showed how far their thinking had

---

[1] *Parliamentary History*, xvi, col. 154.

now moved. ' But suppose Great Britain should be engaged in a war in Europe, would North America contribute to the support of it? '[1] Such a question showed clearly that the British were coming to think of the Americans not merely as auxiliaries in their own territorial wars, but as junior partners in the defence of the empire as a whole. And it was in this fact that the key to the whole taxation controversy is to be found.

The idea of colonial partnership was at once both reasonable and illogical in the 1760s. It was reasonable in that the Americans now numbered about two millions, had been the main beneficiaries of the seven years' war, and were no longer merely struggling tide water settlements. If Britain was now for the first time facing the problems of governing and defending a continent, it had been the interests of the sea-board colonies as much as her own inclinations that had led her into this position: and, on all counts, it was now arguable that the colonists should accept a more responsible position in the empire, and be prepared to undertake a fair proportion of the consequential burdens. On the other hand, the idea of colonial partnership was illogical in that it was bound to be very one-sided. The colonies were expected to remain subordinate in every other respect—subject to the authority of the imperial parliament, bound by the laws of trade, having no share in the formulation of foreign policy. Partnership and subservience were incompatible: and it was characteristic of British imperialism in this period that few men in England saw that this was so.

Thus the policy of taxing the Americans was itself merely the form in which the new British approach to imperial questions was expressed in the 1760s. Underlying it were the fundamental facts. The wars had overburdened the old structure of a commercial empire by making the costs arising from past debts and future defence disproportionate to the profits to be gained from commercial monopoly alone. Somehow the structure must be modified so that, while it still produced its commercial advantages for Britain, it could also give a non-commercial return for a non-commercial investment in American security. It was because few men in Britain saw that the end they were working for could not be achieved by the imposition of taxes without consultation and colonial agreement that the crisis occurred. To achieve colonial

[1] *Ibid.*, col. 153.

partnership within the traditional framework of a mercantile empire would have required new ideas on the nature of the imperial relationship. But the British, obsessed by pride and the principle of imperial authority were unable, until it was too late, to see that this was so.

Retrospectively, we can see that there were broadly two possible ways out of the dilemma. The first would have been to go back to the safe ground of a commercial empire pure and simple, to write off the war-debts as a bad investment, and to attempt to reduce imperial liabilities for the future. And this was the solution most consistently and ably put forward by Edmund Burke. His analysis of the causes of the crisis of the 1760s was accurate and profound. The empire had been founded on commercial principles alone. Monopoly had been its advantage to Britain, and fiscal contributions had never been thought of. It might, of course, have been otherwise: but it was too late now to change fundamentals, and the two principles could not coexist. Taxation of the Americans in a commercial empire he defined with unusual verbal economy as 'A revenue not substituted in the place of, but superadded to, a monopoly; which monopoly was enforced at the same time with additional strictness, and the execution put into military hands.'[1] Therefore, since either the revenue or the monopoly would have to be given up, he proposed that the revenue should no longer be looked for, and that Britain should try to put the clock back to the happy days before 1763.

Probably Burke, and the many who agreed with him on both sides of the Atlantic, were right on this particular point; for at no time in British history has it proved possible to induce old colonies to take on new imperial burdens without receiving compensating concessions in other directions. Yet, to think that such a solution would have been acceptable to the majority of British political opinion at the time would be to underestimate the forces behind the new imperialism. For one thing, the national debt could not be written off, and the clock could not really be put back. More significant still, the idea of colonial support for imperial defence had, by 1774 at least, gained such a hold in Britain that few would now have been satisfied to receive only the limited advantage of the old system of commercial monopoly. Only when war had

[1] *Ibid.*, xvii, col. 1241.

proved that the combination could not be achieved were the British prepared to give up the attempt.

Yet, in 1774, there was still an alternative to going back to the relationship that had existed before 1763. This would be to offer the colonies a new status or some additional advantages to compensate them for the further burden of imperial contributions, and at the same time to obtain these as voluntary payments rather than as arbitrary exactions. At first the most common expression of this policy was to propose the representation of the colonies in the imperial parliament, since this seemed the natural outcome of the argument that no British subject should be forced to pay taxes without his own consent. James Otis, for example, had insisted as early as 1764 that the colonists should be ' represented in some proportion to their number and estates, in the grand legislature of the nation . . . ',[1] and the idea had many later supporters, including Chatham himself. But the project came up against insuperable obstacles. Many in Britain disliked the prospect of a colonial block in the commons, fearing that it would be drawn into the system of ministerial patronage. Burke thought that distance alone made it impracticable. And the theory of ' virtual representation ' seemed to make the proposal constitutionally irrelevant. On their side, the colonists also turned against representation in Westminster. Franklin, who had been ardent for it in 1766, had turned against it by 1774, on the alleged grounds of the ' Corruption prevalent among all Orders of Men in this old rotten State. . . .'[2] In the interval most colonists seem to have decided that they would in any case prefer to contract out of all obligations to share imperial burdens rather than gain representation in parliament. Their decision can be seen as preference for home rule rather than imperial federation; or, perhaps more realistically, as a choice of isolationism rather than involvement in international affairs. Either way, it was clear by the early 1770s that partnership was not to be achieved in this way.

There was, however, another way to achieve the same British end. This would involve acceptance by the British of the full autonomy of the colonies in all domestic affairs in return for continued imperial control of their trade and foreign policy, together with a voluntary contribution by the colonists to common imperial

[1] Quoted by Morison, *op. cit.*, p. 9.
[2] J. C. Miller, *Origins of the American Revolution* (Stanford, 1959), p. 225.

costs. On the colonial side such a system, though without any definite scheme for contributions, was embodied in Galloway's Plan of Union of 1774. But even if this constitutional plan had been accepted finally by Congress, it would be most unrealistic to think that the colonists would have been prepared at this stage of the crisis to commit themselves to permanent contributions to the Exchequer, whatever the inducements held out. Yet, on the British side, the full development of this scheme came only in the mid 1770s: and appropriately it was Chatham, the greatest exponent of the new imperialism, who first put forward a definite plan. In his Provisional Act, put before the Lords on 1 February, 1775, he proposed that the colonists should be granted virtual home rule and given a remedy for all their existing grievances, together with a recognition of congress. In return congress was to be required

> ' to take into consideration . . . the making a free grant to the King, his heirs, and successors, of a certain perpetual revenue, subject to the disposition of the British parliament, to be by them appropriated as they in their wisdom shall judge fit, to the alleviation of the national debt. . . .'[1]

Chatham's scheme caught on quickly in Britain, since it seemed to offer a way of giving both the British and the Americans what they really wanted, neatly coordinating *imperium* and *libertas*. Hence it formed the basis of Lord North's Motion on conciliation with the colonies on the 27th of the same month, and was accepted in this form by parliament.[2] And, although this particular proposal was overwhelmed by the movement to war, the essential idea remained as perhaps the most reasonable of the British war aims. Naturally then, when peace proposals come to be made to congress in 1778, following the Saratoga disaster of 1777, it was to this principle that the British turned. By this time more sophisticated methods of arranging the colonial contributions had been worked out. The commissioners were instructed that, in return for granting the Americans virtually everything they could ask for— short of ' open and avowed independence '—they were to press for voluntary colonial subsidies.

---

[1] *Parliamentary History*, xviii, col. 200.
[2] Printed in M. Jensen, *American Colonial Documents to 1776.* (London, 1955), pp. 839–40.

'The sum required,' they were told, 'will be moderate. It may be taken upon a ratio of their numbers, their tonnage, or exports. The increase of the payment can only be in proportion to the increase of their abilities: and it becomes the interest of Great Britain to promote the industry, the trade, or the population of Our subjects in America.'[1]

The proposal stands as an example of the late eighteenth century instinct for a 'system', self-regulating, logically acceptable, mutually advantageous. It marks also the high-water mark of British imperialist thought in the eighteenth century, and has obvious affinities with the imperial federation movement at the end of the next century. Indeed, the points of similarity between the two are striking and illuminating. In each case the driving force was fear of international danger, coupled with a sense of the smallness of 'little England'. In each period the British reaction was to fall back on the resources of their largely self-governing colonies, to try to induce the colonists, in return for constitutional autonomy, to accept common obligations for imperial defence. The attempt failed on each occasion, for essentially the same reasons. In whatever terms the appeal was made, it was doomed to failure because, at heart, the colonists preferred to opt out of world responsibilities as long as they could rely on being defended in the last resort by the imperial power.

There, however, the similarities end. The contrast lies in the approach to the problem, and the way in which the colonies were handled. At the end of the nineteenth century the British appealed to their colonies as to equals:

'The weary Titan staggers under the too vast orb of its fate. We have borne the burden for many years. We think it is time that our children should assist us to support it. . . .'[2]

Those were the terms of Chamberlain's appeal in 1902. The British in the 1760s were in fact asking for the same help, but failed to see that it could not profitably be expressed in terms of binding legislation. Such an appeal would very probably have failed at any time, as did that made by Chamberlain: to make it only in 1778 was to make certain that it would be rejected.

[1] Harlow and Madden, *British Colonial Developments*, 1774–1834, (Oxford 1953).
[2] *Minutes of the Proceedings of the Colonial Conference*, 1902.

How far the British learned the lessons of their failure to get money as well as commercial profit out of their American colonies is beyond the scope of this essay. But it is at least clear that the essential aims of the new imperialism continued unchanged to at least 1815. It remains to consider briefly two attempts made in the 1780s to achieve the same ends by somewhat different methods: that is, to draw from an empire organized primarily for commerce, additional advantages in terms of imperial defence.

III

It was in Ireland that the specific aim of getting money contributions to imperial defence can best be seen after the failure of the American negotiations of 1778. Indeed, Ireland now remained the only British possession which resembled the American settlement colonies in that it could be regarded as a potential partner in imperial defence. Moreover, there was a certain appropriateness in the fact that the Irish, basing their claim to legislative independence firmly on the offers made to the Americans by the Peace Commissioners in 1778, and, having by 1782 acquired even more than the constitutional status the Americans then rejected, should then have been faced with the same demand for guaranteed fiscal contributions. By 1783 Ireland had achieved a degree of constitutional independence within the empire which had no equal until 1931. By the repeal of the Declaratory Act of 1719, reinforced by the Renunciation Act of 1783, she had gained complete legislative independence, unlimited even by the principle of imperial parliamentary sovereignty. And, before this, she had already gained full freedom in her external trade, coupled with access to trade with British colonies, by British legislation.[1]

These were vast concessions for the British to make: they had made them only because they had no other answer to threats of military action by the Irish Volunteers, and commercial sanction by the Irish Associations, so long as the American war lasted. Yet, once the American war was over, it must be said that leading British politicians did not regret the fact that such humiliating concessions had had to be made so much as the fact that they had

[1] There is a full account of the Irish issues in V. T. Harlow, *The Founding of the Second British Empire* (London, 1952), i, pp. 493 f.

been made unconditionally.[1] The fact was that Irish independence had been rushed through so quickly in the spring of 1782 that there had been no time to negotiate a proper basis for future relations. Two things in particular had been left unsettled—the terms of Ireland's adherence to the navigation acts, and possible Irish contributions to imperial defence costs. It is true that the Irish had adopted all relevant British commercial regulations by a local act in 1782: but this was liable to be modified or revoked unilaterally by the Irish, and so gave no guarantee for the future. No mention whatever had been made of defence contributions. From the British point of view this was the more important defect. Irish adherence to the navigation acts could probably be secured by threats to exclude them from the colonial trade in the future, since their rights there stemmed only from British legislation. But the chance of persuading the Irish parliament to undertake perpetual fiscal obligations for which nothing could be offered in return was very small. How small it was was shown by the failure of an attempt made by the Viceroy in June 1782 to persuade Irish politicians to introduce a bill to the effect that

> ' a share of the expense, in carrying on a defensive or of-
> fensive war . . . shall be borne by Ireland in proportion to
> the actual state of her abilities; and that she will adopt every
> such regulation as may be judged necessary by Great Britain
> for the better ordering and securing her trade and commerce
> with foreign nations, or her own colonies. . . .'[2]

Nor was it surprising that the Irish should reject such proposals. Already the Irish exchequer supported a standing army of 12,000, which had been increased by 3,000 in 1767–8 as the Irish equivalent of the American Stamp Act contribution to imperial security.[3] Moreover, as the Irish continued to contribute to British opulence through their acceptance of the navigation acts and the East India Company monopoly—thus in effect paying a surcharge on their tropical commodities to the British middleman and monopolist—they were conscious of paying their fair share towards imperial

[1] E.g. Pitt to Rutland, 4 December, 1784: ' The manner in which those concessions were unhappily made precluded any return. . . .' Correspondence between . . . Pitt and . . . Rutland . . . 1781–1787, (Edinburgh, 1890), p. 51.

[2] Portland to Shelburne, 6 June, 1782. H. Grattan, Memoirs of the life and times of the Rt. Hon. Henry Grattan, (London, 1839–41), ii, pp. 291–2.

[3] See R. Coupland, The American revolution and the British empire, (Oxford, 1930) for a discussion of this similarity.

costs in the accepted mercantile method. It was therefore evidence of the strength with which the British clung to their new enthusiasm for squeezing an additional bonus from their possessions that within two years of Irish independence an attempt was made to get a guarantee of money contributions to imperial defence. It is also typical of the limitations of British imagination in imperial matters that the attempt was ruined by trying to get too much out of the Irish at one time.

The opportunity arose unexpectedly in 1784 out of a movement in Ireland to obtain better terms in the direct trade with Britain. Irish trade was now technically free, but the markets for her food and manufactures in Britain were hampered by high protective duties, and she was still unable to re-export colonial products to Britain. Moreover, since Irish domestic tariffs were already very low, the Irish had little they could bargain with on the economic level. In this situation William Pitt saw his chance. He more than anyone else in English politics seems to have absorbed the ideas of his father and of his own political patron, Shelburne. Imperial cooperation in defence was in his blood. Hence, his reaction to the new Irish demands was to see them as a bargaining counter for securing substantial fiscal advantages for Britain. Briefly, he was prepared to bring about virtual free trade between the two countries if Ireland would, as he expressed it to the Viceroy, the Duke of Rutland,

> ' give security that her strength and riches will be our benefit, and that she will contribute from time to time in their increasing proportions to the common exigencies of the empire.'[1]

And there, of course, were the essential ideas of the Peace Commission's proposals of 1778: a system under which a money contribution should be guaranteed by the Irish parliament in such a way that it could not later be withheld or altered.

Yet, in its initial form, the proposal was not altogether unreasonable. The Irish had already received political and economic advantages of great value to themselves, and, if anything, the balance of advantage in the imperial relationship now lay with them. And, although the course of the negotiations cannot be followed here,[2] it looked at one stage as if the Irish would accept

---

[1] Pitt to Rutland, 7 October, 1784. *Pitt-Rutland Correspondence*, p. 43.
[2] See Harlow, *op. cit.*, pp. 558–615, for a detailed account.

the principle of money contributions, subject to their own domestic budget being balanced in any particular year before payment was made.[1] This was a considerable triumph for Pitt and Rutland, due to some extent to their moderation in limiting the demand made and accepting Irish amendments. But it was beyond Pitt's power to impose similar moderation on the British parliament, and the course of the proposals through the commons and lords was proof that the British had not learned that to demand too much may involve losing all. Briefly, the original Irish propositions were amended out of recognition. From eleven they were increased to twenty;[2] and two new principles were introduced. First, by clause four, the Irish were to bind themselves never to reject or modify the navigation acts so long as they were retained, even in modified form, by the British. Second, by clause nine, the Irish were to submit to the monopoly of the East India Company as long as this was continued in Britain. In other words, the British parliament, influenced by a storm of protest in the country, could not resist the opportunity once again to demand too much of their relationship with a dependency. Defence contributions alone were not enough without absolute certainty that mercantile advantages also would be gained: a monopoly not substituted in place of, but superadded to, a revenue, to invert Burke's description of the American issue.

As if this was not enough, however, the British parliament also insisted on altering the terms of the proposed Irish subsidy. The new clause omitted the provision that the Irish budget should be balanced before a contribution would be made; and the collection of the Irish hereditary revenues, on which the subsidy was to be based, was to be ' secured by permanent provisions '.[3] In other words, the British would not trust the Irish to stick to the spirit of the treaty to be made: and it was this insult, quite as much as the insistence on perpetual commercial subordination, that killed the whole negotiation. The normally pliant Irish parliament voted by a mere 127–108 for the first reading of the bill embodying the propositions when they were returned to it: as this meant that it

[1] Resolution 11. The sum to be paid was to be the surplus of the Hereditary Revenue over £656,000 in any year, subject to a balanced budget and appropriation by the *Irish* parliament ' towards the support of the Naval Force of the Empire . . .' See Harlow, *op. cit.*, p. 580.

[2] Printed in *Parliamentary History*, xxv, cols. 934–42. The Irish propositions are *ibid.*, cols. 311–314.

[3] *Ibid.*, col. 941–2.

had no chance of eventual success, the Castle dropped it quietly. Once again British imperialism had defeated its objectives by its own excess.

Yet failure did not deter the British from their essential aims. Somehow Ireland must be made secure as a support for British defence as well as an asset for British trade: new methods would have to be devised. Lecky has argued that it was from this time, and largely because of this failure, that Pitt and many others in Britain began seriously to consider the possibility of full legislative union with Ireland:[1] for this, in the fullest sense, would ensure that she would contribute to the ' common exigencies of the empire '. Politically, such a project was not possible in the 1780s. But, after the outbreak of the French war in 1793, with new revolutionary movements inside Ireland to worry the Protestant ascendancy, and the danger of French invasion, the thing became politically feasible. The Union of 1800, on the British side at least, sprang from the same elements of British imperialism as had the taxation of America and the Irish negotiations of 1784–5. And it is perhaps worth noting that when the question of Irish home rule came up again nearly a hundred years later, it was Chamberlain—the chief promoter of imperial integration for common security—who was prepared to split the Liberal party rather than see Ireland as a partially independent state.

IV

After America and Ireland, only the West Indies remained of the old colonial empire as a field to be exploited by the new British imperialism. Here the issues were somewhat different. The islands were already so completely a British economic monopoly, a highly specialized investment in sugar production, that direct fiscal contributions, even if voted by the local assemblies, would in the last resort simply have come out of British profits which were already falling by the 1780s. Accordingly, it was not obvious how they could be made to yield additional advantages in terms of imperial defence, as opposed to British opulence: and it was not until the general situation arising in the Caribbean out of American

[1] See W. E. H. Lecky, *A History of Ireland in the Eighteenth Century*, (London, 1916), ii, pp. 451–2.

independence came to be examined in 1783 that the British saw a way to achieve this.[1]

Fundamentally, the situation was as follows. As economic units the West Indies had relied very heavily on the continental colonies for most of their raw materials—food and timber in particular—on American shipping for the carriage of much of this local trade, and on American markets for much of their produce, such as molasses. The British share in the enterprise had consisted primarily in supplying capital and slaves—which were almost the same thing—and in marketing the sugar in Britain. Thus the islands were as much a part of the American economy as of the British. Now, however, the United States was a foreign country, and, if the navigation acts were strictly applied against the Americans, the islands would be cut off to a large extent from their natural sources of supply. American ships would no longer be able to call at West Indian ports, which could only mean that the costs of all imports would rise, since the alternative was to rely on British ships involved in the long-haul triangular trade with Africa. Moreover, if they were excluded, it was possible that the Americans would retaliate by putting an embargo on British West Indian produce, buying their sugar and molasses only from the French or Spanish islands. In other words, to apply the navigation acts rigidly against the Americans would endanger the prosperity of the British islands. This is turn would affect the profits of the British planters and the British business interests involved in the sugar trade. Obviously, if the profitability of the islands was the main criterion, British policy would have to be to modify the navigation acts so as to allow the Americans free access in their own ships to the British islands, with the right of exporting sugar (otherwise enumerated for direct export to Britain alone) while preserving the direct carriage of exports to Europe in British ships. By these means the dual advantages of the old commercial system —opulence plus the maintenance of a large fleet of long-distance merchant ships as the ' nursery of seamen '—would be retained; and all that would be lost would be the local carrying trade of the Caribbean.

For a time, indeed, it looked as if this sensible policy would be adopted. Shelburne, in particular, seems to have been convinced —possibly in part by his reading of economic radicals such as

[1] There is a detailed account of these events in Harlow, *op. cit.*, 408–492.

Smith and Tucker—that in a case like this economic advantage was best served by modification of the old mercantile principles in matters of detail. His American Intercourse Bill, presented to the commons by Pitt in March 1783 would have given the Americans free access to the British Caribbean possessions. But the bill proved to be a turning point, acting as a catalyst on parliamentary opinion. Because it seemed to throw away one of the essential principles of the navigation acts—the encouragement of British shipping as a basis for naval power—it led to a protest by those to whom the interests of defence seemed even more important than those of opulence. Two men in particular were responsible for the swing of opinion that followed: William Eden and Lord Sheffield. Eden's attack on the bill was made on 7 March, 1783. In it he marshalled all the standard mercantilist arguments against any concession to a foreign state in the trade of the empire: but the crux of his argument lay not in the possible economic losses from allowing the Americans to trade in the Caribbean, but in the foreseeable effect on British naval power. To allow the Americans to carry even the local trade of the islands would lead in the end to their gaining also a monopoly of the trade between the Caribbean and Africa and Europe.

> ' Thus,' he said, ' the kingdom would gradually lose the great nursery for its seamen, and all the means of manning the ships in time of emergency, and would thus decline and languish during peace, and be helpless and dependent during war.'[1]

Here was the classic argument in defence of the navigation acts— the ' nursery of seamen ' gambit, now applied in a context in which a choice might have to be made between the supply of seamen and the wealth resulting from the trade itself. For perhaps the first time the navigation acts could not be expected to supply both without seriously affecting British opulence.

Eden's argument was immediately taken up, and became the staple of a campaign waged against Shelburne's bill. Lord Sheffield entered the fray with an influential pamphlet, *Observations on the Commerce of the American States*, in which he held that

---

[1] *Parliamentary History*, xxiii, col. 607.

' The question is not, at present, whether the British dominions can supply the British West Indies, but whether all the
world can supply them in British shipping.'[1]

On these grounds the campaign was successful. Shelburne's bill
was postponed and later killed. In its place an act, originally
designed merely to repeal the wartime embargoes on American
trade, was so amended that it enabled the Crown, for six months,
to regulate the trade with the United States by Order in Council.[2]
This left the question open: and until the middle of June, 1783,
it still seemed likely that the Americans would be allowed to take
part in the Caribbean trade. Then the tide turned finally. Behind
the scenes the conservatives were bringing pressure to bear on
Lord North, as Fox's partner in the ' coalition ': and perhaps the
most influential of them was William Knox, until 1782 North's
Under Secretary in the Colonial Department. Knox claimed later
that, on being asked for advice on this matter by North, he had
replied that the first principle must be

> ' that it was better to have no colonies at all, than not to have
> them subservient to the maritime strength and commercial
> interests of Great Britain.'[3]

Knox, in fact, was trying to have it both ways. Ideally, he argued,
the West Indies should serve the commercial interests of the
empire by taking all their imports from Britain or British primary
producing colonies such as Canada. As this was, for the moment,
impracticable—since Canada could not yet play its part in the
system—the thing to do was to concentrate on the question of
ships rather than goods, by insisting that only British ships should
trade to the islands, even if they had to carry American goods.

Whether or not Knox had the influence he afterwards claimed,
on 2 July the Government took the crucial step. An Order in
Council was issued which insisted that all trade between the West
Indies and America, as well as between the islands and Europe,
should be carried in British ships. To Knox and his allies this was
victory: and he boasted afterwards that he would like to have the
order graven on his tombstone ' as having saved the navigation of

---

[1] Introduction, p. xxxv.
[2] 23 Geo. III, cap. XXXIX.
[3] Knox, *Extra-Official State Papers* (London, 1789), p. 54.

D

England '.[1] Nor was the decision later reversed. In December 1783 the parent act was renewed, and it lasted in substance until 1825.

What is the significance of this decision for a study of British imperialism in this period? To some extent it may be seen as yet another attempt to squeeze a double advantage out of the commercial structure of the old empire, an ingenious attempt to ensure that the sugar trade made its full contribution to imperial naval defence without affecting its contribution to national wealth: and there were plenty of men who maintained that the two were perfectly compatible, and that the ideal of a self-sufficient empire could still be achieved.[2] But in fact the decision to insist on the shipping monopoly was bound to be at the expense of the commercial prosperity of the islands, and therefore of Britain herself. Those who were directly involved in the West Indian trade—the planters and merchants—had no doubt about the economics of the question, and persistently argued that free trade in free ships with America was essential.[3] This was even tacitly acknowledged by Knox:[4] and in the years after 1784 the facts fully supported their contention. The regulations were consistently evaded in the interests of profit; American ships traded to the islands, often under foreign flags;[5] and, after 1793 under wartime conditions, the British government had to give the island governors permission to allow American ships in openly. In 1794 the British went so far as to offer to allow American ships of less than 70 tons—too small to make the Atlantic crossing, and so to compete in the ' long haul '—to trade to the West Indies: a proposal rejected by the American Senate as inadequate.[6] Thereafter the system stood in principle, though largely inoperative in practice, until 1830.

The conclusion which can be drawn from this episode seems reasonably clear. The British, obsessed with concern for national security in the late eighteenth century, and faced with a choice between the best interests of trade and a policy traditionally held to support their naval power, chose security rather than wealth.

[1] *Ibid.*, pp. 56–7.
[2] See in particular G. Chalmers, *Opinions on Interesting Subjects* . . . . (1784).
[3] *E.g.* Resolutions of the Committee of West India Planters and Merchants, 6 February, 1784. In Harlow and Madden, *op. cit.*, p. 256.
[4] Knox, *op. cit.* Appendix XIII.
[5] For evidence on the extent of American interloping, see Nelson to Sydney, 20 March, 1785, Harlow and Madden, *op. cit.*, pp. 265–7.
[6] Article XII of the Tretay. *Ibid.* p. 275.

But, in doing so, they did not admit that the two were incompatible: and it was still held officially that the maintenance of the West Indian shipping monopoly was in the best interests of commerce as well as of shipping. It was this optimistic belief that the two were perfectly compatible that was most typical of British imperialism in these years, and it was for this reason that the old colonial system survived into the nineteenth century, a monument to the perverse ingenuity of the British in forcing old institutions to serve new needs.

V

How, finally, can this analysis of British imperialism in the late eighteenth century be related to the evolution of British imperial thinking in the nineteenth century? The most obvious change that took place in imperial policy in the thirty or so years after the Napoleonic wars was of course the gradual decay of the mercantile system, with the ending of the British monopoly of the colonial trade after 1825, the steady decline in imperial preference, and the eventual abolition of the intra-imperial shipping monopoly in 1849. Inasmuch as the empire was essentially commercial, the new feature of the nineteenth century was that it was free trading. Yet, as has been argued, commerce had by no means been the only important feature of the old empire: and, if we are to interpret nineteenth century attitudes correctly, it is necessary also to consider whether a change took place in British thinking about the non-commercial aspects of the empire. Here, indeed, the change after 1815 was even more striking. For the moment the race for colonies was over. Britain had once again, as in 1763, emerged with most of the spoils: but this time there seemed no immediate danger of a French war of revenge. In Europe, also, Britain no longer seemed in danger. The British could therefore cease to think of themselves as a small country, competing only with difficulty in international power politics. The colonies no longer seemed necessary for defence, except in that some of them supplied strategic naval bases. Conversely, none of them, except possibly Canada, was now a defence liability for Britain. As a result it was now at last possible to assess the value of the colonial empire without taking defence into consideration.

Thus the key to understanding British attitudes to the possession of colonies in the mid-nineteenth century is not that the empire was free trade, but that, whatever the economic theory now accepted, it was simply and solely an economic empire, from which no collateral advantages were expected. This was the basis of mid-Victorian imperialism. It so happened, of course, that this concentration on the economic aspects of colonies coincided with the general break-up of the older empires and with freedom of trade with all parts of the world. The result, rather fortuitously, was that it became difficult to define the economic advantages to be gained from British colonies which could not be gained equally from other countries: and only the emigration enthusiasts in this period really provided a ' free-trade ' argument for possessing colonies, in that they designated them as unique receptacles for surplus British population. This however was a limited advantage: and the plain fact was that, because the British now felt no emotional concern for colonies as bastions of their own security, the mid-nineteenth century marked one of the lowest ebbs of British imperialist enthusiasm. This had one fortunate result. Because they no longer felt the need to depend on their colonies, the British did not strain their allegiance by trying to squeeze too many advantages out of them. Self-government was conceded to many of them without, as Disraeli later complained, any ' policy of Imperial consolidation ' being agreed on: that is, without obligations being imposed on these colonies regarding tariffs, waste lands and defence.[1] It was this fact more than any other that set the tone of the new imperial system. The settlement colonies grew up in the assurance that membership of the empire was pure gain to them: limited subordination without economic or fiscal obligations, in return for free defence and low-interest loans.

The next major change in the character of British imperialism came sometime after 1870 with the return of some of the typical features of the later eighteenth century environment: an intensive struggle for power in Europe, international competition for colonies, a revival of protectionism abroad, and a decline in Britain's relative military strength. In these conditions, the British reverted to their earlier preoccupation with defence: and this led them once again to look at their settlement colonies as

---

[1] An extract from this speech is quoted in G. Bennett, *The Concept of Empire*, (London, 1953), pp. 257-9.

a source of security, as partners in a common defence system. The danger was, of course, that they would once again try to overload the imperial system to the extent that the colonies, secure still in their geographical isolation, would prefer to secede rather than undertake new imperial commitments. The fact that this did not happen suggests that the new imperialism was more moderate than the old. The colonies were free to reject the new appeal for imperial federation of any kind, and British imperialism eventually transferred its emotional urge for closer association with its colonies to the Commonwealth. It is interesting to note also that economic factors were of minor importance in this new British imperialist movement. Chamberlain tried to harness economic integration to the cause of closer union for defence, and failed. And it was not until 1932 that an imperial tariff re-emerged. Thus, in the modern imperialist movement, the historic order of priorities was reversed. The new imperial policy was political, but it had also to take cognizance of other matters than defence.

Perhaps then, there is a recurrent pattern in British imperialism. Whether or not at any particular time the commercial system of the empire has been protectionist or free trade, the most variable and perhaps decisive factor has been the question of defence. To suggest a broad hypothesis, it might be said that, in times of international stability British imperialism has been moderate, demanding little from the colonies, taking economic interests as the basis of judgement. But in times of political danger the British have tended to fall back on their colonies as an essential make-weight, to hope to gain from them a bonus of security over and above whatever economic advantages they were already yielding her: and it was perhaps this that formed the most characteristic tendency of British imperialism in the late eighteenth century.

MARY BULL

INDIRECT RULE IN NORTHERN NIGERIA 1906–1911

' It is putting it mildly to say that Lugard did not approve of the method and extent to which Indirect Rule had been pushed since he left in 1906.' This was written by Sir Richmond Palmer[1] to Miss Perham,[2] describing the reaction of Lugard when he returned in 1912 to the Northern Nigeria whose government he had created in the first six years of the century. Miss Perham has briefly considered the years between Lugard's two periods of administration as a background to the relations between the Northern officials and himself during his administration of 1912 to 1918;[3] here it is attempted to examine them more fully. What developments had taken place, and why; whose decisions had brought them about; and why should Lugard—and modern critics—disapprove?

Lugard created the foundation of the system of colonial administration which came to be known as ' Indirect Rule '[4] he created it out of a combination of his own character and experience and the situation with which he was confronted in Northern Nigeria. His contribution lay not so much in adopting the ' indirect ' principle, but in his emphasis on ' ruling '; building the native administrations which he found in existence into a structure by which he, with a group of administrative officers numbering 75 in 1906, and with a small but efficient army, could control a territory of nearly 300,000 square miles and a population estimated at seven millions.[5] And he controlled not only the

---

[1] Palmer, Sir Richmond, K.C.M.G., 1877–1958; 1904 Assistant Resident, N. Nigeria; 1908, 3rd Class Resident; 1912–15 Commissioner (later Supervisor) Native Revenue; 1916, 2nd Class Resident; 1918, 1st Class Resident; 1925–30 Lieut.-Governor; 1930–3 Governor, Gambia; 1933–9 Governor, Cyprus.

[2] 17 December, 1949; quoted in Margery Perham, *Lugard: The Years of Authority* (London, 1960), pp. 479–80.

[3] *Ibid.*, Ch. 24; see also Margery Perham, *Native Administration in Nigeria*, (London, 1937, 2nd ed. 1961).

[4] ' Indirect Rule ' is used here to refer to that system of Native Administration first elaborated in N. Nigeria and subsequently applied (with modifications) in many parts of tropical Africa under British rule. It was, of course, a species of a much wider genus for which the phrase indirect rule has also been, rather confusingly, employed.

[5] *Northern Nigeria Annual Report*, 1906–7, p. 99. Population estimates varied widely from year to year; this figure was probably the lowest and the most accurate.

Africans, but also the few Europeans. Northern Nigeria was a
territory in which European influence had been minimal before
British annexation. The paucity of profitable exports had not
encouraged the Niger Company to establish more than a few
riverain trading posts, and Christian missions had remained on a
small scale. Therefore neither of the two groups of unofficials
who, in the coastal colonies of West Africa, had preceded government and were in a position to retain some independence of it,
was to exercise comparable influence in Northern Nigeria.
Lugard's government controlled all land dealings between European and African; it had power to declare any disturbed area closed
to unofficials; and it could deport any undesirable non-native—
European or coast African—from the territory.

The assumption of such powers by a colonial government was
made possible not only by the circumstances of Northern Nigeria
—the almost complete absence of independent European influence
and the authoritative character of Lugard himself—but also by the
changing climate of opinion in England, which was reflected in
both the Colonial Office and the officials who came out to serve
the new government. The combination of the ' new imperialism '
with the spread of socialistic doctrines favoured a more positive
role for government than had been accepted by nineteenth century
liberals—the imperialism of some of the Fabians is indicative of
this[1]—while Cromer and Milner were both providing examples of
how colonial governments could form and execute policies.
Chamberlain's belief in strong government action had been vital
to Northern Nigeria; no other Colonial Secretary could have
extracted the grant-in-aid from the more old-fashioned Treasury
which paid for this protectorate of minor strategic importance.
And because the bulk of his revenue came from the Imperial
exchequer, and he was not bound by the earlier doctrine of self-
sufficiency, Lugard could consider the slow development of the
taxable external trade of secondary importance and maintain the
prohibition on imports of liquors, the duties on which provided the
main revenue of the coastal colonies. The ' new imperialism ',
also, made the career of a political officer in Northern Nigeria
socially acceptable. The creation of the West African Frontier

---

[1] This is illustrated by the minutes of Sydney Olivier, then serving in the
West African Department of the Colonial Office; e.g. on Lugard to Elgin, 17
January, 1906, C.O. 446/52, where he argued the necessity of military expeditions
to establish control.

Force employing officers seconded from other regiments, usually in the hope of seeing some active service, brought what Lugard and others felt to be a better class of Englishman to West Africa than had previously been seen there, and once the South African war ended Northern Nigeria provided one of the more attractive fields for the adventurous spirits amongst the products of the public schools and universities. These men were prepared to devote themselves to their careers, endure discomforts and disease, learn African languages, tour remote and dangerous districts, and aim at understanding the African way of life. They felt themselves capable of deciding how far that way of life should be preserved, and how far altered in the interests of justice or civilisation. If they accepted the principles of ruling indirectly, it was certainly in no spirit of *laissez-faire*.

Neither the Colonial Office nor Lugard, however, was free from nineteenth century assumptions about colonial adminis-tration. Though the Office came to approve of what Lugard had done, each step as he took it was regarded with doubts. When Lugard, in his estimates for the financial year of 1906–7, pleaded for more staff, Antrobus[1] wrote that Lugard must keep to the Colonial Office imposed limit to expenditure of £500,000; that the administration must cut its coat according to the cloth of its revenue; and that 'As Mr. Chamberlain said at one of the last interviews I had with him about N. Nigeria, Sir F. Lugard is trying to do, in the short space of his own administration, work which ought to be spread over 20 years '.[2] And while the officials always supported the policy of ' ruling through chiefs ', they appeared, even at the end of Lugard's term of office in Northern Nigeria, to see little difference between his development of that policy and those variants, as in neighbouring Yorubaland, which exercised only a minimum of control.

Apart from these basic questions of the assumption of unquali-fied control over the whole Protectorate, Lugard differed little from the older officials at home. While he did not support the mid-Victorian belief in the uniformity of human nature which had

[1] Antrobus, (later Sir) Reginald, K.C.M.G., C.B., 1853–1942; 1880–9 private secretary to successive Colonial Secretaries; 1889–90 acted as Governor of St. Helena; 1898–1909 Assistant Under-Secretary of State for the Colonies; 1909–18 Senior Crown Agent for the Colonies. From 1897 to 1909 Antrobus was in charge of the West Africa Department of the Colonial Office, though several reorganizations of business changed his other responsibilities.

[2] Minute on Lugard to C.O., 11 November, 1905, C.O. 446/51.

led British administrators to impose English law and custom on
the first West African colonies, and while he spoke a great deal of
ruling on native lines, he had no doubt that British civilisation had
much to teach, and that native societies must be adapted and made
to learn these lessons. He also believed that British rule should
benefit the British people as well as the African, by opening
Northern Nigeria to British trade, providing a market and a
source of tropical products for those at home. Thus he spent a
great deal of time encouraging the collection of natural products
to be analysed at home; on currency and banking questions; and,
in particular, urging the building of a railway to Kano. He agreed
to a subsidy from his scanty revenue for the British Cotton
Growing Association, which aimed at encouraging the African to
grow cotton for the British market. He could write ' I foresee
with great regret the decline of Kano as a commercial centre when
European goods replace her manufactures, and the exports of
other provinces are diverted by more direct routes to the factories
of British merchants, instead of passing through the hands of her
middlemen and brokers '[1] but he did not doubt that such developments should be promoted by the government.

In administration, above all, he was not dogmatic. His first
thoughts on the form of government for Northern Nigeria began:
' In the earlier stages of British rule it is desirable to retain the
native authority and to work through and by the native Emirs.'[2]
But it is clear that he did not envisage this system as one which
would necessarily be maintained; he was always ready to adapt his
methods in the light of experience. The correspondence between
Lugard and Orr[3] quoted by Miss Perham confirms that Lugard
in 1903 had no fixed principles concerning the extent of the
powers to be wielded by the native authorities. Orr complained
that Residents were being asked to take over administrative
functions which were better left to Emirs; but Lugard believed
that he was only asking Residents to do what was absolutely
necessary, that the control of military and police, and the collection

[1] *Annual Report*, 1904, p. 88.
[2] Perham, *Lugard II*, p. 140.
[3] Orr, (later Sir) Charles, K.C.M.G., 1870–1945; 1889–1902 served in
Royal Artillery in India, China and South Africa; 1903–9 Resident, Northern
Nigeria; 1911–17 Chief Secretary, Cyprus; 1918–19 Intelligence Department,
War Office; 1919–26 Colonial Secretary, Gibraltar; 1926–31 Governor,
Bahamas.

of taxes could not be entrusted to corrupt Emirs of doubtful loyalty.[1] Later, when writing to Girouard[2] on land policy, he said ' You must always bear in mind that my systems were only in gradual course of development. . . . In the interests of the future I would beg you to make no *absolute pledge*; leave a loophole for the experience of the future. You will find that in every agreement made by me, every title of appointment and every settlement of every kind, that I endeavoured always to do this. We cannot forecast the future of a country like Nigeria, and the very ablest and most far-seeing of men cannot forecast what the line of development may be.'[3] Lugard's principles as expressed in his Political Memoranda and later in *The Dual Mandate* were always in favour of Indirect Rule; but when we examine his actions in the years to 1906 it would seem that, had he continued to be in a position to direct the administration, the tendency would have been towards centralisation. He wished to use native administrations, but would have kept a close control over them. He attempted such centralisation when he returned as Governor-General in 1912, but his success was limited—the opposition in Northern Nigeria and in the Colonial Office had become too strong, and the war was too great a distraction.

When Lugard resigned in August 1906, he had already convinced Lord Elgin, the Secretary of State for the Colonies, that a railway was needed in Northern Nigeria, and that the Treasury must be persuaded to help find the money. This fact determined the choice of his successor. Elgin wanted more expert advice on its route and method of construction, and so appointed as the new High Commissioner (whose title was soon changed to that of Governor) Sir Percy Girouard for one tour only in order to advise on railway construction. The letter offering him the appointment spoke first of the various railway proposals on which Lord Elgin sought his advice, and only then mentioned the other responsibilities of governing Northern Nigeria.[4] At the end of his

[1] Perham, *op. cit.*, pp. 185–6.
[2] Girouard, Major-General Sir Percy, K.C.M.G., R.E., 1867–1932; 1896 Director of Sudan railways; 1898–9 President, Egyptian Railway Board; 1899–1902 South African War; 1902–4 Commissioner of Railways, Transvaal and Orange River Colony; 1907–9 Governor of Northern Nigeria; 1909–12 Governor, East Africa Protectorate.
[3] Lugard to Girouard, 12 April, 1908, Lugard Papers, MSS. Brit. Emp. s63.
[4] C.O. to Girouard, 22 December, 1906, draft in Lugard to C.O., 20 May, 1906, C.O. 446/54.

single tour it was hoped that arrangements for amalgamating the
two Nigerias might be made, and probably Girouard was not
expected to make a contribution to the administration of the
country. But Girouard was a man of more active and wide-ranging
mind than the Office at this time appreciated.

However, when considering Northern Nigeria during the years
1907–12, the dominating fact of the construction of the Baro-
Kano railway must not be forgotten. Everyone concerned,
whether in Britain or Nigeria, whether official or unofficial,
believed in the necessity for its construction. Above all the
administrative staff of the Protectorate were conscious of the time
and money being wasted by trekking on foot with human carriers
through the tsetse belt which separated the river from the northern
plains where animal transport was possible. There was also the
strategic factor: officials did not forget the time taken in 1906 for
the troops of the W.A.F.F. to march from the Benue to the northern town of Satiru where a revolt had annihilated the local forces
and could have been the signal for a concerted rising of the emirates. The Niger Company, the British Cotton Growing Association, and the trading interests of Southern Nigeria added their
voices.[1] The officials of the Colonial Office were already convinced
of the general desirability of developing colonies by means of
railway construction, and supported Lugard's arguments concerning the benefits of this line, both in development of trade and
in administrative economies. The new Liberal ministers of
December, 1905, Elgin with his Indian experience and Churchill
with his passion for construction, were quickly won over. Churchill, in a memorandum arguing the case for a railway, wrote: ' Until
that communication is provided we are encamped in Northern
Nigeria rather than in permanent occupation; and a jogging string
of pack animals is an impossible backbone on which to throw the
weight and strains of so extensive and elaborate structure of civilized

[1] See, for example, the pamphlet published by the B.C.G.A. (No. 10, May,
1906) which gave an account of the deputation to the Prime Minister of that
month, requesting Imperial funds for the railway, and quoted speeches by Elgin
in the House of Lords (Parliamentary Debates, Lords, 10 May, 1906, IV. 156,
1435–43), and by Churchill at Liverpool, 5 May, 1906, in favour of a railway
(enclosed in C.O. to Treasury, 28 February, 1907, T.1. 10675/15732/1907);
Lord Scarbrough to C.O., 9 July, 1906, C.O. 446/58, advocating routes for the
railway; resolution from the Associated Chambers of Commerce, forwarded to
Lord Elgin, 26 March, 1907, C.O. 446/69, urging the government to proceed
with the construction of railways and roads in the colonies generally, and in
Northern Nigeria in particular.

government already in existence.'[1] The Treasury—or more particularly Asquith, as this was the only matter concerning Northern Nigeria in these years to be decided by the Cabinet— was finally persuaded to give financial aid.[2]

Girouard did all that the Colonial Office could hope for. He sent his report on the transport policy for Nigeria soon after his arrival in the Protectorate, supporting Lugard not only on the importance—indeed urgency—of railway communication, but also on the advantages of the route to Kano, the agreed terminus, from Baro, the highest point on the Niger navigable, in the two-month season of high water, by ocean going vessels. He thus favoured the river and rail route from the sea as against an all-rail connection to be made by extending the Lagos railway northward.[3] Girouard also supported Lugard's proposals for the construction of the line by the Public Works Department of Northern Nigeria with all possible assistance from other departments, rather than by the usual colonial practice of construction by a British firm of Consulting Engineers under the supervision of the Crown Agents for the Colonies. There can be little doubt that Lugard's advocacy of the rail-river route, and of the ' departmental ' method of construction, were influenced by his desire to keep his control of Northern Nigeria unfettered by any possible restraints from either Southern Nigeria or from the Crown Agents and their engineers. Girouard and the Residents whom he consulted were also aware of these factors. The construction methods, in fact, ably served the declared aims of speed and economy; the succeeding Governor, Sir Hesketh Bell,[4] wrote in 1910:

' The economy and celerity that have characterised the construction of the Baro-Kano line have been almost entirely due to the tact, zeal and enthusiasm shown by every official who has been

[1] 18 July, 1907, copy in C.O. 446/69.

[2] The campaign by the Colonial Office to convince the Treasury is best seen in the Treasury file, T.1. 10675/15732/1907, which contains all the official letters from the Colonial Office, with the Treasury minutes upon them, and also unofficial letters from Elgin to Asquith (28 February, 1907) and from Churchill to Runciman (August, 1907).

[3] Girouard to Elgin, 30 May, 1907, C.O. 446/63; printed in *Further Correspondence relating to Railway Construction in Nigeria*, Cd. 4523, March 1909, p. 53.

[4] Bell, Sir Henry Hesketh, G.C.M.G., 1865–1952; 1882 entered Colonial Service, West Indies; 1890–3 Gold Coast; 1894 Receiver-General, Bahamas; 1899 Administrator, Dominica; 1906–9 Governor, Uganda Protectorate; 1909–12 Governor, Northern Nigeria; 1912–16 Governor, Leeward Islands; 1916–25 Governor, Mauritius.

connected with the work. Every department in the Service has had a hand in it, and we all feel that it is *our* railway. The lack of serious difficulties in connection with the labour supply must be ascribed to the personal influence exercised by the political officers over the various tribes, and to their humane methods.'[1]

It did, however, cost the time of the existing staff, not only of the Public Works Department but of Girouard who personally supervised much of the early work, and of the Residents in the Niger, and later in the Zaria and Kano provinces, who were engaged in arranging labour supplies. It was the organization of railway labour that the Northern Nigeria officials were most anxious to keep under their own control when questions arose of the extension of the Lagos railway into Northern Nigeria, and of government versus private construction of the line to the Bauchi tin mines. Though the Yorubas of Ilorin were to some extent abandoned to the influence of Africans from Lagos, the political officers desired to control all relations between all other Africans and the outside world.

The decision on the route was not so happy, but some of the difficulties were the responsibility of the Treasury. With memories of the Uganda railway all too clear in their minds, the officials there refused either to grant or to raise the money ($£1,230,000$) themselves—' economy is safeguarded by not giving our proconsuls power to draw on the public purse '.[2] They forced the Colonial Office to raise the money by a loan on Southern Nigerian credit, the Treasury repaying the interest charges to the southern government. To secure the agreement of Sir Walter Egerton, Governor of Southern Nigeria, to this scheme, Elgin promised him that the railway from Lagos should be extended into Northern Nigeria, to cross the Niger at Jebba and link with the Baro-Kano railway.[3] The all-rail route proved more attractive than the Baro-Niger route, and the Colonial Office came to feel it had been mistaken to allow both;[4] while the entry of the line from Lagos into Northern Nigeria, and the assumption by Egerton that the whole system

[1] Bell to Crewe, 30 May, 1910, C.O. 446/90.
[2] Minute by Chalmers on C.O. to Treasury, 26 July, 1907, T.I. 10675/15732/1907.
[3] Egerton to C.O., 3 August, 1907, Cd. 4523, p. 90.
[4] ' I agree with Sir W. Egerton in thinking it very unfortunate that the construction of a line from Baro was decided upon ' minuted Antrobus on Egerton to Crewe, 27 July, 1908, C.O. 520/63.

should be controlled by Southern Nigeria, was resented in the north.[1]

Yet, while Girouard spent much of his time at the railway construction camp near Baro, supervising the unloading of steamers and peppering the Colonial Office with sometimes incomprehensible telegrams demanding more men or materials, he was still able to consider the general problems of native administration. Although he had not previously held an administrative post, he came to Northern Nigeria with some clearly defined ideas on the subject. Girouard had spent the previous ten years directing railways in Egypt and the Sudan, under Cromer and Kitchener, and in South Africa, under Milner. In South Africa he had married the daughter of Sir Richard Solomon, Attorney-General of the Transvaal and a constitutional expert. His views reflected these influences, particularly that of Cromer; he believed in the beneficial effect of strong, paternalistic European rule in Africa, which would allow African societies to develop ' on native lines ', rather than in attempts to mould them in imitation of European societies. Thus he became a ready convert to the system which was being enforced in Northern Nigeria: the preservation of the Muslim emirates and the control by the Residents of all influences brought to bear upon them.

His appreciation of this system of administration was undoubtedly enhanced by the fact that it was being practised by an enthusiastic and intelligent group of Residents. He described them to Lugard as ' a loyal and devoted staff, devoted to their work, and may I say it, devoted to you and the memory of your work '.[2]

Five of these men had considerable influence on the development of Northern Nigeria. Major Burdon[3] was the senior, and

[1] ' There is a tendency on the part of Sir W. Egerton to look upon it [the future amalgamation of S. and N. Nigeria] as though it were a sort of annexation by S. Nigeria ' minuted Strachey on Egerton's proposals that the completion of the railway link should be followed immediately by the amalgamation of governments (on Egerton to Crewe, 31 January, 1910, C.O. 520/91). Yet Strachey also thought the Northern criticisms exaggerated: ' I am inclined to think that the N.N. people are too much disposed to be terrified at the advent of the railway from the south ' (on Bell to Harcourt, 25 September, 1911, C.O. 446/100).

[2] Girouard to Lugard, 25 January, 1908, *Lugard Papers* MSS. Brit. Emp. s.63.

[3] Burdon, Major (later Sir) John Alder, K.B.E., 1866–1933; 1897 Niger-Sudan campaign; 1898–9 Commandant, Royal Niger Constabulary; 1900 Resident, Northern Nigeria; 1903–6, 1909–10 Resident, Sokoto; 1910–15 Colonial Secretary, Barbados; 1915–25 Administrator, St. Kitts; 1925–31 Governor, British Honduras.

was in charge of the senior emirate, Sokoto. Burdon was the most whole-hearted supporter of Fulani rule; an expert in the Hausa language, he spent much of his time learning the history and genealogy of the Fulani ruling families, and as far as possible left the administration in their hands. Lugard had never sympathised with this degree of separation between the European Resident and the mass of the people, and was somewhat critical of the amount of time Burdon spent in his office. Temple also suggested later that there had not been enough touring and direct supervision in Sokoto. But the confidence which developed between Burdon and the Sultan of Sokoto was acknowledged by all to be an important factor in the acceptance of British rule by the Fulani, and especially in the Fulani loyalty to the British during the Satiru revolt.

The most able of the Residents was usually held to be Charles Temple.[1] His father had held the highest posts in the Indian Civil Service, and the son had spent a number of years in the Consular Service before going to Northern Nigeria. His personality, assured, charming, but strict with subordinates and Africans, made him esteemed by governors and the Colonial Office (where he was a good friend of Charles Strachey),[2] and he devoted much more thought to the nature and object of British rule in Africa than was common at this time. In these years, when he was administering Bauchi, Sokoto and Kano provinces, his ideas were less dogmatically in favour of preserving the existing administrative systems than they became when he wrote his book.[3] Girouard described him as a supporter, but not an uncritical supporter, of indirect rule, and his temperament made him far more inclined than was Burdon to direct personally, and to attempt to improve, the administration of his province. But he held strongly that the Resident must have the greatest possible freedom from the central government in dealing with the native authorities.

The third of those who were regarded as the best of the

[1] Temple, Charles Lindsay, C.M.G., 1871–1929; 1898, 1900 and 1901 Acting Consul, Paraguay; 1899 Vice-Consul, Manaos, Brazil; 1901 Resident, Northern Nigeria; 1910–13 Chief Secretary, N. Nigeria; 1914–17 Lieutenant-Governor, Northern Nigeria.

[2] Strachey, (later Sir) Charles, K.C.M.G., 1862–1942; 1885–99 Foreign Office (concerned with West African Protectorates); 1900 Colonial Office; 1906 Principal Clerk, West Africa Dept.; 1909 Principal Clerk, Niger Department; 1913–14 travelled in West Africa; 1919 represented the Colonial Office at the Peace Conference; 1924–7 Assistant Under-Secretary of State for the Colonies.

[3] C. L. Temple, *Native Races and their Rulers* (Cape Town, 1918).

Residents[1] was Captain Orr, who was for a number of years in charge of Zaria province. Orr was the closest friend and greatest admirer of Lugard, and the correspondence between them which is preserved in the Lugard Papers shows that he was concerned with the nature of British administration. But his devotion to Lugard's ideas as expressed in the Political Memoranda made his contribution less individual. Both Burdon and Orr were appointed by Girouard to direct the secretariat, where they were his chief advisers in administrative matters, though both asked to return to their provinces.

Two of the junior Residents, both of whom had been marked out by Lugard for rapid promotion, made important contributions in these years which will be discussed later. One was Richmond Palmer, who, placed in charge of Katsina emirate. a division of Kano province, was able to appoint a co-operative Emir and to conduct the most thoroughgoing reforms of the native administration—in particular he developed the Native Treasury. Girouard was a little concerned at the extent of his reforms and of his aim of transforming the ruling class into government officials, but in other emirates Palmer came to accept the orthodoxies of indirect rule. The second was Hanns Vischer[2] who was accepted, even in 1906, as the man with the greatest interest in, and sympathy with, the native outlook, and whose appointment as Director of Education was of the greatest importance to Northern Nigeria's future, and the educational future of all British colonies.

One of the first decisions which Girouard had to make illustrated the direction in which the Residents wished to alter the administration. Soon after Lugard's departure Wallace[3] had recommended, with enclosures from senior Residents supporting —or inspiring?—the proposals, that the European police system, or Constabulary as it had recently been renamed when giving it a more military type organisation, should be abolished; that in the

[1] In, e.g., a minute by Fiddes on Girouard to C.O., 22 May, 1909, C.O. 446/87.

[2] Vischer, (later Sir) Hanns, 1876–1945; 1900–1 C.M.S. Hausa Mission; 1903–8 Resident, N. Nigeria; 1906 crossed the Sahara from Tripoli to Bornu; 1908–15 Director of Education, N. Nigeria; 1915–18 seconded to War Office; 1923–9 Secretary of the Secretary of State's Education Advisory Committee, Colonial Office; 1926–45 Hon. Secretary-General, International Institute of African Languages and Culture.

[3] Wallace, Sir William, K.C.M.G., 1856–1916; 1878 joined Royal Niger Company; became one of the Agent-Generals; 1900–1910 Resident-General and Deputy High Commissioner, Northern Nigeria.

E

larger emirates law enforcement should be left to the Emir's
unarmed police, or *dogarai*; and that what armed police were
needed in pagan areas should be directly under the control of the
Resident.[1] The Colonial Office was doubtful; matters which
appeared to affect the safety of the Europeans and the existence
of government stations were taken very seriously, and the matter
was held over for Girouard's report. This report[2] warmly endorsed
the proposals, but the officials were still worried; they considered
the factors influencing the men. The friction which had arisen
between Residents and Constabulary officers responsible to a
central Commandant made the former anxious to abolish the
latter; while the economies which this would effect, by throwing
the cost of law enforcement in the emirates onto the native
administrations, would naturally appeal to Girouard, struggling
desperately to frame estimates which would keep expenditure
within the £500,000 limit. Sanction was not given until Girouard,
on leave early in 1908, had personally convinced Lord Elgin.
Lugard, commenting from Hong Kong, queried the decision—he
felt the *dogarai* were 'impregnated with the old looting and
bribery and forced levy traditions'; he preferred European
efficiency and justice to the preservation of native institutions.[3]
The detachments of the W.A.F.F., which remained posted in the
provinces giving the Residents their necessary backing of force,
did not seem to have presented any problems to Residents; the
officers, on temporary secondment, were not brought into contact
with the Native Administrations and would have had no opportunity to disturb the Resident's political influence.

Girouard, however, did not respect the powers of the Emirs
because he trusted their loyalty: on the contrary. In his con-
fidential despatch giving the political reasons for a railway to
Kano, he stressed the possibility of a combination of the emirates
against the British. The situation was complicated, he argued,
by the fact that the Fulani were themselves conquerors; they were
not selected by the people, and were now dependent on British
support. This temporarily kept them loyal, but was not conducive
to the development of good government. He instanced the
Satiru revolt: this had clearly been planned for some time, so that

[1] Wallace to Elgin, 1 November, 1906, C.O. 446/55.
[2] Girouard to Elgin, 16 October, 1907, C.O. 446/65.
[3] Lugard to Girouard, 2 April, 1908, *Lugard Papers*, MSS. Brit. Emp. s.63.

either the Sokoto leaders did not know of the plans, and were thus dangerously out of touch with the people, or they knew of them but did not choose to warn the British, which took much of the value from their loyalty during the actual revolt. He felt this lack of loyalty was natural: ' It is only a repetition of experience elsewhere in the Empire where Mohammedan populations are ruled, and where even in those who have acquired great prosperity such as India and Egypt, an undoubted dislike for white and Christian rule outweighing with the people all benefits which may have accrued from it.' The dislike could only be overcome by the lapse of time during which ' the native institutions were to be retained and utilized for the government of the people through the agency of their own chiefs '. Unnecessary interference with the chiefs, especially by means of military expeditions, could only retard the development of peace and prosperity, and in an accompanying note to Antrobus, he wrote: ' Constant worrying patrols, even in the pagan countries, and attempts at injudicious taxation, will not do much good, and I am putting my foot down on both heavily.'[1]

A tour of the northern provinces at the end of 1908 made Girouard even more convinced of the suitability of the type of administration that was being practised. ' The general principles of administration advocated by Sir F. Lugard have been loyally carried out and his admirable series of Political Memoranda have been interpreted as, I think, he would have desired '. He found only one Resident, Palmer at Katsina, critical of the system. Palmer considered that the Fulani paid only lip service to British aims, and took the Resident's advice only through fear; while Lugard's ideal of the Resident as an adviser to the Emir with political rather than administrative functions was impossible. The people knew that the white men were the rulers, and the enforcement of the laws and ordinances of the Protectorate gave the Residents functions far in excess of that of mere residential adviser.

---

[1] Girouard to Elgin, 30 May, 1907, C.O. 446/63. A.C.G. Hastings, in *Nigerian Days*, p. 118 describes how, when as an Assistant Resident in Bauchi he subdued a hostile pagan group after a brief military encounter, he was discomfited at being censured, rather than commended, by Girouard. He therefore risked his life by demanding submission from the neighbouring group, having entered their village with only a small police escort; but he attributed his success to the fact that this group knew of the lesson their neighbours had been taught.

But Girouard, while granting some of these points, could see no better alternative.[1]

All that he saw in Northern Nigeria convinced Girouard that his most important task was to devise a land law which would prevent the disturbance or undermining of the existing society by any of the evils which had beset other British dependencies in which English land law had been applied. He had become interested in land questions, and had been studying the problems and attempted solutions in India, before he left for Northern Nigeria.[2] In his memoranda and despatches on the subject he referred to B. H. Baden-Powell's *The Land Systems of British India* (1892), and to Theodore Morison's *The Industrial Organization of an Indian Province* (1906). Morison, and perhaps Josiah Wedgwood (later Lord Wedgwood) who was a personal friend,[3] seem to have converted him to the doctrine of the nationalisation of land, and the imposition of the ' single tax ' on land. He wished to avoid creating on the one hand a landlord class, and on the other a freeholding peasantry who could mortgage and thus lose their land. The unjustified sale by chiefs of tribal lands, and the bringing of land disputes before courts applying English Common Law, must also be prevented. A Northern Nigerian law, he considered, should declare all land to be national land; there should be no freehold, but the use of the land should be granted according to custom. And in return each occupier should pay an ' economic rent ' which would provide the main income of the state, that is, the ' single tax '.

Soon after arrival in Northern Nigeria Girouard sent a memorandum to Residents asking for information on existing customs concerning land tenure and taxation. The replies confirmed his belief that private property in land was unknown, and that what he considered to be a feudal type of system existed in the emirates by which the supreme rights over land was vested in the Emir—previously in the Sultan of Sokoto—and delegated by

[1] Girouard to Crewe, 17 February, 1909, enclosing report of his northern tour, C.O. 446/82. Palmer later quoted from a letter he had received from Girouard at this time, which argued the desirability of upholding Fulani rule. *See* Sir Richmond Palmer, ' Some Observations on Captain Rattray's Papers ', *Journal of the African Society*, vol. XXXIII, January, 1934.
[2] C. W. Orr, *The Making of Northern Nigeria* (London, 1911), p. 190.
[3] See Strachey's comment on a Parliamentary question of Wedgwood's, that Wedgwood was a single taxer who had been raising land questions in and out of Parliament for some years, and was a friend of Girouard. 27 May, 1908, C.O. 446/78.

him through the various grades of chiefs down to the village head who allocated the use of the land in his village to the cultivators. The Residents also agreed that the system of taxation, which was being consolidated in the emirates from the existing Muslim taxes mainly on the produce of the land, but which was imposed as a poll tax in pagan areas, could be gradually transformed into a land rent.[1] He sent these conclusions to the Colonial Office, suggesting that, as neither he nor his administrative staff had had previous experience of the subject, an expert committee be appointed.[2] The officials were enthusiastic at such a statesmanlike attempt to settle the basic questions of land tenure, and the committee was soon formed, under the chairmanship of Sir Kenelm Digby, of officials of the Colonial Office, Council of India (Sir Digges La Touche and Theodore Morison) and Northern Nigeria (Temple and Orr, then on leave). Josiah Wedgwood was added at his own request. The members considered Girouard's memoranda, and Lugard's memorandum on taxation, interviewed Residents then on leave and commercial representatives, and came to conclusions which fully endorsed those of Girouard. Their Report[3] recommended a proclamation to the effect that ' the whole of the land of the Protectorate is under the control and dominion of the Government, and that no title to the occupation, use, or enjoyment of any land is valid without the assent of the Government ' and that it should also be declared that such control and dominion should be exercised ' with due regard to lawful customs proved to exist at present in the province or district where the land is situated '. The other recommendations on tenure concerned the protection of the occupant against government and individuals, and the principles for the grant of leases to non-natives.[4]

The Committee then went on to deal with revenue. While approving Lugard's measures of continuing the existing taxation but simplifying it into a single annual payment, they recommended

[1] Memorandum by Girouard, 2 November, 1907, in *Northern Nigeria Lands Committee: Minutes of Evidence and Appendices*, Cd. 5103 (1910), p. 4–27.

[2] Girouard to C.O., 24 April, 1908, C.O. 446/80. Girouard later told Lugard that he urged the appointment of a Colonial Office Committee so that the policy would appear to emanate from the Office and thus make later repudiation more difficult. Girouard to Lugard, 25 April, 1909, *Lugard Papers*, MSS. Brit. Emp. s.63.

[3] *Report of the Northern Nigeria Lands Committee, and Despatches Relating Thereto*, Cd. 5102 (1910).

[4] *Ibid.*, p. xxiii.

that in future taxes on agricultural produce be kept separate from those on trade and crafts, and be developed into an economic rent by which government could share in the increasing value of land. They recognised that such an alteration in the basis of the tax could not be made until staff was increased and land surveyed,[1] but even the political officers who spoke in their evidence of the difficulties such assessments would involve did not question that the aim of developing an economic rent was desirable. The Committee also recommended that, in the interim, the Resident should follow Lugard's policy of assessing a village as a whole, and leaving it to the headman to distribute the tax among individuals according to their wealth, rather than make individual assessments. It was agreed that a poll tax was the only possible form for the more primitive pagan societies, but the arguments in favour of a general system under which each man (or hut) should be taxed equally were discounted. This position was taken by Orr and Gowers,[2] who had had more experience of pagan areas, on the grounds that extortion by headmen was checked by it being widely known how much was due from each man.[3] The ex-Indian officials, supported strongly by Temple, stated that in the Muslim areas at least, the village officials should be given the responsibility of individual assessment, though political officers should always be ready to hear grievances.[4] The Committee also recommended, in agreement with Girouard's suggestion, that there should be an officer at Headquarters to coordinate assessment policy, though they warned of the disadvantages of appointing an Indian official, since Northern Nigeria should develop its own system in accordance with the customs and sentiment of the people.[5]

The main recommendations concerning land were incorporated into the Land and Native Rights Proclamation, No. 9 of 1910, which declared all land to be national land, with no right of freehold, and all rights of occupancy to derive from the government, which delegated its powers in most areas to the Native

---

[1] Ibid., paras. 44–6, pp. xiv–xvi.

[2] Gowers, (later Sir) William Frederick, K.C.M.G., 1875–1954; 1899–1902 British South Africa Company; 1902 Resident, N. Nigeria; 1921 Lieutenant-Governor, N. Nigeria; 1925–32 Governor, Uganda; 1932–8 Senior Crown Agent for the Colonies.

[3] Memorandum by Orr, Cd. 5103, pp. 55–6; and Minutes of Evidence, paras. 1078–9, pp. 100–1.

[4] Cd. 5102, para. 49, p. xvi.

[5] Ibid., para. 51, p. xvii.

Authority. But many of the recommendations, especially those concerning revenue, were left to be enforced administratively.

In what way did the findings of this Committee express, or influence, the development of Indirect Rule? The views of its members derived as much, if not more, from collectivist theories current in England at this time than from Northern Nigerian experience; the theorists saw in Northern Nigeria the field in which their theories could be applied. The emirates were considered as a feudal type of society, the pagan areas as exemplifying primitive forms of socialism, and the aim was to preserve both from an influx of European individualism which, it was beginning to be thought, had done so much harm in India, and to a lesser extent in the West African coastal colonies. An ordered society of status rather than contract was to be preserved, in which a paternalistic British government should provide the superior level, regulating the pace and nature of change, economic, social and political. The Native Administrations, however, whether the Emirs and their hierarchy, or the chiefs and elders of pagan communities, should retain two of the basic functions of government —the right to allot the use of the land, and the right to collect taxation.

The land measures were essentially designed to protect the *status quo*, and did not really alter the situation created by Lugard's earlier measures. He had wished to preserve the customary rights of the people with regard to land, and declared that non-natives could only lease land through the government. The question of the sale of land, or rather of the right of user, was, however, open to debate; Lugard was sufficient of a Victorian to consider that a system by which individuals could buy and sell such rights was a development in accordance with economic progress; the Committee did not. Palmer gave evidence that such sales were common in the city of Kano, as contracts between individuals without reference to the Emir's government, and that they were developing in the densely populated farmlands around Kano. He recommended that such sales be recognised, but that the government should receive the proceeds.[1] Lugard advocated a similar system of premiums to be paid to the government on the transfer of land, and also argued that provision should be made to alter village or

[1] Cd. 5103: Memo. by Palmer, 24 November 1907,, pp. 34–5; Minutes of Evidence, paras. 187–90, p. 69; para. 268, p. 71; para. 276, p. 72.

tribal boundaries in accordance with population changes.[1] This was a version of the problem of peaceful change, faced by all superior authorities who attempt to impose peace and order without full control of administrative and judicial procedures. In fact, the measure left the balance of power in land control to be worked out between British and African officials; Lugard, when later giving general approval to the measure, stated that, in his control of the land, the Native Authority should be supervised and guided by the British staff towards the encouragement and protection of small holdings and permanent improvements, and the curtailment of shifting cultivation.[2] Later criticisms of the land system of Northern Nigeria apply more to the lack of such administrative control by British officials, and perhaps of amendments to the law, than to its original passage.[3]

The taxation proposals were far more revolutionary. Lugard had introduced considerable changes, both in British colonial policy and in Northern Nigerian practice, but he could claim that his procedure was based on the existing Muslim system. The Colonial Office, fearful since the Sierra Leone Hut Tax disturbances of 1898 of imposing direct taxation in West African colonies, had been persuaded by this argument, combined with the fact that there seemed no other way of ensuring that this prosperous but largely self-sufficient agricultural territory could begin to pay for its own administration. Many of the local officials came to accept Lugard's more sweeping notions of the benefits of direct taxation,[4] in particular two ideas: first, that only by paying taxes does the individual or group really acknowledge the authority of the government, and second, that only by personally assessing villages does a political officer really get to know the people and the country. They argued that Muslim rulers had imposed regular taxation, and most pagan tribes were familiar with the idea of paying tribute to an overlord; it was necessary for political as well

---

[1] Memorandum by Lugard, enclosed in Orr to C.O., 5 October, 1910. C.O. 446/95. Temple and Orr had shown the draft proclamation to Lugard when all were in England on leave during 1910, and Lugard, just before returning to Hong Kong, sent this memo. to Orr, who forwarded it to the C.O. The Office were doubtful about this procedure, and while considering Lugard's points to be interesting, decided that the proclamation could not be reconsidered.

[2] Lugard, *Dual Mandate*, p. 301.

[3] *E.g.* Perham, *Native Administration*, p. 315.

[4] See Lugard, Memo. No. 5: Taxation (1906), printed in Cd. 5103, p. 112, esp. para. 3; Lugard, *Dual Mandate*, p. 232 ff; Perham, *Lugard II*, pp. 165–6, 315.

as financial reasons for the British administration to control the system and make it equitable. Lugard's system provided for two main innovations in the emirates: the consolidation of a number of dues into a single annual tax, and the assessment of villages by British officers. The village headman was to be responsible for the division of the total tax to which the village had been assessed between individuals, and for its collection. He passed the receipts up through the hierarchy of the Emir's government, and the Emir and Resident decided the proportions to be made over to village and district heads.[1] The evidence before the Committee gives most interesting information on how the system was actually being worked, and the means by which the Resident gradually extended his control, means which varied considerably from province to province. For Sokoto, Temple spoke of his methods of assessing villages, and the political skill needed to extract information from native officials;[2] for Kano, where the Muslim system had been most fully developed, Palmer stated that the headmen continued to collect the traditional amounts, the Resident, in consultation with the Emir, supervising from above;[3] for Bornu, Hewby described annual gatherings of headmen and their consultation with Shehu and Resident over the amounts due from each.[4]

The changes, then, though giving the British official a direct role in the functions of the Emir's government, were being introduced gradually in accordance with the conditions of each province, and would appear to the people as adaptations of the old, rather than as entirely new, systems. The basic principle, that a regular proportion of the crops grown should be given to the headman as the share of the government, remained. To introduce instead a system based on the amount of land cultivated meant a far more fundamental alteration. All land, it was recognised, would have to be surveyed; problems presented by shifting cultivation solved, rates worked out for different classes of land. How an ' economic rent ' was to be determined was never discussed. These were practical difficulties: the real surprise at such an aim being accepted by Girouard and the Residents is caused by the fact that to organize such a system must entail direct rule by the British, and could never be represented as ' ruling on native

[1] Lugard, Taxation Memo., paras. 38–43, Cd. 5103, pp. 121–2.
[2] Cd. 5103, Minutes of Evidence, paras. 609, p. 84 ff.
[3] Ibid., paras, 204, p. 69 ff.
[4] Ibid., p. 60.

lines '. Though Africans might be trained to operate such a system—and classes to train mallams as surveyors were amongst the first instituted at the Nassarawa schools[1]—they would have to be taught European methods of keeping land records, calculating taxes, judging between different classes of land. Yet a beginning was made in Kano, it appears, and was contemplated in Ilorin,[2] before the whole concept dropped into obscurity. For Lugard disapproved; to the practical disadvantages he added the argument that to declare a rent upon land would lead the African—and other critics—to assume that the government was expropriating the land.[3]

The Report of the Committee could perhaps be said to have had more practical effect in London than in Northern Nigeria. Apart from the ' single tax ' aim it did little more than express the policy and practice with regard to land and taxation which was being followed in Northern Nigeria. It was the Colonial Office which was converted to the desirability of formulating both general policies and comprehensive laws on land tenure suitable to conditions in Africa, and in 1912 the West African Lands Committee was appointed, under the same chairman, to deal with the problems in the other West African colonies. A great deal of evidence was collected for the Committee before it was dissolved in 1915 owing to the war.

Girouard did not appear to have given much thought to the question of what should be done with the revenue, once collected, and accepted Lugard's decision that the amounts should be divided equally between Emirs and the central government; the Sultan of Sokoto keeping three-quarters of the proceeds of his territory as recognition of his superior status, and pagan administrations keeping, mostly, only a quarter. Wallace considered the matter needed attention; in a private letter to Strachey he referred to his correspondence with Burdon at Sokoto who ' nearly went daft because I sent a circular to the Residents asking their views on the subject of payment to the Emirs and suggested that they [the Emirs] should receive no further advance on the large sums now paid them until the Government's share had reached a third of the

---

[1] Annual Report, 1910–11, p. 17.
[2] Annual Report, 1910–11, p. 36–7, and 1911, p. 28–9; see also Memo. by Palmer on Taxation in Ilorin Province, enclosed in Temple to Harcourt, 18 August, 1911, C.O. 446/99.
[3] Lugard, *Dual Mandate*, pp. 237 and 291.

whole. He accused me of being a direct ruler, etc., and wrote me a 70 para. minute. . . . Far better had Sir Percy attempted to settle an important matter such as this instead of raising a land question for which there was no hurry and which could easily have been settled by applying the same law to the natives as was then in force against non-natives viz. that neither could obtain freehold in land.'[1]

Girouard had, however, given his permission for one of the most important experiments of these years—Palmer's development of the Native Treasury at Katsina. He persuaded the Emir to provide a budget for his share of the revenue, converting his retainers into salaried officials.[2] The idea dated back to Lugard and was accepted by all the Residents—none of the concepts of Indirect Rule envisaged a Native Administration whose finances were not open to British supervision. When this question had arisen in the evidence before the Land Committee, and Temple was asked his opinion of the desirability of the members of the Emirs' government becoming salaried officials, he had replied ' We are all agreed on that point '.[3] The Committee had approved the principle,[4] and it would seem that Palmer began the system in 1908, though it was not reported officially to London until the Annual Report of 1910–11.

This interval was probably due in some part to the change of governors: in 1909 Girouard was appointed Governor of East Africa and was succeeded by Sir Hesketh Bell, who came from governing Uganda. Bell was a more orthodox Colonial official than his predecessors, and was content to follow a policy which was showing itself to be so successful, and to be guided on all matters concerning native administration by his Residents, Temple in particular. The finances of the Protectorate, however, were a matter of concern to him, and the question of the Emirs' share of the revenue was one of the few subjects which he took up of his own accord. In his despatch accompanying his estimates for 1911–12 he discussed the methods of dividing the land revenue between Emir and government. In Bornu, he reported, it had

---

[1] Wallace to Strachey, 8 March, 1910, filed with Wallace to C.O., 31 May, 1910, C.O. 446/95.
[2] Palmer gave an account of the early development to Miss Perham; *see Native Administration*, p. 71.
[3] Cd. 5103, Minutes of Evidence, para. 683, p. 88.
[4] Cd. 5102, para. 54, p. xvii.

been insisted that the Shehu pay over the total amount, and then
receive back the Native Administration share, distributing it
under the Resident's supervision. But in most other emirates the
Emir had been required only to pay over the government share.
The latter system, he considered (and quoted the agreement of
Temple and other senior Residents) ' makes it appear that the
whole of the taxes raised on land are the property of the native
Ruler, and that the proportion payable to the British government
is in the nature of a *tribute* paid in consideration of protection '.
Bell desired to have the total revenue listed as part of the Protectorate revenue, and the share retained by the Native Authorities
treated as grants in aid of Native Administrations. Lugard and
Girouard had both desired that the native administration officials
should be paid regular salaries, he wrote, and the creation of
Native Treasuries should now make this possible. The Residents
assumed that the Native Administrations needed all the revenue
that they could raise, but Bell seemed here to consider that fixed
salaries would make possible fixed grants to Native Administrations, while all increases in revenue should swell the finances of
the central government. But he considered that ' the question is
one that will require the most delicate treatment, and its adjustment will affect in a great degree, the relations which will
exist in the future between the Native Chiefs and the Government.'[1]

In his first Annual Report Bell described the development of
the Native Treasuries, and spoke of the extension of the system
from Katsina and Kano to the rest of the Protectorate. It should
regulate the expenditure and consolidate the rank and authority
of the Emirs and chiefs, and should make the judiciary less liable
to corruption. He admitted, however, that it could hardly be
expected to be popular with Emirs who thus lost their unfettered
control of the revenue.[2] The development of Treasuries meant, in
fact, that the Resident, who had taken on the responsibility of
raising the revenue, now assumed the responsibility of spending it :
by introducing western methods of estimating and accounting,
in however rudimentary a form, he made the treasury clerks
responsible to him, not the Emir. The Emirs were allowed salaries
which, by the standards of chiefs in other parts of Africa, were

[1] Bell to Harcourt, 19 December, 1910, C.O. 446/92.
[2] Annual Report, 1910–11, p. 4.

large; this enabled them to live in traditional splendour, keep large households, and presumably bestow favours where they desired. But all expenditure outside this allowance had to be approved by the Resident. His control over emirate funds was thus established, but the control of the central government over the Residents proved more difficult; Bell was unable to devise a satisfactory financial division and Lugard's attempts at control were later thwarted.[1]

In common with all reformers aiming to create an improved society and government, the administrative officers considered that attempts to transform adult men into efficient, honest and disinterested rulers were not likely to be rewarded, and pinned their hopes on the next generation. Education of the young, and particularly of the sons of chiefs, should implant the proper ideals of truth and service to their people, as well as loyalty to the British crown. This was one of Lugard's primary aims, and though the necessity of first establishing a stable administration, together with the lack of funds, did not permit him to create a system of government education, his ideas were followed, at least at first, by those who did.[2]

Consideration of education in African colonies in these years was impossible to divorce from consideration of the position of missions, for nineteenth century evangelism had played so great a part in the opening of Africa to Europeans, and British government had so frequently arrived after the missions had opened their schools. The government's role in education had been seen, during the latter part of the nineteenth century on the West African coast, as assisting mission schools by subsidy and inspection. But by the twentieth century attitudes were changing, and mission education had to face severe criticism. The scientific theories of the period, and especially the popular versions of Darwinism, laid stress on the racial differences between Africans and Europeans, and asserted that attempts to educate a race of black Englishmen would only lead to the corruption of the

---

[1] Perham, *Lugard II*, pp. 480–5.
[2] The London University Ph.D. thesis of Miss Sonia Graham (Mrs. Parkinson), entitled 'A History of Education in relation to the development of the Protectorate of Northern Nigeria, 1900–1919, with special reference to the work of Hanns Vischer ' (1955), discusses the whole question very thoroughly and, using mission as well as government records, is able to give a picture of the progress of European education in pagan as well as Muslim areas.

African nature. Africans should be encouraged to develop ' on
native lines ' and not be treated as identical with the European.
The missions themselves were suffering from a lack of self-
confidence in their methods of education, and were sensitive to the
criticism that their boys respected neither traditional nor British
ideals.

Lugard was not dogmatic in his attitude to missions; his
experience covered a wide section of Africa and he had come to
believe that the character of the missionary was the most important
factor in judging the value of a particular mission. It was therefore important that he was impressed by the character of Dr.
Walter Miller, the leading member of the group of Church
Missionary Society men who wished to work among the Hausa in
Northern Nigeria. So, while Lugard found it necessary to prevent
the C.M.S. from opening stations in Kano, their main objective,
on grounds first of the safety of the missionaries and later because
of his pledge to the Emirs not to interfere with their religion, he
regarded this prohibition as temporary. In 1903 the C.M.S.
opened a station in Muslim, but non-Hausa, Bida, with the con-
currence of the Emir, who in 1904 sent his sons to their school.[1]
Lugard stated that at his special request a class for teaching
mallams to write in Roman character instead of Arabic had been
instituted. In 1905 Miller's Hausa mission transferred to the
city of Zaria, and Lugard wrote enthusiastically of its progress and
prospects.[2] In the same report he discussed his aims for education
in Northern Nigeria. He regarded four types of education as
necessary—first, for the mallams, already educated along Koranic
lines, who should be taught Hausa in the Roman script, English,
arithmetic and geography to fit them to be officials in the native
administrations and teachers in primary schools; second, for sons
of chiefs who should be boarders in a school where they would be
brought up in an ' atmosphere of loyalty to the King, and imbued
with ideas of truthfulness and honesty, so that the next generation
of native rulers may be enlightened and loyal, without necessarily
foregoing their own religion, or imbibing ideas of European dress
and habits unsuited to their environment, which would cause
them to lose influence and caste among their Mohammedan
subjects; ' third, general primary schools on a secular basis; and

[1] Annual Report, 1903, p. 18, and 1904, pp. 124–5.
[2] Annual Report, 1905–6, pp. 118–19.

fourth, cantonment schools for children of government clerks, mostly Christians from the coast.[1]

Lugard conferred with Miller about implementing these aims, and in September 1906 (after his resignation had been accepted) he wrote to the Colonial Office recommending that Miller's proposal for a school in Zaria for mallams and sons of chiefs, drawn from the Hausa areas as a whole, should be supported by the government and given a small subsidy. Miller had promised to co-operate with the aims of the government and with the local Resident, had agreed not to proselytise in school hours, but to encourage his pupils to keep Muslim observances. Yet, Lugard, reported, Miller ' relied greatly on my personal influence both with the Emirs, and with Residents, to obtain the pupils and he fears that the former and some of the latter may not view the proposals with favour '. Lugard went on to say that of course if the government could open its own schools the difficulties caused by Christian missionaries teaching Muslims would disappear; but that Northern Nigeria did not have the money for this, and the only man in the administration capable of running such schools would be Hanns Vischer. Elgin and Churchill were both concerned that Muslims might be antagonised, yet they decided that Lugard's judgment was to be trusted and that the Northern Nigeria government should be instructed to assist Miller's schemes.[2]

Miller had reason to fear the effect of Lugard's departure. Wallace reported that although he had secured the consent of the Emirs of Kontagora, Katsina and Zaria to sending their sons to Miller's school, they were clearly unwilling to carry out their undertaking, and he enclosed letters from Residents stating that they considered it unwise to ask Emirs to send their sons to another city to be educated by Christian missionaries. Miller's defence of his proposals was also enclosed, but his tone had become less tolerant, and his reference to the support commanded by the C.M.S. in England did not please the Colonial Office. Elgin regretted that he had ever sanctioned the scheme, and government support for it came to an end.[3]

Miller opened a day school along the proposed lines in May,

[1] Annual Report, 1905–6, pp. 119–20.
[2] Lugard to C.O., 26 September, 1906, C.O. 446/60.
[3] Wallace to Elgin, 1 April, 1907, with enclosures from Miller (6 January), Temple (11 January), Festing (21 January) and Palmer (26 January), C.O. 446/62.

1907, with fifteen boys from Zaria, and he continued his mallams' school. Official reports became less enthusiastic about the success of the school, numbers declined, and in 1910 it became a conventional C.M.S. school with teaching aimed at conversion to Christianity.[1] Missions and mission schools in pagan areas were however officially encouraged by the government, whether from a real belief in their utility or from the desire to divert them from Muslim areas. There were a number of stations opened along the Niger and Benue, and in the pagan areas of Bauchi, by the C.M.S. and the Sudan United Mission in particular, but the region was difficult to penetrate, as a result of both geographic and human factors, and success in these years was slight.

Girouard went to Northern Nigeria with a mind already influenced against allowing Christian missionaries to enter Muslim areas and ready to accept Lugard's ideas of government education. Soon after arrival he circulated a memorandum on education amongst the Residents which enclosed a speech of Cromer's arguing for the exclusion of missions from the Muslim Sudan, and Girouard, supporting this, stated that he was 'absolutely opposed to their [the missions] having any educational functions with or without government assistance. . . . The way to the future regeneration of these peoples will best be opened by the teachings of the missionaries now working in the guise and garb of the ordinary British officer, civil and military'. He reported to the Colonial Office that the Residents were unanimous in their support of this position; yet they all agreed that government education had become a necessity, especially as 'the imminent advance of the railway, bringing in its train 20th century Europe to 10th century Hausaland, imperatively necessitated that the latter shall be prepared by education, as far as time will allow, to meet the changes the former will thrust upon it '.[2]

One attempt at government education had been made. Burdon, when Resident at Sokoto, had opened a school in 1905 in which boys, mainly sons of leading families who had already received some Koranic education, were taught Roman script and English subjects by a mallam whom Burdon himself had taken to England for training. Girouard regarded the school as a successful experiment, having in 1907 thirty-six pupils, and stated that a similar

---

[1] See Graham, op. cit., Ch. III.
[2] Girouard to Elgin, 31 October, 1907 (with enclosures), C.O. 446/65.

scheme had been proposed for Katsina but that no teacher had yet been found.[1]

Further consideration of the question led Girouard to agree with Lugard that education in Muslim areas should be placed in charge of Hanns Vischer, the young Resident of Swiss origin, who first came to Northern Nigeria as a missionary, and who had already become prominent for this journey across the Sahara from Tripoli to Bornu in 1906.[2] He was a brilliant linguist, and Girouard reported on his suitability for the position because of his sympathetic insight into African minds, and his fluency in the Arabic, Hausa, Kanuri and Fulani languages.[3]

The Colonial Office had no criticisms to make of Girouard's proposals, and agreed that Vischer should tour Egypt, the Sudan and West African coastal colonies before formulating his plan. This tour took place early in 1909;[4] Vischer found much to criticise in the English-style education offered in Egypt and Lagos, but he was warm in his praise of the educational system in the Sudan. There the methods had been ' sytematically adapted to the conditions of the country and the feeling of the people ' by developing the existing Muslim schools. The success he attributed basically to the high standard of the staff, who nearly all ' held scholarships at some University at home while several of them are Gold Medallists. Such men will of course readily study the condition of the people they have to deal with and learn to see and think from the Native point of view '.

Vischer then stated his aims for Northern Nigeria:

' 1st. Develop the national and racial characteristics of the natives on such lines as will enable them to use their own moral and physical forces to the best advantage.

' 2nd. Widen their mental horizon without destroying their respect for race and parents.

' 3rd. Supply men for employment under Government.

' 4th. Produce men that will be able to carry on the Native Administration in the spirit of the Government.

[1] *Ibid.*
[2] See Graham, *op. cit.*, Ch. IV.
[3] Girouard to Crewe, 22 July, 1908, C.O. 446/74.
[4] Vischer's reports of his tour, of his general scheme for education in Northern Nigeria, and of his progress to date were enclosed in Bell to Crewe, 30 March, 1910, C.O. 446/89. There was no official report to the Secretary of State on education between Girouard's proposal to second Vischer in July, 1908, and this report on schools already established in March, 1910.

F

' 5th. Impart sufficient knowledge of Western ideas to enable the native to meet the influx of traders, etc., from the coast with the advent of the railway, on equal terms.

' 6th. Avoid creating a " Babu Class ".

' 7th. Avoid encouraging the idea readily formed by the African that it is more honourable to sit in an office than to earn a living by manual labour, by introducing at the earliest opportunity technical instruction side by side with purely clerical teaching.'

For his types of schools, Vischer followed Lugard's proposals. Working at Nassarawa on the outskirts of Kano, he had established by March, 1910, a school for mallams and one for sons of chiefs. The 35 mallams from several of the emirates he taught himself; they were being trained as teachers for elementary schools, and as officials for the native administrations. The 31 chiefs' sons were receiving most of their lessons from the more advanced mallams; a four-year course was planned, with two years of teaching in the vernacular and two years in English, in which they should receive a sound education in the three R's ' along with such special instruction as may be found necessary to train men able to understand and carry out the duties of the Native Administration under the Government '. As teachers became available, elementary schools were to be founded, or rather adapted from existing Koranic schools, throughout the country, whose brighter pupils could continue at primary, technical and agricultural schools. A secondary school was to be established when pupils were available. Vischer's funds were extremely limited; the education estimates of the central government for 1910–11 allowed £1,795 which covered only the salary and allowances of Vischer and one assistant, Urhling-Smith, whom Vischer had persuaded to transfer from the Sudan. All other funds had to come from the Native Administrations and from fees; the Emir of Kano was paying £1,000 which was to cover the costs of African teachers, buildings, religious instructors and subsistence for mallams and apprentices. Men of the leading families were to pay fees for their sons, and it was intended that the elementary schools should be supported by fees and the local Native Administrations. The cost of equipment and of salary for a European instructor was the major obstacle to the establishment of a technical workshop.

When forwarding these reports, Bell declared himself whole-heartedly in favour of the policy of excluding missions from the Muslim areas, and of developing education along the lines proposed. ' I am informed by those who know the country well,' he wrote, ' that, in spite of all our efforts to impress upon the chiefs and peoples of the Moslem territories our earnest desire to work with them for their own welfare, all our efforts are viewed with the greatest suspicion. The Fulani especially appear to entertain a deeprooted distrust of our intentions, and it is, perhaps, only natural that they should hate us for having broken their power, and reduced them to the condition of practical impotence in which they now find themselves. They fear that schools organized by Europeans are an indirect attack on their religion, and it is believed that a considerable period must elapse before they are brought to realise the honesty and disinterestedness of our efforts.'[1]

In these proposals the emphasis of the ' on native lines ' policy was placed on the methods of education; the content was to be mainly English, and it was definitely intended to train boys for employment with the central as well as the local governments. The native administrations, with such officials, should develop along English lines of efficiency, honesty, and ordered finances. Vischer, as well as Lugard, considered that the schools for chiefs' sons should be modelled on the English public school, and although such a policy helped to preserve the Fulani as a self-conscious ruling élite, the method could hardly be regarded as ' on native lines '. However much the missionaries were criticised for destroying respect for traditional authorities and behaviour, and the need declared to be the adaption rather than the uprooting of customary life, there were no doubts expressed that the succeeding generations of Africans should be educated to adopt many of the ideals and techniques of western civilisation. The real difference from missionary education lay in the fact that it was the political officer who determined what should be preserved and what adapted, and that his decisions were based on principles less explicit than those of the missionaries. The authority of the Residents was built into the system from the beginning; Bell recommended that Vischer and his assistant remain as seconded political officers rather than have a separate departmental structure created for them, for ' it has been represented to me, both by the

[1] Bell to Crewe, 30 March, 1910, C.O. 446/89.

Resident of Kano Province [Temple] and by the Director of Education that, in view of the close connection which the officers of the Education Department would have with the natives, it is very advisable that they should, if possible, both be in some degree under the supervision and control of the Principal Administrative Officer of the Province in which they work.'[1] The schools being established in other provinces (Bauchi, as well as Sokoto, had its own school for ' chiefs' sons ') were directly under the control of the Residents. Therefore, as the opinion of the Residents tended to harden, in the following years, against the introduction of almost any European influences, the educational system was directly affected. When Temple wrote on Northern Nigerian education in 1918 he expressed very different opinions from those of ten years earlier: ' I regret to say that classes have been formed recently with the avowed object of training pupils to become clerks. This I need hardly say appears to be directly opposed to the system of Indirect Rule through Native Administrations and the policy of assisting the native to develop on his own lines.'[2]

Girouard, then, was concerned with establishing policies for land tenure, taxation and education which would recognize African practice in these fields, and adapt rather than undermine it. Bell supported the policy; and both Governors relied to a large extent on the advice of the Residents. On the question of establishing what African practice was, the Resident was unchallenged. In the problems of day-to-day administration Residents were still guided by Lugard's Political Memoranda; neither Governor reported any of the problems of native administration in which there was no financial content in other than very general terms. One of the more surprising omissions from the official correspondence is that of the Kano troubles in 1908. When Girouard reported on his northern tour of early 1909, he stated that Kano was the most restless of the emirates; ' political troubles ' had been caused by lack of continuity in officials there, and by the tendency which had grown up for British officials to deal directly with native subordinates, thus decreasing the power of the Emir.[3] Strachey gave further information when the question arose of

[1] Bell to Crewe, 30 March, 1910, C.O. 446/89.
[2] Temple, *Native Races*, p. 222.
[3] Girouard to Crewe, 17 February, 1909, C.O. 446/82. His solution was to move Temple from Sokoto to Kano.

invaliding the former Resident, Dr. Cargill: ' Major Burdon tells me that he cannot account for his [Cargill's] erratic behaviour while in charge of Kano on any other supposition than that he was not all right mentally. He authorised an assessment of part of the Kano province on an absurdly high basis, and the attempt to enforce it led to bloodshed and gave Sir P. Girouard serious misgivings at one time as to the safety of our position at Kano. There were also other curious incidents, such as the destruction of all the old provincial records, which seems an extraordinary thing for a sane man to do.'[1] The Annual Report for 1907–8 mentions that in Kano Province the military was called upon to render assistance on six occasions, and that the telegraph was wilfully cut several times, yet gives an overall picture of peace and progress in the province.[2] The Colonial Office did not remark on the lack of official information on such troubles in this most important of the provinces.

In 1910 Temple was promoted to the new position of Chief Secretary and from January to August 1911 administered the government while Bell was on extended leave. His greater interest in, and knowledge of, provincial administration was immediately demonstrated to the Colonial Office. In particular, he began to send extracts from the Provincial Reports, with his own comments upon them, to the Secretary of State.

The reports from the major emirates were mainly accounts of more thorough assessment for taxation, the establishment of Native Treasuries, the increasingly efficient working of native courts and emirate police. A reflection of Temple's policy would seem to be shown in the stress each Resident placed on the need for political officers to spend much of their time touring, though when the report from Ilorin spoke of increasing decentralisation of administration to allow officers to spend more time in the districts, Temple pointed out the need for political officers on tour to take care not to settle complaints without reference to the Emir.[3] The Resident of Zaria told of the time spent in educating the District and Village Heads in their new roles, and Temple expressed the view that this was the most important task of the

[1] Minute on Cargill to C.O., 19 October 1908, C.O. 446/80.
[2] Annual Report, 1907–8, p. 39.
[3] Temple to Harcourt, 31 July, 1911, enclosing extracts from report on Ilorin Province, C.O. 446/98.

political officer.[1] The views of the Residents on Fulani rule differed, however, according to personality and to local conditions. Palmer, at Kano, was now the most enthusiastic on Indirect Rule: ' The more the machinery which controls this large emirate of 2,000,000 people is studied, the plainer, I think, it will appear that an alien administration could never satisfactorily replace it, or exercise that moral control over the less advanced members of the community which, founded on common beliefs and the traditions of centuries, make the wish of their Emir law.'[2] But from Yola came the report that despite the cooperative attitude of the new young Emir, the Yola Fulani were lazy, and the District Heads weak and inefficient. Native courts outside the capital needed close supervision to guard against corruption.[3] And from Bornu, Hewby who had been in charge since 1903 was, Temple considered, unduly pessimistic concerning the Native Administration. He stated that the Shehu and chiefs were not really more useful than they had been eight years before; they showed no initiative or zeal for progress. Extortion by District Heads was rife, and many of the Courts untrustworthy.[4] There was no suggestion from any Resident, however, that any changes in the system of administration were needed.

There must have been many points of contact between Resident and Emir which were not mentioned in these reports. There was, for example, the staffing of native administrations. It was accepted that the Emir had control of all appointments, but his right to dismiss men he considered to be lacking in loyalty to him was equally important to the maintenance of his power. A fascinating account of how the Emir of Zaria maintained his authority in this field has been given by Dr. M. G. Smith,[5] but the solution of these problems was left, it would seem, for each Resident to solve according to local conditions. The requirement that District Heads should live in their districts which dated from the inauguration of Lugard's rule must still have been causing disputes, but this, also, finds no mention in these reports.

[1] Temple to Harcourt, 17 July, 1911, enclosing extracts from report on Zaria Province, C.O. 446/98.
[2] Temple to Harcourt, 17 March, 1911, enclosing extracts from report on Kano Province 446/98.
[3] Temple to Harcourt, 20 July, 1911, enclosing extracts from report on Yola Province, C.O. 446/98.
[4] Temple to Harcourt, 26 July, 1911, enclosing extracts from report on Bornu Province, C.O. 446/98.
[5] M. G. Smith, *Government in Zazzau*, (London, 1960), pp. 207–22.

The reports from the pagan areas showed a different emphasis. Assessment and collection of taxation were still the main functions of political officers, but the work was done by getting in touch with each small group individually, and not through an existing machinery. Temple disagreed with the Resident of Kabba's statement that each family among his primarily Igala and Idoma people was a law unto itself, and requested him to do more to discover what held the tribes together and to use such machinery in administration.[1] It was admitted by the Resident of Muri that in the administration of the Munshi (as the Tiv people were then called) indirect methods were the aim and not the reality.[2] And in Bassa province, where Temple praised the rapid growth of effective administration, he did not comment on the report that while it had been attempted to rule through local tribal elders, alien District Headmen had had to be appointed in most districts who had proved much more successful.[3] Revenue figures were commonly taken as the yardstick by which to measure the success of the administration, both because they indicated progress towards financial self-sufficiency, and because of the general belief that only by paying taxes did the African acknowledge himself to be under the control of the government.[4] The riverain pagan areas were the chief source of Northern Nigeria's exports —wild rubber, palm oil and kernels, and shea butter and nuts formed almost half the exports for 1910–11[5]—and the reports stress the value of closer administration as making possible an extension of trade, though the increases in these years were in fact slight. These reports on the mainly pagan provinces indicate that a division was growing up between the Muslim and pagan areas both in the staff and the methods, and that the larger northern emirates were the prestige posts. Indirect rule might be argued as the aim for the southern section, but direct methods were recognized as the necessary expedient. The status of posts in the emirates increased under a natural momentum: only the five northern provinces of Sokoto, Kano, Bornu, Bauchi and Zaria

[1] Temple to Harcourt, 17 July, 1911, enclosing extracts from report on Kabba Province, C.O. 446/98.

[2] Temple to Harcourt, 17 July, 1911, enclosing extracts from report on Muri province, C.O. 446/98.

[3] Temple to Harcourt, 6 June, 1911, enclosing extracts from report on Bassa Province, C.O. 446/98.

[4] *E.g.* Report on Muri Province, *loc. cit.*

[5] Annual Report, 1910–11, pp. 12–13.

were to have First Class Residents (an alteration of Lugard's earlier proposals of reorganizing the whole Protectorate into eight large provinces, each under a First Class Resident) and these men were the main advisors to the Governor.

One of the results of this increasing division between the two parts of the Protectorate was that the senior Residents were willing to allow European missionaries and traders much greater opportunities in pagan areas than in the emirates; for example, Temple favoured proposals for the exploitation of the forests in Bassa province by European concessionaires.[1] There would seem to have been a number of reasons for this: that the riverain areas, especially along the Benue, were those which the Niger Company had already penetrated, and whose exports were important; that there were not the strong native authorities whose collapse would disturb large areas; that pagan social organization was thought less worthy of protection. Temple's arguments for encouraging missions in these areas later came to be: ' The primitive pagan is a very robust fellow mentally as well as physically. . . . There is little danger of his losing his characteristics readily . . . it requires nothing short of the full weight of Government machinery to create a decadent condition in the case of such robust constitutions as these.'[2] But in these earlier years he was not concerned to preserve pagan characteristics. When reporting the deposition of a chief on the Bauchi plateau who, on conversion to Christianity, refused to carry out the customary rituals, he praised the acceptance by the convert of the consequences of his new religion. ' This spirit—in view of the ultra-conservative nature of the Pagan as regards most of his tribal customs—should it spread, may lead to great results in the near future, and mean a very much more rapid advance up the ' steep slope of civilization ' than has ever been hoped for on the part of these primitive peoples.' It was the new Parliamentary Under-Secretary, Lord Lucas, who commented ' I hope it will be a lesson to all future chiefs '.[3]

The Colonial Office, in fact, had become complete converts to the idea of Indirect Rule and the necessity of preserving customary institutions—possibly they were more enthusiastic than the men

[1] Temple to Harcourt, 6 June, 1911, enclosing extracts from report on Bassa Province, C.O. 446/98.
[2] Temple, *Native Races*, p. 216.
[3] Temple to Harcourt, 1 June, 1911, C.O. 446/98.

who dealt with the practical difficulties. Though there had been criticism of Lugard's swift assumption of authority over the whole Protectorate, his political settlement with the Emirs had always been approved.[1] The years of comparative peace and order which followed showed the advantages of a system in which full sovereignty had been explicitly assumed from the inception of the Protectorate over one in which treaties with native rulers left the extent of British powers in dispute, and where the rights of the government in, for example, Abeokuta, were constantly being challenged by African lawyers and such bodies as the Aborigines Protection Society. Other aspects of Lugard's system which had been regarded at first with some doubt had been proved to work well; for example, the introduction of direct taxation and the control of the administrative officers over the Native and Provincial Courts.[2] Above all, the system was admired for its efficiency and economy. But a major reason for the Colonial Office encouragement of the exercise of such large powers by administrative officers was the lack of pressures towards any other system. The Niger Company, and the lesser traders, were content to work within the system, for there was no prospect of quick returns to be gained if there were greater freedom from administrative regulation. The boom in tin mining in 1910 which led to the establishment of a large number of companies and the influx of a considerable number of Europeans caused the Office a number of problems; but the fact that the tin was on the remote Bauchi plateau, inhabited by small pagan groups amongst whom the full doctrine of Indirect Rule had never been possible, meant that the native administrations of the major part of the Protectorate were unaffected. But even here, though the Colonial Office at first regarded favourably proposals that private capital should build a

[1] *E.g.* after the Satiru revolt proved the loyalty of the emirs, Antrobus wrote: ' The management of these native chiefs is Sir F. Lugard's strong point.' On Lugard to Elgin, 28 February, 1906, C.O. 446/52.

[2] When Wallace, as Acting High Commissioner after Lugard's departure, proposed that the duty of reviewing Provincial Court sentences should pass to the Chief Justice while he (Wallace) was on tour, Cox, the C.O. Legal adviser, stated that he had always considered that this should be a duty of the Chief Justice. But Antrobus defended the practice of review by the High Commissioner which, he said, had been decided upon in 1898 by Lugard, Goldie, Wingfield and himself. ' It seemed to us then that it would be impracticable, and probably dangerous, to give to a judicial officer the power of revising everything that the Residents might do in their judicial capacity; especially as judges in a Colony are not usually as discreet and wise as one would wish them to be.' Minutes on Wallace to Elgin, 1 November, 1906, C.O. 446/55.

railway to the mines,[1] they were quickly converted by Northern
Nigerian protests to the necessity for such a line to be built and
controlled by the government—in particular, no-one but a
political officer should recruit the necessary labour.[2] In general,
the Office expected the economic development of the Protectorate
to be slow, and were willing to place political considerations,
aimed at ensuring peace and order most economically, over
economic ones.[3]

While it was the clear system of control exercised by Lugard
and his officers over both African and European which first
impressed the officials, during Girouard's governorship they were
increasingly enthusiastic about the idea of ruling ' on native
lines ', of preserving and adapting the indigenous political systems,
and taking care not to allow the erosion of the Native Authorities.

An early example of enthusiasm for the positive role of government in controlling social and economic change was the reaction
to Girouard's proposals for the establishment of a Committee to
advise on the land law. ' We have undoubtedly a great opportunity
in Northern Nigeria. We have caught our land system young
there, and now is the time to confirm it in a straight and proper
growth and to profit negatively by the experience of the older
West African Colonies, and both negatively and positively by the
experience of India.'[4] When Vischer's proposals for education
came before the Office, Strachey considered them ' so reasonable
and so well thought out that the S. of S. need have no hesitation
in sanctioning them as a scheme of which the details are to be
filled in in the future.'[5] When in 1910, not only Girouard but also
Burdon and Orr, the senior Residents, had left Northern Nigeria,
enthusiasm became concentrated on Temple. It was Strachey

[1] Minutes by Fiddes and Crewe (Strachey disagreeing) on A. Reutlinger to
C.O., 7 April, 1910, C.O. 446/95.
[2] Bell argued the case for government construction most strongly in Bell to
Crewe, 30 May, 1910, C.O. 446/90; his arguments were used in the C.O.'s
application to the Treasury of 14 November, 1910, draft in C.O. 446/95.
[3] *E.g.* Antrobus wrote: ' Northern Nigeria is not, like Southern Nigeria, a
country with great wealth of indigenous products which have only to be collected
and with an adequate population to collect them. It is a country which must be
developed by agriculture, and it has at present a comparatively scanty population.
Now that tribal wars and slave raiding have been stopped, the population will
no doubt increase; and in 15 or 20 years we may hope that there will be a larger
population and a flourishing cotton industry. But we cannot hasten that result
by spending money extravagantly now.' On Lugard to C.O., 11 November,
1905, C.O. 446/51.
[4] Minute by Butler on Girouard to Crewe, 24 April, 1908, C.O. 446/80.
[5] Minute on Bell to Crewe, 30 March, 1910, C.O. 446/89.

who proposed his appointment as Chief Secretary—' Sir H. Bell is badly in want of somebody at headquarters who really knows something about N. Nigeria from personal observation and actual work in the provinces.'[1] Cox agreed that he had been impressed, when sitting with Temple on the Lands Committee, with his ' caution, sagacity and tact. What he does not know about Nigeria is, I should say, not worth knowing.' And Crewe endorsed ' I have heard excellent accounts of Mr. Temple on all sides '.[2] When Temple acted as Governor, his forwarding of provincial reports was encouraged,[3] his steps to enforce prohibition in Muslim areas supported over Bell's protests,[4] and his conduct of the administration summed up as: ' There can be no question as to the manner in which Mr. Temple discharged his duties as Acting Governor. He has covered almost every subject of import- ance in his despatches, and put many questions before us in a new and convincing light. He must have worked exceedingly hard: he at any rate gave the Dept. plenty to do and think about during the months of August and September when we were short- staffed.'[5] And the final commitment to Northern Nigerian policies came when the amalgamation of the two Nigerias was being discussed: ' I think we are all agreed that it would be a serious mistake to entrust the task of amalgamation to anyone who was strongly imbued with S. Nigerian ideas.'[6]

Yet the Colonial Office could not claim to have initiated any part of this system of rule. The officials did not see their role as one of administering the colonies, but only of supervising their administration, and while a number of matters were queried, and a watch kept on such politically awkward questions as that of punitive expeditions, the supervision did not bear heavily on the Nigerian government. A close control was exercised over the finances of the Protectorate, but since Lugard had devised his structure for the very limited funds available, lack of money did not affect the method in which it was operated. One difference of

[1] Minute on Bell to Crewe, 2 May, 1910, C.O. 446/90.
[2] Minute on Bell to Crewe, 27 August, 1910, C.O. 446/91.
[3] Harcourt wrote ' Very interesting and useful ' and agreed to the suggestion that the N. Nigerian government be asked to send provincial reports regularly; on Temple to Harcourt, 15 March, 1911, C.O. 446/96.
[4] Temple to Harcourt, 18 February, 1911, C.O. 446/96; and Bell to C.O., 1 May, 1911, C.O. 446/103.
[5] Minute by Anderson on Bell to Harcourt, 7 September, 1911, C.O. 446/100.
[6] Minute by Fiddes on Bell to Harcourt, 25 September, 1911, C.O. 446/100.

opinion between Office and Governor in these years arose out of the officials' greater concern to protect the emirates from outside influences. Their objections to allowing missionaries to enter Kano were much stronger than those of Bell and the Residents; the London officials feared a religious war while those in Northern Nigeria merely disliked the idea of a group developing which would not acknowledge the Emir's authority.[1]

The year 1906 had provided two important events for Northern Nigeria. One was the departure of Lugard which allowed a new relation to grow up between Governor and Residents, one in which the senior Residents came to form a group on whose experience the two succeeding Governors were forced to rely, and who, because of this freedom to express their opinions (both verbally to the Governor and practically in their administration) came to develop a doctrine of Indirect Rule which meant not only rule through native chiefs but ruling on native lines. The other event was the Satiru revolt; a revolt in which the people attacked both the Fulani and the British systems, and therefore drew the two systems together in its suppression. Dr. Smith argues that the suppression of this revolt marked a turning point in British-Fulani relations; it showed both groups that they were interdependent for the maintenance of their rule. The relationship changed from ' superordination based on force to a near parity based on common interests ' and a tacit agreement grew up that force would not be used.[2] On the British side, this was due partly to the local government's fear of provoking a combination of the emirates, and their desire to establish peaceful government and avoid the expense of military expeditions, and partly to the pressure from the Liberal Secretaries of State to avoid ' punitive expeditions '. This dependence of the British on Fulani rule served to limit the political pressure on these states, and increased the bargaining power of the Emirs and their resistance to British demands for change.

[1] Minutes on Bell to C.O., 15 July, 1911, C.O. 446/103, and on Bell to Harcourt, 19 December, 1911, referring to opinions of Arnett, acting Resident of Kano, C.O. 446/101.   When Temple discussed government exclusion of missions in *Native Races*, pp. 214–17, he stated that it was the undermining of native authorities and the artificial Europeanisation of the African which he feared. If the missionary would encourage obedience to the native authority and to sanctioned tribal customs and manners, his presence would be welcomed by Emirs, chiefs and Residents.
[2] M. G. Smith, *Government in Zazzau*, pp. 205–6.

Lugard's system had been to force the Emirs to acknowledge British sovereignty and then establish a defined chain of political responsibility from the Governor through the Residents to the native administrations. But such a clear line of command was not compatible with the equally important necessity of maintaining the prestige, and to some extent the power, of the Emirs. The political relation between Resident and Emir had to be worked out in each individual case, and once the first shock of conquest was over, the Emirs learnt how to use their advantages. The Residents, similarly, learnt to use the demands of the Emir, and the need to uphold his prestige, as a lever against too much control from Government House. Above all, what was done by the native administration did not come within the formal pattern of the colonial administration, and did not have to be justified by reference to ordinances or executive orders. Temple, in his defence of Indirect Rule, lays stress on these points. Where there is Direct Rule, he argues, 'the responsibility for every action taken is clearly traceable right through from the district officer or Resident who took such action through the senior officers of the Government of the Colony up to the Secretary of State for the Colonies' who is accountable to the House of Commons; this leads to a centralised system which denies any initiative to the man in closest touch with the native. But he is not held accountable to anything like the same degree for actions performed by a native authority.[1] Temple then goes on to state the case for limiting the control of headquarters over the Resident. ' Clear and distinct instructions as to the general trend of the policy he should, I think, receive, and, I need hardly add, carry out strictly. But outside interference with the *mode* of carrying out that policy, and as to what action should be taken in a special case, can rarely, if ever, be of assistance to him.'[2] Such interference, or reference to headquarters, lowers his prestige with the Emir and the Emir's prestige with the people. The Resident should be judged not by particular actions but by the general well-being of the community.[3]

The circumstances of the years between Lugard's departure as High Commissioner and his return as Governor allowed the Residents a great deal of this freedom from central control.

[1] Temple, *Native Races*, pp. 56–7.
[2] *Ibid.*, p. 69.
[3] *Ibid.*, pp. 64 and 69–70. Miss Perham, in *Lugard II*, pp. 474–6, discusses Temple's view of Indirect Rule as given in this chapter.

Girouard and Bell both admired the system of Indirect Rule and wished to maintain it, but lacked the personal experience of its working, and the length of office to gain this experience, to direct it in detail. Girouard was fascinated by the concept of rule on native lines, and so avoided interference with the Residents on principle. He did try to keep in touch with them by the increasing telegraphic network,[1] and proposed a Residents' conference for October 1909—' a long-cherished project of my predecessor '[2]— but this was abandoned after his departure. Bell was inclined to give greater priority to economic development than to principles of administration, but he had neither the substantial period of office nor the force of character needed to establish strong control over the Residents. As has been stated,[3] he outlined a scheme for greater powers for the Protectorate government over Native Administration funds, but this never came to fruition.

Thus each Resident was able to strengthen his position in his province. Control of revenue assessment and of the Native Treasury, gave them the most important means of dominating the Emir; also, there was the detachment of the W.A.F.F. as a reminder of the armed might of the British government. But the control of appointments to and dismissals from the native administration staff, of the police and of the native courts, depended on the relations between individual Residents and Emirs. The Residents also depended on personal influence, rather than direct commands, to encourage such measures as development of roads, schools, export crops (cotton and groundnuts) and sanitary regulations.[4] To preserve the balance of power, they could insist that the decision when to press such reforms must be left to their personal judgment; for the Resident to act as a channel for commands from the Governor would destroy the basis of administration.

By 1912 this interpretation of Indirect Rule had developed from a useful administrative method to a political dogma, with Temple as its leading exponent and most of the Residents as its disciples. It was this transfer of authority from Governor to Residents which, Miss Perham has shown, Lugard found so

[1] Girouard to Elgin, 22 July, 1907, C.O. 446/64.
[2] Girouard to Crewe, enclosing report of northern tour, 17 February, 1909, C.O. 446/82.
[3] See above, p. 68.
[4] See Temple, *Native Races*, pp. 68–71.

difficult to accept.[1] But he was unable to alter it, nor did he shake the enthusiasm of the Colonial Office. The doctrine of Indirect Rule spread throughout British tropical Africa; even though the absence of the large centralized and administratively advanced emirates meant that modifications were required and central governments kept more power, the principle of ruling through native chiefs on native lines strongly influenced the development of British Africa.

[1] Perham, *Lugard II*, pp .469–88 and 505–11.

ELIZABETH CHILVER

NATIVE ADMINISTRATION IN THE WEST CENTRAL CAMEROONS[1] 1902-1954

This is an account of the work of European political officers in a small part of West Central Africa between 1902, when a German imperial military station was built in Bamenda, and 1954, when the Southern Cameroons obtained its first instalment of local political autonomy. The area lies between the Fulani emirates of Adamawa and the northern edge of the equatorial forest, on the fluctuating boundary of two administrative philosophies.

The politics of an area the size of Wales, with the population of less than half a million, will appear rather parochial. The larger issues of policy studied by Margery Perham in *Native Administration in Nigeria* (1937) and *Lugard: the Years of Authority* (1960), and the influence of the Permanent Mandates Commission and the Trusteeship Council will merge rather more shadowily than they would if the scene had been viewed from the Resident's desk in Buea rather than from the divisional officer's trestle table in the old German fort at Bamenda. For most of the period of British colonial rule the bulk of political life in Bamenda which can be recorded consisted of the dialogue between a handful of alien officers and those spokesmen of the ruled they chose to listen to. This dialogue was transmitted upwards to the Resident, the

[1] This essay is largely based on the scrutiny of some papers in the Buea archives and the divisional and Native Authority registries in the former Bamenda province. In the former, correspondence between the German military station and the Imperial Government in Buea between 1908 and 1914, and some Assessment and Intelligence reports were consulted. Copies of the latter have recently been transferred from the Secretariat, Lagos, to the Federal Nigerian archives. In Bamenda annual and quarterly reports, and files relating to Native Administration and chieftaincy matters were consulted. In 1960 the most important provincial and divisional files no longer in current use were being transferred to Buea, recoded and card-indexed under the supervision of Mr. E. W. Ardener. I am grateful for the help of the Committee for Commonwealth Studies in the University of Oxford and of the authorities and missions of the former Southern Cameroons in the course of two brief visits in 1958 and 1960, in the company of Dr. P. M. Kaberry. Her studies of the sociology of the Bamenda area date back to 1945, and she has generously allowed me the use of her files and note-books. I am greatly indebted to Dr. M. D. W. Jeffreys for help in the collection of material.

G

Secretary for Native Affairs, the Lieutenant Governor or Chief Commissioner, the Governor, the Secretary of State for the Colonies, and to international agencies, losing its particularity and the momentum of shared experience along its route. The directives and circulars which flowed down to the divisional officer had to be translated into the local idiom of the compromise between administrative policy and chiefdom or village politics whenever they involved the ruled directly. The divisional officer was the node of this system of political communication which persisted unchanged until 1949.

German foundations, 1902–1915

' The little bit I have got to take over,' wrote Lugard to his wife in March 1916, ' will give me as much work as a much larger area.'[1]

The ' little bit ' of Kamerun allotted to the United Kingdom by the Allies fell into three zones: a strip of coast with a high, fertile, volcanic hinterland, a narrow belt of rugged forest, and the western part of the montane grassfields that continued into the French sphere. Each had presented their German conquerors with rather different problems of military occupation, economic exploitation and district administration. The western coastal zone had, since 1896, become the main centre of a highly capitalized plantation industry which had radically changed the initial pattern of economic penetration from the coast by European trading houses, German and English, and their native allies. The inland forests were colonized by the plantation industry here and there, but retained something of their original character, given them by the middlemen of Duala and Calabar and their up-country trading partners—that of a zone of small scale forest exploitation delivering its palm oil and kernels, some wild rubber, ivory and hardwoods to factors and native traders. The redirection of the products of the forest zone to ports under German control seems to have arrested the development initiated, in the nineteenth century, by the entrepreneurs of Calabar. The grassfields to the north of it, and divided from it by a dramatic escarpment, were linked to the plantation area and the ports by difficult lines of communication, passing through corrugated forested country. The first long-distance ox-wagon trek from the Nkongsamba

[1] Margery Perham, *Lugard: the Years of Authority* (London 1960), p. 545.

railhead to Bamenda and Kumbo was made in 1912 by Telschow, a German settler: even then it could not be made without one stretch of porterage.[1] The first motor car only reached Bamenda, from across the French zonal border, in 1925. But the routes to the coast, provided they were policed, were passable by travellers, including Europeans who could command carrier labour. In the course of their occupation of the grassfields, largely included in the German military district (*Bezirk*) of Bamenda,[2] the Germans had constructed a useful internal network of wagon-tracks and marching roads with forced and tax-labour. These for the most part ran close to earlier trade-routes and interconnected the hinterland stations and posts. Nevertheless the grassfields, partly hemmed off from their pre-colonial outlets to the Benue and Cross Rivers, lay for the most part outside the main currents of hinterland development in the western regions of Kamerun; these flowed from Duala and Kribi to Bamum and the Ngaundere highlands, a prospective area of European pastoral settlement.

The western grassfields were first traversed in 1889 by Eugen Zintgraff, seeking an overland route to Adamawa. They were a disappointment to the German trading firms, since they were devoid of worthwhile surpluses of palm oil, not significantly blessed with resources of ivory and rubber or indeed with any natural products except kola which repaid the heavy costs of collection and transport to the coast. But they were, by Central African standards, quite thickly settled except in areas recently swept by Fulani or Chamba slave-raids. Their main exploitable commodity was manpower. From 1896 onwards labour, at first provided by the chiefdom of Bali-Nyonga under contract to the Westafrikanische Pflanzungsgesellschaft Victoria, began to reach the plantations. The newly-established concession company, the Gesellschaft Nordwest-Kamerun, considered, in 1900, that the main commercial prospect for them in the grassfields was labour-

---

[1] *Amtsblatt für des Schutzgebiet Kamerun* (1912), 200.

[2] The German *Bezirk* included Bamum and parts of the Bamileke region, later included in the French mandated area, Kentu and Western Gashaka, later administered by the British as parts of the provinces of Benue and Adamawa. For a discussion of political and administrative boundaries see J. R. Prescott, ' Les régions politiques des Camerouns Anglo-Français', *Ann. Geog.* (Paris), lxviii (1959), 263–7 and J. C. Anene; ' The Nigerian-Southern Cameroons Boundary ', *J. Hist. Soc. Nigeria*, ii (1962), 186–195. The German boundaries are best followed in Max Moisel, *Karte von Kamerun* (Berlin, 1913) 1:300,000, Sheets E1, E2, F1, F2.

recruiting. Indeed, after a regular military station was commissioned at the beginning of 1902 in Bamenda, the provision of
labour was its main *raison d'être*, overshadowing all other attempts
to develop the region by the establishment of cotton trials, the
upgrading of local stock, or the encouragement of small plantations
on the mensal lands of chiefs. Since the western grassfields were
of minor commercial interest the triangular competition between
traders, planters and government for labour which raged elsewhere
was here, rather, a covert competition between the Station and the
planters complicated, in the last years of the régime, by the
demands of railway construction.[1] A large part of the long-
distance trading activity in the north of the region was in Hausa
hands, a small-scale trade demanding far less in the way of porterage than was required, say, in the main areas of rubber exploitation.
A German firm established in Kentu for ivory and rubber collection had failed by 1913 in the face of Hausa competition, supported
in the rear by the Royal Niger Company. The ivory and rubber
of the more easterly regions was exploited by the Hausa agents
of German and British firms with factories in Bamum, Yoko,
Yaunde, Ngambe and Garua.[2]

The early stages of labour-recruitment seem to have taken
three forms, a small voluntary supply of adventurous volunteers
to the Westafrikanische Pflanzungsgesellschaft Victoria and to
Government service, a larger flow of penal labour rounded up in
punitive expeditions or extracted from defeated villages, and
another provided by chiefs either under contract to licensed
recruiters or to stave off their visits and those of military patrols.

The most heavily recruited area in the Bamenda military
district lay in the south-west, within easy patrolling distance of
the station; this was also the area dominated by the small state of
Bali-Nyonga, the main native labour contractor. To the east lay
the larger state of Bamum, a state based to some extent on the
productive use of captives taken from surrounding peoples, able to
supply the carrier and other labour demanded of it without doing
too much violence to its traditional political structure. Initially

[1] See Harry R. Rudin, *Germans in the Cameroons*, 1884–1914 (London, 1938),
pp. 316–7.
[2] See F. Thorbecke, *Im Hochland von Mittel-Kamerun*, ii, (Hamburg, 1916),
p. 75 ff. for the competition between the British-supported Hausa trade from
the Benue and the German firms. The kola trade remained partly in local
hands.

the German military administration established close relations with them both.

Between 1901 and 1909, when the scandals of labour recruitment and mortality in the plantations had at length given rise to stricter labour regulation, the military complement of the Bamenda station was frequently engaged in battles with the surrounding peoples. Some of these arose out of the refusal of chiefdoms to provide labour to the station, others out of friction between labour contracting chiefdoms and their satellites. By 1909, however, the region had been sufficiently brought to order for a start to be made with the collection of poll-tax, at a rate of 6M. per able-bodied male commutable to 30 days tax labour, and 10M. for clerks, craftsmen and better-paid employees.[1] By 1914 the military station had established an orderly, if superficial, administration over most of the large area it controlled. The main posts in the area were connected by bridle-paths or wagon-roads maintained, as a legally-enforceable obligation, by the villages through which they passed. Some villages had been forced to move nearer to roads for this purpose, and to enable official or commercial carrier-parties and caravans to be provisioned at fixed prices. Along these routes were rest-houses, maintained by chiefs with public labour, and courier or 'flag-posts' provisioned by them. The majority of chiefs had been issued with ' books ' establishing their status as official tax-collectors in receipt of a 10 per cent rebate or as minor agents of Government to be protected from the depredations of neighbours or unruly carrier parties. The more important ones were obliged to keep ' deputies ' resident at the station to whom orders and instructions or exhortations to plant new crops or prepare for the arrival of vaccinating teams could be given. Around the station itself, alongside the cosmopolitan *Schutztruppe* company, a society of interpreters, messengers, carrier headmen, road foremen and domestics had grown up. This group of men was the focus of news, rumours, intrigue, interpretation of German intentions and innovations from the coast. Close as they were to the German administrators, with whom many established mutually beneficial and often warm relationships, they controlled the access of petitioners and complainants to them.

---

[1] Directions to stations on methods of tax-collection are contained in ' Bekanntmachung des Gouverneurs zur Ausführung der Steuerverordnungen ', *Amtsblatt* (1909), 55–6.

Among them were some gifted men, on whom the *Stationsleiter* relied for intelligence, and to whom the conduct of inquiries and negotiations was often delegated. They were, possibly, a more effective instrument of social change than any other element of the German presence except the missions. There were two of these—the Basel Mission, which had established itself at Bali in 1903, and the Society of the Sacred Heart of Jesus which reached Nso, in the east of the *Bezirk*, in January 1913.

The Roman Catholic Mission was welcomed by the military administrators, who had criticized the Basel Mission for its failure to provide German-speaking native clerks and agents for the station. By 1910 the Basel Mission had established two middle, two girls elementary, and nine vernacular village schools in the *Bezirk*, with an enrolment of over 700.[1] The new Roman Catholic Mission, assisted by Grassfielders returned from the coast, had laid the basis for a large elementary school in Nso with over 100 boys and several others had just been started when the first world war broke out. Both missions emphasized craft training and the subsequent British administration relied heavily on the carpenters, locksmiths, and masons they produced.

The elaborate system of native tribunals introduced in the coastal areas between 1891 and 1896 were not extended inland.[2] As in other military districts chief's courts were left undisturbed to deal with civil pleas and less flagrant criminal matters, except insofar as poison-ordeals, enslavement and brutal punishments were formally forbidden. In Bamenda, little seems to have been known of their composition, jurisdiction and procedure, in contrast with the more developed areas. The Station Commander and those Europeans deputed by him to act as justices exercized a comprehensive jurisdiction, civil, criminal and administrative. They sat with native assessors, usually appointed for a year. The assessors, whose functions were interpretative and advisory, were often drawn from chiefdoms or villages not concerned in a dispute;

---

[1] The establishment and early development of the missions are described by Wilhelm Schlatter, *Geschichte der Basler Mission* 1815–1915 (Basel, 1916), 279 ff., and Pater Joh. Emonts S.C.J. *Ins Steppen-und Bergland Innerkameruns*, 2nd edn. (Aachen, 1927) passim. Official German education policy is dealt with by M. Schlunk, *Die Schulen für Eingeborene in den deutschen Schutzgebieten* (Hamburg, 1914), p. 59 ff.
[2] Hesse, 'Eingeborenenschiedsgerichte in Kamerun', *Kolonial Zeitung* (1896), p. 299 ff., and Winkelmann, 'Die Eingeborenenrechtspflege in Deutsch Ostafrika, Kamerun und Togo,' Zt. *vgl. Rechtswissenschaft*, liii, 189 ff.

consequently the customary law, protected in the *Schutzbrief*, was applied in a diluted and generalized form, influenced or modified by German law. On tour the officers of the station settled outstanding disputes and received complaints in open-air moots of chiefs and elders. The station officers' courts and moots were one of the more popular features of the German regime; the latter were often occasions for ceremony and the exchange of gifts. The effectiveness of the station courts was, of course, limited. At any distance from the station and even quite close to it, ordeals were still carried out, suspected witches disposed of, and persons sold into slavery. In the small chiefdom of Bamessong, for example, its chief had ordered his regulatory[1] society to dispose of 7 relatives before the station was brought into action in 1909 by complaints; in the large chiefdom of Nso, conquered in 1906, two of the major councillors and other noblemen were convicted of witchcraft or *lèse-majesté* and executed between 1908 and 1911: only one of these executions seems to have come to the knowledge of the station. It was inevitable that many of the cases brought before the *Stationsleiter's* court were the result of delation to those native agents closest to him.

In the early years of administration, between 1901 and 1909, a systematic occupation of tribal areas preparatory to a thorough labour assessment and manpower allocation could not be carried out. The reduction of Bafut, for example, took two expeditions and numerous patrols which left chaos behind them but little else, until the exiled chief was restored to his people in 1909.[2] The administrative follow-up of the initial ' punishment ' of particular tribes was constantly postponed by calls on the station Company to take part in more distant expeditions, such as the suppression of the Anyang revolt in 1904–5.[3] In 1904 the understaffed station had been directed to simplify its *Befehlsapparat* by the formation of

[1] A characteristic feature of traditional political organization in the greater part of Bamenda and adjacent areas was the regulatory society, a closed association staffed by appointed officers and controlled by the chief. It had police and, frequently, judicial functions and was usually closed to princes whose ambitions it checked. See P. M. Kaberry, ' Retainers and Royal Households in the Cameroons Grassfields ', *Cahiers d'Etudes Africaines*, forthcoming.

[2] See Arnold Rüger in H. Stoecker (ed.), *Kamerun unter deutscher Kolonialherrschaft* (Berlin, 1960), p. 197; the official estimate of Bafut casualties here quoted was 1062. In addition over 600 prisoners and penal labourers were taken during the first punitive expedition.

[3] For a list of punitive expeditions between the end of 1904 and the beginning of 1907 see *Amtsblatt* (1909), 1.

larger tribal units wherever possible: consequently a number of
rebellious villages were displaced and put under the authority of
the Bali-Nyonga ruler, others under one of the Meta chiefs. To
judge from surviving chief's books and tax-lists the practice was
often extended in the wake of the German advance. Moreover
staff shortages, the result of frequent military activity, compelled
the use of other intermediaries, such as the Basel Mission in Bali
and Bamum, and local European or coloured factory managers.
In 1908 the station, under the leadership of Hauptmann Menzel,
was beginning to question these practices which, on the one hand,
had involved it in military support of the ' high chiefs ' it had
created, and on the other, diminished its capacity to control local
political affairs.[1]

If one high chief was stripped of some recent vassals, however,
the Imperial Government in Buea was not disposed as yet to
encourage the ' premature dissolution of traditional states '. It
was not until 1912 that considered new instructions were issued
by Governor Ebermeier to the Bamenda station and the neighbouring military station of Banyo.[2] These instructions called for
closer and more direct administration and gave notice of the
impending division of the Bamenda station's huge district into
three; these measures were to be taken in preparation for increased
European settlement and the replacement of military by civil
administration. In the Governor's view the possibility that the
Bamenda native would soon ' be able to earn money in his own
province as well as at the coast ' would inevitably loosen traditional
political associations, and this was to be welcomed. The *Stationsleiter* was told that the practice whereby chiefs had a lien on the
earnings of plantation labourers for tax-purposes and their view
that the prolonged absence of their subjects on the coast was
treasonable must be opposed; the support given them by the
station in their ' communal ' view of economic activity and their
request for the repatriation of absent tribesmen must cease. These
attitudes were, in the Imperial Government's view, detrimental
to the economic freedom of the individual. Station commanders

[1] IC51n: Imperial Military Station to Imperial Government (half-yearly
Report), 2 Oct., 1908; a special report from the Station Commander dated
Duala, 7 May, 1909; and an historical appendix to the annual Station report for
1910–11 dated 21 June, 1911 (Buea Archives).
[2] Governor Kamerun to Imperial Military Station Bamenda (copied to
Banyo), Buea, 10 July, 1912 (Buea Archives).

were instructed to ' impress on the mass of the population that tax is a tribute owed to the Government, which had replaced the chiefs, who no longer have any claim to tribute '. The working-out of the new policy was difficult, for how was the station to fulfil increasing demand for labour, both in the plantations and on the railway, and expand its own activities without reliance on and rewards to the chiefs in its rear? In 1913–14 military posts had been established in Wum and Kentu, but some pockets still remained completely unpatrolled in the north, north-east and extreme west of the district. The *Stationsleiter*, conscious of the shortcomings of official policy, reported that fifteen villages had run over the border to British Takum because they had been complained of to the station and feared reprisals, because of the activities of deserters, soldiers and customs-men, and because they feared labour recruitment. Nearly 11,000 men had been recruited in that year through regular channels, of whom 2,000 were destined for the plantations and railway; more could not be recruited without grave economic and social damage. As it was ' the flower of Bali youth ' had been sacrificed to the plantations' interests. Whatever might be said in Germany, the *Stationsleiter* asserted, there was nothing voluntary about this recruitment: the chiefs decided who was to go. Some alleviation for the south-west of the *Bezirk* could be expected with the opening-up of Wum, but the prospects of local earnings from local establishments had receded with the discovery of tse-tse fly in the relatively under-populated south-east of the district.[1]

The Imperial Government in Buea distrusted the station commanders for their reliance on military measures, their tendency to maintain closer communication with the *Schutztruppe* command than with the civil authority, and their lack of interest in economic development.[2] The station commanders, in the years after 1908, had become increasingly bold in their scorn of the labour recruiters,

[1] Annual Report of the Imperial Military Station Bamenda, 1 April, 1913, to 31 March, 1914 (Buea archives). The rounding up of labourers was often carried out by *basoge*, armed retainers maintained by the bigger chiefs with official sanction. For a brief account of an important chief's role in tax-collection and recruitment under the German régime, viewed from an African standpoint, see E. M. Chilver and P. M. Kaberry, ' Traditional Government in Bafut ', *Nigerian Field* (1963), forthcoming.

[2] Governor Kamerun to Imperial Military Station Bamenda, Buea, 27 Oct., 1912; Governor Kamerun to Secretary of State, Reichskolonialamt, No. 390, despatched simultaneously (Buea Archives).

had managed to get prompt approval to the closing of unadministered or restive areas to trade caravans, and made no bones
about their irritation with the Basel Mission for furthering the
claims of particular chiefs. They grew more ingenious in present-
ing to the Imperial Government at Buea the consequences of its
policies and the disagreeable alternatives open to it to compel
fulfilment of them. The station staff, some of whom were
associated with the district for as long as five years, became
increasingly involved in the logic of the peoples they ruled,
though oddly incurious, still, about the covert institutional background to it.[1] They might well have taken courage from the new
winds that started to blow at the time of Solf's visit to the protectorate. The application of a new administrative model to some
of the interior districts had occurred to the German Colonial
Secretary, the ' system en vogue in Northern Nigeria ', and he had
already begun to discuss this with Governor Ebermeier when he
wrote to Lugard for a copy of his *Political Memoranda* and for
further information in the autumn of 1913.[2]

Direct administration 1916–1921

The first British attempt to penetrate the grassfields was a
failure. A British column was overrun in September 1914 at
Nssankang and the advance from Takum was held. The German
victory was followed by the punishment of some chiefs whose
loyalty seemed doubtful, but no serious trouble developed in the
Bezirk. In early October 1915, General Cunliffe[3] decided to move
against Bamenda from the north-east and south-west and on
October 22nd Bamenda station was occupied by Major Crookenden's[4] four companies. A detachment of two hundred rifles
was left behind to garrison the station while Crookenden moved
on to join forces with other detachments moving up from Chang
and down from Banyo. The retreating German forces, led by two
former station commanders, managed to withdraw their forces

[1] In contrast with the Residents of German Adamawa and the civil administrator of the neighbouring Ossidinge *Bezirk*, Dr. Alfred Mansfeld, who was
prepared to use the Ngbe regulatory society as an auxiliary instrument of government, cf. his *Urwald-Dokumente* (Berlin, 1908), pp. 160–161.
[2] Eberhard von Vietsch, *Wilhelm Solf* (Tübingen, 1961), pp. 369–370.
[3] Cunliffe, Brig.-Gen. Frederick H. G., C.B., C.M.G. (died 1955); entered
army 1889; W.A.F.F. 1904; Commanded Nig. Regt. 1914.
[4] Crookenden, Maj. J.; served N.Nig.Regt. of W.A.F.F.; H.Q. Nig. Regt.
1918; Lt.-Col., 2nd in Comm. 1922.

and to inflict damage on convoys and patrols.[1] Before they left they instructed chiefs not to involve themselves in a ' whiteman war ' and to accommodate themselves to the British as best they could.[2] If Bamenda was spared the devastation suffered by the Banyo district, it was disorganized by military impositions— carrier duties and the commandeering of food—and suffered from the usual deprivations of the stoppage of trade. The cash savings of more important chiefs had been borrowed by the isolated German officers, and little new money, save commandeering notes of limited negotiability, was put into circulation.

By early December the line Kuti-Fumban-Ngambe-Yoko was securely held and Bamenda station's temporary importance as a staging point in a military supply route up the Cross River called for a civil administrator. One was spared from the depleted Nigerian service. On January 1, 1916, G. S. Podevin[3] crossed the divisional boundary into Bamenda from Calabar, calling in ' big men ' as he trekked to the station, examining their chief's books, recording their former tax liabilities, and the considerable number of men away with the German forces as carriers and soldiers. His first tasks were the formation of an intelligence bureau and the selection of informants, interpreters and messengers to repair the gap in information arising out of the disappearance of the German station records, the uselessness of the military intelligence handbook and the failure of General Cunliffe's Moslem agents to collect any information of value. In spite of its closeness to the Nigerian border little was known of the region, and no attempt had been made to collect what had been published by way of ethnographic and linguistic research in learned journals; the local knowledge of the missionaries had been dissipated with their deportation by the military. As Podevin's rough ideas of tribal distribution improved, messengers were despatched to bring chiefs into the station with their books. Day to day decisions, governed by the simple policy of maintaining ' the principles of Native Administration as practised by the Germans' was based

[1] F. J. Moberly, *Official History of the War: Military Operations, Togoland and Cameroons*, 1914–18 (London, 1931), pp. 340 ff.; Erich Student, *Kamerun's Kampf*, 1914–1916 (Berlin, 1942), pp. 45 ff. and 278 ff.

[2] H. Martin (ed.), *Histoire et coûtumes de Bamum redigées sous la direction du Sultan Njoya* (Duala, 1952), p. 215.

[3] Podevin, G. S.; apptd. to the Political and Admin. Dept., S. Nigeria 1909; assumed duty as District Officer, 2nd Cl. in Bamenda in Jan. 1916; died at Bamenda.

upon these books, any other correspondence individual chiefs might have preserved and the impression of authority they gave.[1]

By and large the submission of the chiefs was ready, and even an occasion for the competitive display of retinues and regalia. But the chiefs of a few towns, though declaring themselves willing to meet political officers on their own ground, refused to come in. There was, Podevin reported, considerable unrest in Bali country. Here, it was believed, the foundations of German administration had been shaken by European officers and N.C.O.s on the line of communications during the interregnum. These, ' dabbling in Native affairs' had made individual bargains for food and carriers with breakaway village-heads in return for informal recognition. The example was catching and other breakaway attempts had been made in Meta and Bikom. In March-April 1916 a military patrol had burnt the recalcitrant village of Bamunum and destroyed the farm houses of the rebellious chiefs.

In early March 1916, the French and British spheres of administration were partially delimited though Bamum and Chang, later to be detached from the British occupation area, remained under temporary control; the north-eastern boundary remained indistinct and the area near it was unadministered save for a couple of visits by a French tax-collecting officer. The delimitation was followed by a proclamation by the Governor-General establishing the basis of administration, namely the Laws of Cameroons, ' so far as known ', and failing these the Laws of that part of Nigeria in which the administering officer had previously held his appointment. Two months later the Native Courts Ordinance of 1914 and the Native Authorities Ordinance of 1916 were applied by proclamation.[2]

Of these, and indeed of an earlier military proclamation which would have given him the legal powers he sought to make the possession of firearms illegal, Podevin had no knowledge until long after the event, for no Gazettes reached him for six months after he assumed responsibility for his territory. This during 1916, included the old Ossidinge *Bezirk* and most of the former Bamenda *Bezirk:* the population of the latter according to the last German

---

[1] Bamenda Station Diary, Jan. to Mar. 1916.

[2] *Proclamation* issued by General Dobell, No. 10 of 17 March, 1916; *Proclamations issued by the Governor-General relating to the British Sphere*, B 2027/1624 of 2 April, 1916. and B. 1094/1610 of 10 June, 1916. Podevin's previous experience had been in the northern districts of the Southern Provinces.

count was roughly estimated at 414,000. At the end of the year Kentu and Wum passed temporarily into the Muri province; in fact they were left virtually unadministered.[1]

To carry out his civil duties Podevin was assisted by a Lieutenant with a small patrol in Bagam, an area later transferred to the French zone, an assistant in Kentu with some interpreters, an assistant in Ossidinge, with no clerical support whatever and at headquarters two policemen, two interpreters and 12 messengers. A garrison company of the 3rd Nigeria Regiment was only available to furnish escorts and men for police duty. In the last year of German administration the main station had had three commissioned military government officers, supported by a paymaster and two N.C.O.s used for a variety of administrative tasks, two Medical Officers, three European P.W.D. officers, three native clerks, three interpreters, 50 messengers and various other grades. At the Wum sub-station a commissioned officer, a N.C.O., two clerks, three interpreters and 30 messengers were the establishment; in Kentu one commissioned officer, three clerks, two interpreters and 40 messengers. At the agricultural station near Fumban, an Agricultural Officer with supporting clerical staff and an escort exercized certain delegated administrative powers. Ossidinge had been a fully staffed and efficient civil station, with a detached police post supervising its unruly northern border.[2]

Recruitment for the plantations caused Podevin most concern. He had collected evidence, which he forwarded to the Resident, that the plantation managements had broken their contracts with some of the 2,300 labourers recruited with his help. But in spite of evidence that they had failed to pay wages or issue stipulated rations, a recruiter was sent up with a supporting letter from the Resident. Podevin refused to let him recruit until the fifteen hundred odd pounds owed to labour in the division had been paid. In the argument with the Resident which followed, Podevin threatened to lay his case before the Governor-General. The plantation managers were proceeded against, under German law,

---

[1] For the subsequent transfer and administrative vicissitudes of Kentu and Gashaka, see A. H. M. Kirk-Greene, *Adamawa, Past and Present* (London, 1958), p. 82.
[2] *Report on the British Sphere of the Cameroons* (1922), p. 35; Imperial Military Station Bamenda to Imperial Govt. Kamerun, 20 June, 1913 (Buea Archives). Of the estimated population, over 82,000 were ascribed to Bamum, Podevin to Resident, 25 May, 1916 (Bamenda papers).

and Podevin received orders in September 1916 that he could stop recruiting.[1]

A promise given by the political officer to the labourers had been broken; Podevin's anger with his superior officers was increased by what he regarded as another breach of trust, the proposal that poll-tax should be levied at the official rather than the local exchange value of the German mark: the last proclamations had fixed it at 9d. but he found that its purchasing power was 6d. in Ossidinge and 2d. in the African Association's factory at Ikom, the nearest factory now active. Internally it still held to its old value as a local currency. No answer was received to his proposal that the mark should either be guaranteed or redeemed, but by the end of 1917 its official value was allowed to fall to 7d. In making his protests Podevin felt obliged to insist that he was far from being ' soft with natives ': his case was based on the notion that pledges given by political officers should be upheld, and that the value given in return for a recognized currency by European traders was ' simply cheating '.

Some intermittent consideration was being given in Buea to the form of administration in Bamenda. There seemed to be little disposition, as yet, to trust the divisional officer's advice. One Resident considered that some of the larger chiefs could run their own Treasuries and bring smaller chiefs into their scope.[2] But, like his German predecessors, Podevin pointed out that their authority could not be restored without the use of force: and this could not be entertained at the time. In 1917 he was instructed to raise the tax-rate: he opposed his orders with such resolution that the Governor-General finally approved the rate he proposed. Another Resident pressed him to train native clerks so that a network of Native Courts in Southern Provinces style could be established. The first instructional court was set up at the station under his supervision in 1917 and in the following year two more were set up at Bali and Bagam. By now he had the help of an assistant divisional officer, who visited the most accessible eastern parts of the division for the first time to restore the abandoned wagon-roads to use. In November 1918, the influenza epidemic

---

[1] Bamenda Division: Reports upon labour supplied to the Plantations in 1916; Depositions by Vatung and others of Kumbo, 15 Nov., 1916 (Buea Archives); Quarterly and Annual Divisional Reports, 1916 and 1917 (Bamenda papers); Bamenda Station Diary, 1916, 1917, passim.

[2] Resident to Sec. Southern Provinces, 5 Dec. 1916 (Bamenda papers).

reached Bamenda, and Podevin, already ailing, died in early December. Over 15,000 deaths were believed to have resulted from the epidemic in the Division.[1]

His successor, Major Crawford,[2] retransferred from war-service in East Africa, was deprived of his assistant. He was virtually penned to the area round the station from which he emerged for five days' touring. The complicated task of recording and repatriating internees in a division shaken by a major epidemic fell to him. Perhaps fortunately he had only one court and Treasury to supervise. The Bali court had to be closed because the ruler, dissatisfied with the treatment of his suzerainty claims, boycotted it;[3] the Bagam court, under the supervision of a detached military patrol, dissolved because the notables concerned in it had been involved in a human sacrifice at the burial of their king: they were hanged. The writ of the station ran as far as military escorts could be provided or where the influence of friendly chiefs was substantial, as in Nso where, despite the fact that only one administrative visit had been made to it, tax was regularly collected and brought to the station. No major disorders followed the epidemic, as they did in Duala and its hinterland: the divisional officer recorded a friendly disposition on the part of the chiefs who visited him.[4]

The breakdown of administration in 1919 was to some extent repaired in the following year. Three divisional officers and an assistant were sent up at various times and the use of force was conceded. In August part of the disturbed area, Bagam, was handed over to the French. A patrol action was set on foot against the villages which had refused the jurisdiction of the Bali court in both its judicial and tax-collecting capacity, but was fruitless. Other patrols visited the Widekum borderland, the Wum district and the area between Wum and Kentu. Many villages were visited for the first time since the occupation by a resolute civil officer, N. C. Duncan.[5] For the first time since 1916 it was

[1] For an account of the epidemic see G. Martin, *L'Existence au Cameroun* (Paris, 1921), pp. 125–162.

[2] Crawford, H. R. H.; apptd. Political and Admin. Dept., S. Nigeria 1906; Resident 1921–26.

[3] I am indebted for this information to Mr. Max Fohtung, court clerk for Bali at the time.

[4] Report, Bamenda Division, for the year ending 31 Dec., 1919 (Bamenda papers); Quarterly reports from Bagam patrol (Bamenda papers); Bamenda Station Diary, Feb. to Dec. 1919.

[5] Duncan, N. C.; apptd. District Officer, S. Provinces 1914, formerly Lieut., S. Nigeria Regt.; invalided 1925.

possible to detach officers to describe, in more detail, the political geography of parts of the division and the effects of five years of underadministration.[1]

Experiments in indirect administration

Between 1916 and 1920 no Residents had been at their posts long enough to master the human detail of the Province. They and their miserably exiguous staff were chiefly concerned to carry out international and Nigerian obligations—the identification and valuation of enemy property, the repatriation of soldiers and civilians, the construction of a rough and ready rationing system, the maintenance of the plantations and wharves; the influenza epidemic intervened to disorganize their work.[2] The divisional officer in Bamenda was 14 days away, linked only by a roundabout military telegraph line to Buea and to the Cross River line of communication by mailrunner. Even though some apparatus of government was restored in Bamenda in 1920 policy was in confusion. Within a few months of one another contradictory instructions were received in the Division. The first, issued by Resident Davidson,[3] laid it down that the whole Cameroons Province was to be run ' on the former Southern Nigeria principle '. The second, issued shortly after the Milner-Simon Agreement had settled the zonal boundaries, laid it down that ' the principles of Indirect Administration ' were to be applied: it had followed the recovery of the remaining German correspondence relating to Bamenda.[4]

The new instructions merely established a negative policy: the ' old Southern Nigeria System ' was to be abandoned. But which of the precepts of Sir Frederick Lugard's *Political Memoranda* were to be applied; and which were applicable in the situation? The removal of the divisional officer from the presidency of the

[1] Hitherto the only substantial accounts of local political organization received were from Lt. L. W. G. Malcolm, in charge of the Bagam patrol, subsequently curator at the Welcome Museum. The material collected by him was pvblished in learned journals, and is listed in M. McCulloch, M. Manoukian and I. Dugast, *Peoples of the Central Cameroons*, Ethnographic Survey of Africa (London, 1954), pp. 52–4.

[2] The Nigerian Civil Service had been depleted by a third in 1917, Colonial Annual Reports, No. 1030, *Nigeria*, 1917, p. 24.

[3] Davidson, James; apptd. Political and Admin. Dept. S. Nigeria, 1901; Sen. Resident and Member of Legislative Council 1921–26.

[4] Report on the Bamenda Division 1920; Report supplementary to the preceding with accompanying minutes and correspondence, 1920; Memorandum, Resident to D. O. Bamenda, 15 April, 1921 (Bamenda papers).

Native Courts, a *sine qua non* of Northern and Southern applications of the doctrine, was hardly applicable in Bamenda where divisional officers were called upon to introduce a new institution rather than reform an old one. Moreover, were the courts to be based on the principle of wide representation and consent as to the boundaries of jurisdiction, as laid down in Memorandum No. 8, or were ' village chiefs of influence and character ' to be encouraged to take control of a village-group, as a former Resident had proposed, and as Memorandum No. 1 seemed to imply? The second course had already involved the use of force in two districts. The existence of a ready-made poll-tax system, a population broken in to its collection by chiefs, and the remuneration of chiefs by means of a ' tax-dash ' appeared to provide better opportunities for a more advanced form of native administration than could be attempted in the south-eastern forests. But experience had shown that the choice of tax-units was a delicate matter. What had already been organized could not be easily abandoned since pledges had been given. The German ' books ' and the authority they were locally held to confer had been recognized during the period of status quo administration. The Bali king's special position and stipend had been retained; they now turned out to be based on an incomplete record of German transactions with him. During the brief ' Southern Nigeria ' period two more inter-tribal courts had been established, and their development into the old Southern all-purpose regulatory institutions had begun. If they were to be dissolved, what was to replace them?

The reasons for the muddle in Bamenda seemed patent to the energetic Resident, F. H. Ruxton[1]—lack of definite policy, contradictory instructions, lack of staff, the chaotic state of law, want of communications, want of markets. The ideological contradiction between Native Courts under direct administration with no tax, and Native Courts under indirect administration with tax had passed unnoticed. The gradual reorganization of Native Courts, based on tribal units, and free from interference of foreign clerks should, he thought, be the first step. The material upon

[1] Ruxton, Maj. U. FitzHerbert, C.M.G. (1873–1954); Army Serv., Worcs. Regt. 1895–1911; Roy. Nig. Co., 1898–99; Col. Civ. Serv. 1901: Intell. Div., Admiralty 1915–18; Asst. Milit. Att., Berne 1918; Brit. High Comm., Constantinople 1919–21; Lt.-Gov., S. Prov. Nigeria, 1925–9.

which to build administratively was, he believed, superior in Bamenda, ' owing to Hamitic influence being at work on the Semi-Bantu population '.

His divisional officer was prepared to go further. ' Work ', he wrote, ' was begun on the old Southern Nigeria system with its attendant use of uniformed Government officials, Police and Court messengers; the last I have heard described as the backbone of the Administration! The success or failure of the District Officer under this system is gauged by the amount of revenue extracted from litigants; every endeavour is therefore made to encourage persons who have the slightest petty dispute with their neighbour to seek redress in the Native Court. Looking at the cause lists, it will be seen that the majority of cases should easily have been settled privately without recourse to litigation. The Native Court Clerks inspired by the same High Ideal must in my opinion have been persuading the chiefs to fine for almost every offence as no attempt at inflicting Native punishment was made.'[1]

The divisional officer proposed that alien clerks should be removed from the courts and local clerks appointed, that ' law-courts on the plan of the Old Bailey ' should be abolished, that the chiefs' retainers and tribal regulatory societies should be employed in place of court messengers and police, and that he should be allowed to make mission teachers and pupils understand that their religion did not excuse them from allegiance to chiefs.

The inquiries he and others had undertaken in the spirit of Lugard's proposals for the collection of records about each tribe of importance, had so far revealed ' about ten groups ' upon which a Native Administration could be based: Map 1 illustrates the conjectured political areas which had emerged from inquiries. The divisional officer hoped to persuade village heads in each group to acknowledge a district head. Later two or three groups with the same executive, judicial and marriage customs might be amalgamated. He could report that the poll-tax system in force was nominal. Owing to ' the commonsense of the chiefs ' it had developed into a graduated tax under which some might pay one shilling and others ten, reminiscent of the system of lump sum assessment successfully introduced in parts of Northern Nigeria. The discs issued to payers as receipts merely provided unnecessary

[1] Memorandum covering Annual Report, Bamenda Division, 1920 (Bamenda papers).

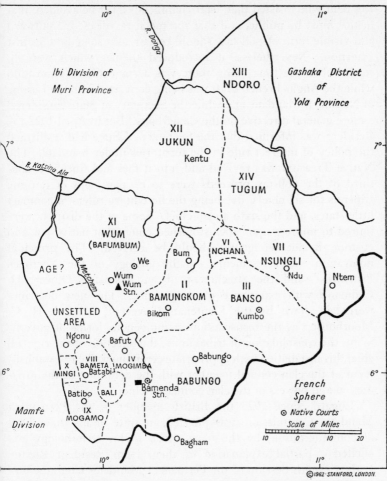

Sketch Map showing projected political areas (after W. E. Hunt) 1922.

arithmetic for his clerks; the chief should receive a bulk receipt, ' since it is the Fong (chief) who imposes and receives tribute '.[1]

This bold project of social engineering, importing the flavour of Memorandum No. 5 into an area so recently viewed as Southern, was treated with a mixture of caution and sympathy by the

[1] Despite instructions from the Imperial Government, the German poll-tax had never been more than a district quota, revised from time to time by a count of heads and roughly adjusted according to trading activity to judge from accounts collected by Dr. Kaberry and myself from elderly notables.

Resident who insisted that 'star chambers' must be avoided, that justice must be public, and that the metal tax-discs, the outward and visible form of poll-tax, should remain as a safeguard against extortion. Nevertheless, it introduced themes which were to recur.[1] For the time being there was a standstill to innovation while the Anglo-French draft was being converted into the League of Nations B Mandate, and while the Secretary of State considered a more general directive on the Cameroons. But in April 1922 the Resident was informed that the Secretary of State had reaffirmed the policy of indirect rule in the territories under mandate. The Native Treasury was revived and into it fees and fines and one-third of the poll-tax proceeds were to be paid; out of it came stipends for six chiefs, five being the hereditary rulers of compact little states, and the sixth a clan chief. Some of the districts were toured to impress upon the astonished chiefs that native law and custom, if not repugnant, should be revived. The principal innovation was assessment 'on the analogy of the Northern Provinces' and the attachment of an Assessing Officer, H. Cadman,[2] with experience of its practice. The new doctrines were laid down by the Lieutenant-Governor, Lt.-Col. H. C. Moorhouse,[3] as the resuscitation of indigenous forms of government, the consolidation of tribal units, the selection of the rightful chief, his installation with appropriate ceremonial, the re-establishment of the clan council together with the definition of the jurisdiction and powers of the clan council or chief.

Lugard, since 1923 the British member of the Permanent Mandates Commission, was puzzled, in spite of his inner lines of communication, by the turns given to his terminology and elicited a partial explanation of them from Resident Ruxton at the Seventh Session of the Permanent Mandates Commission.[4]

[1] Provincial Report, 1921; Memoranda, D. O. Bamenda to Resident, 13 and 19 Jan., 1922; Resident to D. O. Bamenda, 25 Jan., 1922, and 17 Feb., 1922; 'Report on Native Institutions', D.O. to Resident, 24 Jan., 1922 (Bamenda papers).

[2] Cadman, Hal; apptd. District Officer, S. Provinces, 1912, and later was detached for assessment work among the Tiv; died in Bamenda Division, 1924.

[3] Moorhouse, Lt.-Col. Sir Harry (1872–1934); R.A. 1891–1908; Chief Assist. Col. Sec. S. Nigeria 1908; Prov. Cr. 1911; Sec. S. Prov. Nigeria 1914; Lt. Gov. 1921–25; Spec. Cr. to the Solomon Is. 1928.

[4] Permanent Mandates Commission, *Proceedings*, 7th Session, 5th Mtg. 21 Oct. 1925. Lugard's question reflects the rather contradictory proposals of the Grier (1922) and Tomlinson (1923) reports on Native Administration in the Eastern Provinces, discussed by Margery Perham, *Native Administration in Nigeria* (London, 1937), pp. 201–3.

What, he asked, were the mutual relations of clan councils, salaried chiefs and Native Court areas? The new system, Ruxton explained, was at an embryonic state and the terms had different connotations in different areas. In the Victoria Division the German system of Native Administration, with its courts and Government-appointed chiefs had had to be retained since indigenous forms of Government had been overlaid by the plantation system: the Bakweri tribe seemed to him ' a very uninteresting people '. In the forest divisions a basis for Native Administration was being sought in councils of clan elders, some of whom would receive stipends. Other members of the Commission were uninterested in the minutiae of small-scale administration, and thought that the preoccupation of the Nigerian Administration with it was overdone. Some thought that the absence of agricultural extension work and compulsory crop schemes and the laxity of labour discipline argued a hand-to-mouth policy. The Resident's view that economic development simply required law and order, roads and taxation, rather than a positive policy favourable to European investment and colonization would, M. Rappard remarked, have satisfied Adam Smith. Other representatives thought the trust reposed in indigenous authorities misplaced: on the Mandatory's own evidence sasswood trials occurred, cannibalism ' on a very small scale ' was admitted, and women were accumulated as capital. Was it enough to hope for the gradual influence of the missions? Was it proper to entrust tax-collection to chiefs and allow them the legal right, to turn out unpaid labour, confusingly described as both voluntary and compulsory, for village public works?[1] Ruxton defended his charges from the accusation of savagery, pointing to the recent belief in witchcraft in Europe. He remained unshaken in his main thesis that the moral welfare of the inhabitants of the Cameroons meant the development of their political capacities: his place at the table, he hoped, would eventually be taken by a native.

Meanwhile the legal confusion which had inhibited divisional officers had been removed. Under the British Cameroons Order

---

[1] *Ibid.* 6th Meeting. The rights of recognized Native Authorities to sue tax-defaulters and village corvée defaulters for refusal to obey authority were laid down in the Native Revenue and Native Authority Ordinances. They had also been covered by local German legislation.

in Council of 1923 the Southern mandated territory was administratively integrated with the Southern Provinces of Nigeria. In 1924 and 1925 the British Cameroons Administration Ordinances under which Nigerian Laws were applied by order with local modifications, provided the territory with a comprehensive law: under these the Northern Nigerian Land and Native Rights Ordinance was applied.

The other Northern Nigerian importation was its system of tax-assessment, under which tax quotas were fixed as a percentage of an estimate of the gross income of villages based on yields per acre, the annual value of livestock, wage income, and the disposal of crop surpluses and manufactures at local market prices. It was a hardy attempt, given the absence of continuous crop estimates by experienced revenue clerks, field to field records and reliable market information, in a mountain country where farm plots were scattered on a long fallow system. Rule of thumb substitutes were found in the measurement of the yield of model plots and the periodic collection of prices of foodstuffs and imported goods at the main markets.[1]

The original Assessments also proposed the form and jurisdictional area of the Native Court and Native Authority, sole or conciliar, or, where they had already been established, reported on their work and on internal arrangements for tax-collection. They invariably contained historical and ethnological chapters, and descriptions of the main features of the political system, customary law and land tenure.[2]

The Assessment tours usually took thirty or forty days. One such tour, which took 111 days, provoked admiration in some superior officers for the evidence it gave of *rapport* with remote villages, and irritation in others for the neglect of routine judicial work it entailed. A proposal to publish it as a model for Southern Nigerian purposes provoked a long argument between Northern and Southern-minded secretariat officers which rivalled the report in length.[3]

---

[1] For a critique of the system see *Report of the Commission on Revenue Allocation* (Lagos, 1951), p. 122 ff.

[2] The only Cameroons Assessment to be published is B. G. Stone, *Assessment Report, Victoria Division*, (Lagos, 1931); a Bamenda Assessment of 1934 was circulated to members of the Permanent Mandates Commission.

[3] Mbo Assessment Report, and accompanying Minutes by Sir Hugh Clifford, Captain (later Sir Walter) Buchanan-Smith, W. E. (later Sir William) Hunt and others, Nov. 1923 (Buea archives).

Indeed, as more settled conditions gave rise to more burden-some routine, full-dress Assessments could never be repeated since the exercise involved the absence from the station of a divisional officer and also of other irreplaceable staff—clerks, interpreters and experienced station messengers. Consequently other devices—special reports and touring notes—kept the political information reasonably up-to-date. After the recon-sideration of Native Administration in Sir Donald Cameron's[1] governorship substantial Progress, Intelligence and Reorganization reports took their place. The large chiefdom of Nso, for example, was assessed twice, in 1922 and 1934 and between 1936 and 1938 was the subject of frequent special inquiries. The so-called Nsungli area was assessed in 1923, was the subject of a lengthy Intelligence Report in 1934, a Progress Report in 1936, and other *ad hoc* inquiries. Since continuous economic assessment was impracticable, the tax quota system was regarded as too arbitrary and replaced after 1933 by a poll-tax.

The first round of Assessments gave the lie to the *simpliste* views held in 1921. They displayed an uncomfortably varied range of political systems in the division. Most of the 12,000 Ngi (Ngie, Mingi), for example, had a common speech and common legend of origin; their remote villages were distinct political units and appeared to be presided over, rather than ruled, by clanheads, some of whom claimed a genealogical seniority over others, assisted by family-heads. Their liveliest institutions, a witch-finding system and a title-society, were believed to be too closely associated with repugnant practices (cannibalism was reported) to be harnessable to administration. Bali-Nyonga, on the other hand, was a compact secular monarchy with a well-developed system of appointive offices but no clearly defined council. The 14,000 Meta, seemingly of the same origin as the Ngi, were militarily formidable and combined the outward marks of village chiefship with the same fundamental structure as the Ngi. The Nso chiefdom was a sacred monarchy with a Tikar dynasty, a hereditary council of state, a regulatory society, and local military clubs with public functions. Bikom was another sacred monarchy, with a matrilineal dynasty and both patrilineal and matrilineal

[1] Cameron, Sir Donald, G.C.M.G. (1872–1948); Col. Civ. Serv. Brit. Guiana 1890–1904; Mauritius, Act. Col. Sec. 1904–7; S. Nigeria 1908; Act. Col. Sec. 1912; Sec. to Central Govt. Nigeria 1914; Chief Sec. 1921–4; Gov. and C.-in-C. Tanganyika 1925–31; Gov. and C.-in-C. Nigeria 1931–35.

villages. Wum was perhaps the hardest to grasp and use: it was a federal association of ward chiefs, often at loggerheads, one of them a ritual primus; each of them had one or more tributaries. Dynastic succession was matrilineal in most wards. Some institutions, or rather names for them, seemed to be widespread, but their powers and functions varied.[1]

The Assessing Officer's first task, the demarcation of a political area, was the most difficult and posed the most fundamental questions, perforce left unanswered in the general statements of policy. How far back in time were the principles to guide administrative consolidations to be sought? How much of the German consolidation was to be undone? How far were former sovereignties to be recognized if they upset well-entrenched claims? Once recognized, were the customary regalities, insofar as they were not repugnant, to be enforceable in the Native Courts?

Some of the difficulties of consolidation, as well as the influence on divisional officers of overlapping waves of administrative doctrine, can be illustrated by a comparison of the two main efforts to organize the Meta, or Menemo as they later came to be called. Their first experience of British rule was unhappy. Two Meta villages had, after a punitive expedition, been resettled on Bali land by the Germans, and placed under the Bali chief for tax and corvée. During the British invasion they decamped. In 1916 a military patrol was sent after them by Podevin, in accordance with his general instructions to preserve the status quo: the German *Schutzbrief* to Bali in his possession showed them to be ' subjects '. For four years the village-heads refused to come in to the station and were protected by other villages. In 1920 another patrol was sent against them, and destroyed crops and huts without result. But before operations were resumed, the divisional staff began to doubt the basis of its case.[2] The assistant divisional officer, C. J. Gregg,[3] walked the disturbed area alone and exposed himself to danger in an effort to start negotiations. He was

[1] See P. M. Kaberry, ' Traditional Politics in Nsaw,' *Africa*, xxix (1959), 366–83, and P. M. Kaberry and E. M. Chilver, ' The Traditional Political System of Bali-Nyonga,' *Africa*, xxxi (1961), 355–71; F. Carpenter: Report on Kwifon, 1936; B. (later Sir Bryan) Sharwood-Smith, Assessment Report on the Ngemba and Mogamaw speaking families, 1925; E. G. (later Sir Gerald) Hawkesworth, Notes on Clans in the Wum area, n.d. 1926? and other reports listed in McCulloch, Manoukian and Dugast, *op. cit.*

[2] Bamenda Station Diary, March, 1920.

[3] Gregg, C. J. A., R.E.; appted. Southern Provinces 1920, and resigned, as District Officer, 1932.

successful. The leader of the rebellious villages, one Tabi, trusting Gregg's word that he would get a fair hearing, came in. After local Meta opinion had been sounded, the fearless Tabi was recognized as ' clan head' and as President of a Native Court established in November 1922. The choice of Tabi as Clan Head was confirmed by the subsequent Assessment tour. Tabi was described to the Assessing Officer as the lineal descendant of the founder of the clan, the disposer of disputes between heads of other branches, and the only Meta chief with the right to receive compensation for murder and absolve persons from blood guilt. But two leading Meta chiefs stayed away from Tabi's court, one of them being the chief recognized as paramount by the Germans. They accused Tabi of demanding a tribute of game and wine and of using the court to enforce his demands: he was, indeed, behaving like a Bali or Tikar chief. Tabi's difficulties were put down to ' a misunderstanding of Native Administration principles' and he was admonished. The two recalcitrant chiefs were persuaded to attend the new court and pay their tax through Tabi. But as soon as the Assessing Officer's back was turned the quarrel broke out afresh. It became clear, in the following years, that payment of tax through another chief was regarded as a demeaning symbol of subjection, and could not be used to build up a Meta political unit. One of the chiefs, it was discovered, belonged to another clan and owed no ' natural' allegiance. But nothing could be done about him as he was in the wrong place. The Native Court was maintained, and despite these quarrels it worked quite well.[1]

When the Intelligence Report of 1933 came to be written the meticulous reports of C. K. Meek on Ibo Government and law had received a wide circulation and consolidated official sympathy for conciliar government and village courts. The new investigator asked different questions and got different replies. There was no such unit as the Meta clan, and consequently no Clan Head. There was no single chiefly line. There were five genealogically-related local groupings but the basic political unit was the village under the headship of the representative of its founder-lineage. This fact had already been recognized for tax-collection purposes, since it had proved impracticable to collect tax except through

[1] C. J. Gregg, Assessment Report on the Meta Clan, 1923; Annual Report‹ Bamenda Division, 1925 (Bamenda papers).

village-heads. The 'rightful chief' recognized by the British held an important ritual office: he had been put forward by the Meta in order to reach a workable compromise with the whitemen. The former German nominee was an important man too; he was the biggest village-head, whose predecessors had adopted the paraphernalia of Tikar chiefship not so long ago. The solution proposed was a council of village-heads and elders and a central court, both presided over by the divisional officers, and five minor courts, one each for the local groups; this was partly to legalize and bring under control the 'palace-jurisdictions' which had covertly persisted. The proposals were never carried out in full because persistent staff shortages made the supervision of so many small courts impossible.[1]

Genealogies were used in support of the consolidation of tribal units in the first intensive rounds of political inquiry and tax-assessment. In the south-western, 'Widekum', areas they took the form of family-trees of the main speech or local groups showing the connections between the founder-lineages of villages. The two Meta family trees collected show quite marked differences. But it is unlikely that the reporting officers were hasty or misinformed: it is far more likely that the family trees they collected represented either contemporary political relations expressed in family-ties or agreed modifications of them. In the first tree the seniority and political attributes of one village-head was stressed because they represented a claim to be released from the domination of another tribe. Once this had been achieved, other claims could be made to seniority with an eye to fiscal independence.

A broader form of genealogical inquiry, involving the tracing of dynastic interrelations, was used in the areas with centralized chiefdoms. Shared traditions of origin from a mother chiefdom might, it was held, imply a common customary law and a disposition to combine in Native Courts or councils. Dynastic links might be rephrased by informants when a limited aim in relation to tax-collection or courts had been achieved. One case, which took up many pages in divisional files, will illustrate the process. During the German period Ntem had been assigned to Banyo Station. After 1919 it was assigned to the British sphere and placed under the administration of the Fulani District Head of Gashaka,

---

[1] C. H. Croasdale, Intelligence Report on the Menemo-speaking families, 1933; Supplement thereto by V. K. Johnston, 23 Dec. 1935 (Bamenda papers).

a chieftain of the Banyo royal house. This little chiefdom had once been more important but was reduced to a small village by repeated Fulani slaving, and its chiefship had been temporarily usurped by nominees of the Banyo lamido. The principle that communities should not be forced to accept alien chiefs had been established in the south-west of the division and was now asserted in the northern border areas. Its chief did not relish an association with a Fulani superior. As early as 1921, divisional officers had considered the attachment of Ntem to Yola Province indefensible. Moreover, it could not be visited by the divisional officer and received no benefits in return for tax. During 1923 the Nsungli area of the Cameroons Province, less remote from Ntem, was assessed. The aged Ntem chief then claimed a dynastic connexion with a Nsungli chief and accepted his leadership. This move was assumed to mean that Ntem was a cadet chiefdom of the Nsungli one. Once Ntem was detached from Yola and associated with the Nsungli chief's court and tax-agency, and once the old chief was dead, there were mounting complaints about the Nsungli chief's claims to seniority. In 1932, the Ntem area was assessed, and reported on again in 1933 and 1936. A different tradition of origin, supported by some neighbouring chiefs, and a lengthy king-list were produced. Since the Nsungli chief by virtue of his assumed family-headship had been given a court it seemed evident to the Ntem chief that, once he had established his pedigree, he should have one too. The area was organized after assessment and the Ntem chief was made a president of a local court. The Lieutenant-Governor was not altogether pleased. The reorganization had, he thought, been based on ' sentiment ', since there was not enough work to keep the little court busy. The divisional officers were perhaps more conscious than he of the merits of petty justice on the complainant's doorstep rather than at the end of a back-breaking trek.[1]

But as information about the traditional politics of the Bamenda peoples accumulated, ' sentiment ', in the sense of respect for the claims and institutions of the tiniest villages, was difficult

[1] Papers relating to Nsungli Clan Assessment, 1923; E. H. F. Gorges, Kaka-Ntem Assessment, 1932; F. W. Carpenter, Intelligence Report on Mbaw, Mbem and Mfumte areas, 1933; R. Newton, Progress Report on the Mbaw, Mbem and Mfumte, Native Court Area, 1936; Divisional Annual Reports, 1933 and 1934; Tour Notes, 1933 and 1934 (Bamenda papers). The claims of Ntem and the political use of genealogies have recently been discussed by M. D. W. Jeffreys, ' Some historical notes on the Ntem ', *J. Hist Soc. Nigeria*, ii (1962), 260–76.

to avoid. The discussions with chiefs, village heads, their councillors and retinues, governed by a code of courtesies laid down in a provincial circular, became more captivating as divisional officers mastered the traditional constitutional principles underlying succession disputes, suzerainty claims, boundary cases and cases about the possession of regalia. Between them and the traditional authorities there arose a common ground of political argument and respect for one another's capacity for the use of precedent and the extension and adjustment of principles to meet new cases. Some divisional officers found that their advice in the settlement of domestic political disputes was sought: they were sometimes cast in the local rôle of *tafon*, titular father to the chief. Some issues which occupied their attention must have seemed a little mysterious to a distant Secretary for Native Affairs unfamiliar with the local constitutional idiom. Sub-chief Y, for example, had been caught wearing a regal necklace of leopards' teeth: what made the offence worse was that he was claiming the right to have the regulatory society, *ngumba*. Chief X, the ruler of a miniscule conquest state which claimed Y, sent members of his own regulatory society to snatch the necklace from the sub-chief's neck, but this manner of settling the matter was clearly liable to lead to an affray. The divisional officer had to intervene. The experts of the Native Court pronounced that the necklace was a lesser matter; the sub-chief must surrender the paraphernalia of *ngumba*. This he did, save for one object, the society's lictor-mark, *mabu*. Another point now had to be determined: were *ngumba* and *mabu* separable or inseparable? The court pronounced them inseparable and suggested the exchange of *mabu* for the necklace. The necklace, when it was returned, was alleged by sub-chief Y to have some teeth missing, so, he claimed, the settlement was void. At this point the patience of the divisional officer began to crack: the sub-chief was told to come into the station for a talk. This command, involving an 85-mile walk and some face-losing hanging about in the petitioners' corridor, secured a temporary lull in the dispute. But sub-chief Y had another shot in his locker. In accordance with the general policy of associating hamlet-heads with tax collection, rather than allowing it to fall, where developed chiefdoms existed, into the hands of retainers, the tax-discs sent out from the station had been parcelled up into batches corresponding to the sub-groupings of a village-area or chiefdom evident in the tax-lists. It had been explained that permission to receive tax-discs did not involve any change in constitutional relations between their recipients and Chief X. But the change was disturbing. Chief X wrote ' I wish to counted all my people in peace. I no want to separate them, like last year 1934. Please find the tax-list of 1932 and 1933. You will see (my) people are not separate. I wish (to keep) all my sub-chiefs (named). I wish to stay with them in peace as before. Because they are not My Family, they are my chiefs since long time and I wish to join all the total numbers of taxable in one place as before, and I will allow them to get their 10 per cent for tax and I will make list, show how many each chief pay his tax. Because if D.O. separate the tax discs from Bamenda before send to me to give them, so they will not hear (obey) me. They always said (will always say) D.O. make us free, we are not under X chief again '. And so it turned out: sub-chief Y emboldened by the receipt of tax-discs, though foiled in the matter of the necklace and *mabu*, asserted himself by bringing a carved stool to court and refusing Chief X the customary share of game.[1] The belief that a subordinate tax-collection agency implied political recognition by the colonial power died hard, and divisional officers and their Cameroonian staff were obliged constantly to restate the principles of tax-collection, and to refuse to entertain claims for jurisdictional separation which were solely based on a sub-chief's delegated authority as a minor fiscal agent, even if it dated from ' Kamenda ', ' Damasi ' or ' D.O. Houseboy ', the Paul Bunyans of the pioneer periods of German or British administration[2]. Even more likely to lead to disturbances were intertribal boundary disputes. These, whether settled administratively with the consent of the parties concerned or by means of the inquiries provided for in the Inter-tribal Boundaries Settlement Ordinance of 1933, required prompt action, long marches as often as not, and considerable patience in the unravelling of the evidence presented: as some of the surviving Land Record Books and Inquiry Reports show, a familiarity with particular traditional patterns of tribute and homage was necessary

---

[1] Tour Notes, 1934, 1935; Nsungli Area Progress Report, 1936 (Bamenda papers).

[2] Namely ' Kommandeur ', usually Hauptmann Hans Glauning, Lt. Adametz and Mr. E. G. (later Sir Gerald) Hawkesworth (ob. 1949), one of the most impressive divisional officers of the ' twenties; subsequently Governor of British Honduras.

if the intention of witnesses was to be understood and if they were to be cross-examined effectively.

The programme of research into native institutions stimulated by the inquiries into the Aba riots and the subsequent despatch from the Secretary of State of 1930 involved no new departure in the Division: officers had conducted them when they could be spared. But if the leading theme of the inquiries of the 'twenties had been the search for and maintenance of legitimate authority, the element of consent was stressed in those of the 'thirties.[1] The shift in emphasis had Lugard's full approval in the Permanent Mandates Commission.

The cross-current of Christianity

The first inspection of the division by a Lieutenant-Governor took place in 1932. A younger man than others before him, Captain Buchanan-Smith[2] was able to face the 300-mile trek on foot that his tour involved. In his statement at the 24th Session of the Permanent Mandates Commission he admitted that the northern model of Native Administration had been followed ' rather slavishly ' and that there was little room, in the current system, for the Christian and educated members of the community. The new trend towards decentralization might seem chaotic but it would, he believed, give more scope to schooled men in the management of local affairs. Even schoolboys, he suggested, might take a share of the work in the smaller Courts and conciliar authorities proposed. This was a far cry from the early 'twenties when scribes and literate hangers-on were shooed out of meetings with chiefs and elders by the divisional officers, in an effort to increase chiefly prestige and self-confidence. Buchanan-Smith also reported that Monsignor Rogan[3] in charge of the prefecture

[1] C. K. Meek's Introduction to *Law and Authority in a Nigerian Tribe* (London, 1937) lucidly expresses the new outlook. See also *Annual Report, Southern Provinces, for the year* 1932 (Lagos, 1933), pp. 2–3.

[2] Buchanan-Smith, Sir Walter (1879–1944); Brit. N. Borneo C.S. 1903–8; Asst. Dist. Cr. S. Nigeria 1909; Acting Cr. Lands 1912, 1914; Nig. Regt. 1914–18; 1st Cl. D.O. 1918; Resident 1921; Act. Sec. S. Provinces 1923, 1925; Sen. Resident, Cameroons 1926; Act. Lt. Gov. 1928–9; Lt. Gov. S. Prov. 1930; Admin. Govt. 1930, 1934; Ret. 1935; Admin. Govt. of Seychelles 1939; Member N. Rhodesia Copperbelt Commn. 1940.

[3] Rogan, Mgr. Peter, D.D., O.B.E. (1886–   ); Asst. to the Pontifical Throne; joined St. Joseph's Society for Foreign Missions, in Liverpool, at the age of 14; Ordained 1909 and served as missionary priest and resident Chaplain to the Forces in Kenya 1909–1925; Prefect Apostolic of Buea 1925–39; Bishop of the Diocese of Buea, 1939–61.

of Buea, had intervened to allay the conflicts between the adherents of the Roman Catholic mission and the pagan chiefs, which had, hitherto, been a regular feature in the Mandatory's reports.

The intertwining of mission questions with reforms in Native Administration policy was not accidental. During the period of German administration there had been a rough division of missionary activity in the area. The Basel evangelicals had centred their work in the west and south-west, the Sacred Heart Fathers in the east. In 1920, after a preliminary tour by Father Shanahan, the Fathers returned to their station in Nso.[1] Their arrival was followed by disorders and persecutions of mission adherents in the Nso and Bikom chiefdoms which required the intervention of the Resident: yet, curiously enough, it was precisely the rulers of these two chiefdoms who had most warmly welcomed Father Shanahan's proposals to reopen the mission. The return of the Fathers had been preceded by the repatriation, in 1919, of the interned soldiers and military carriers from Fernando Poo. These, during their internment, had been indoctrinated by the Roman Catholic chaplains; some 900 Grassfielders were baptized and 1,500 had joined the catechumenate between 1916 and 1919. The eastern districts of the division had been called upon to send carriers to Fernando Poo; many of these were men who had been in contact with the mission. During their brief stay in Fernando Poo, over 800 sought baptism in the internment camp. The chaplains had reinforced the military *ésprit de corps* of the camp by their instruction; many of the repatriated men were enthusiasts, uncompromisingly contemptuous of traditional *mores*. The divisional files of the 'twenties contain frequent references to their high-handedness.[2] The local groups of faithful, held together by a few remarkable catechists, such as Peter Wame of Babungo and Paul Tangwa of Kumbo, were thus powerfully reinforced by men whose loyalties were elsewhere and with whom the divisional staff had had no contact. Moreover the eastern districts were scarcely visited until 1921, and the reabsorption of the internees coincided with a period when these districts were left to their own devices. The arrival there of the Fathers polarized local sentiment between the minority of new men looking to the mission and the

[1] John P. Jordan, C.S.Sp., *Bishop Shanahan of Southern Nigeria* (Dublin, 1949), pp. 170–72; Joh. Emonts S.C.J., *op. cit.*, pp. 403 ff.; F. W. Migeod, *Through the British Cameroons* (London, 1925), p. 115.
[2] See also *Evangelische Heidenbote* (1927), 100.

traditional authorities looking to the divisional officers for support. Even to-day literates refer contemptuously to unlettered pagans as ' N.A. ', and pagans to literates as ' Bara ' or foreigners.[1]

The Fathers, one with local, others with Belgian Congo experience, were unfamiliar with British colonial practice; their arrival, moreover, was shortly followed by a swing in the sentiments of officers towards some of the current Northern Nigerian interpretations of Indirect Rule.[2] The divisional staff became impatient with the mission's interventions in favour of Christians who had offended against custom and its appeals for the speedy punishment of pagans. ' For them,' wrote one divisional officer in 1921, ' all Native Administration is comprised in the word Juju '.

The stay of the ' French Fathers ', as they were locally called, was brief: the division of the German territory required a new and compatible ecclesiastical reorganization and this was carried through in 1923, when the Mill Hill Mission (St. Joseph's Society for Foreign Missions) took over their establishments in the British sphere. Tension between Christians and pagans lessened somewhat, but minor disturbances and friction continued. A convinced Roman Catholic laity, sustained by six years of doctrinal teaching, angered by the petty persecutions of those they mocked as ' bushmen ', and vindicated in the British courts was in no mood to welcome the justice of the Native Court.

The main issues around which friction occurred were the rights of chiefs to reserve girls for their households, their rights to recruit pages, sometimes from particular social categories, the channel of tax-payments and the flight of wives and wards to the mission to learn doctrine. The right of chiefs to girls was as undisputable a mark of regality as their allegiance tributes of leopards. Adultery and even unchaperoned conversation with a chief's wife or the wives of certain other titleholders was treated both as an abomination and as treason. Boys, recruited as royal attendants or boy-servants of the regulatory society for a term of years, became the messengers and executives of the chief or the society; the encouragement offered to them to leave the chief's

---

[1] B. T. Sakah, ' The Influence of Western Civilization on the Nso ', roneod, 1962 (International African Institute MS. collection).

[2] See Margery Perham, *Native Administration*, pp. 329–31. The swing in sentiment cannot be ascribed to denominational or ' Northern ' loyalties, for the Resident at the time was a Roman Catholic and the divisional officer had previously served in Eastern Nigeria.

service to attend catechism classes and avoid contact with pagan practices more obviously undermined chiefly authority, if it was done without chiefly consent. The flight of royal wives and wards provoked even more widespread anger and scandal; the majority of pagans regarded it as a deliberate reversal of the social order. Their forcible recovery was, of course, prohibited by the divisional staff who were, by and large, obeyed by the chiefs. The runaway women were believed, quite unjustly in the majority of cases, to be living by harlotry.[1] Their subsequent marriages to Christian converts, without the consent of their lineage-head, led to family estrangements, and to bitter cases in the Native Courts over compensation for adultery which presented reviewing officers with difficult problems in equity.[2]

The difficulties over the channel of tax-payments was associated with these revolutionary reversals of custom. The collection of tax by lineage-heads or royal retainers, indeed by those with whom the converts were most likely to be in conflict over desertions from the family-compound or the palace, was sometimes resisted.[3] Christians or learners who had congregated around or fled to mission establishments were emboldened by the protection these gave to appoint their own collectors, or to protest, sometimes with justice, against over-assessment under the ' commonsense ' schemes run by the chiefs or the permitted schemes which followed the brief attempt to introduce lump sum assessment officially after 1929. The channel of tax-collection was the ark of the covenant of the earlier models of Native Administration, and proposals by Fathers-in-charge to collect on behalf of their flock as a whole were firmly rejected. The political object of lump-sum assessment was the association of the smallest constituent units of a Native Authority area with collection, because of the education in co-operation and responsibility the process was believed to confer. The Roman Catholic lay communities were not officially recognized as such units. Indeed their tendency to evolve their own systems of self-government and organize

[1] From the mid 'twenties onwards, the Fathers would usually despatch the royal runaways and their Christian partners to a more distant mission, a practice which mollified the chiefs.

[2] By the time the Nigerian Marriage Ordinance was applied, the demand of native Christians for it was lukewarm. See the discussion of the question at the 26th Session of the Permanent Mandates Commission, 3rd Mtg.

[3] In 1929 some chief's retainers were recognized as *dogarai* or chiefdom police, cf. *Annual Report, Southern Provinces* (Lagos, 1929), p. 17.

I

prestations and subscriptions was alarming to divisional officers. The separation of the Christians from the pagan community was most acute in Bikom where the lack of communication between the palace and the Christian quarters of the larger villages was almost complete. The Fathers, of course, counselled moderation in speech and traditional courtesy to pagan lords, but in Christian eyes their authority replaced the chief's.[1] Originally the Fathers had forbidden their converts to join all indigenous societies, not only the regulatory societies but the military clubs which, in some chiefdoms, organized local public works; the Christians were concerned with their own, perhaps more onerous, public works, the building of churches, mission schools and catechists' houses. The Christians themselves desired separation for spiritual reasons: they were fearful of the temptations of traditional offices, which some could have filled, and of assaults on their faith. Moreover in two of the large chiefdoms in which they were strongest, the rulers were aged conservatives, of whom an understanding compromise with new forces, except under direct administrative pressure, could not be expected.

By contrast, the accommodation of the Basel Mission to traditional authority was relatively peaceful, and the main troubles it met with arose out of competition for its services. The Basel flock, though sustained by flying visits from members of the Paris Evangelical Mission and contacts with the Native Baptist Church, had been left without a resident missionary till 1925. A visiting missionary in 1921 reported that the old centre of missionary activity in Bali was divided by factions but that a strong movement existed in the Meta, Ngemba and Bafut areas.[2] As in the Catholic-influenced east, local catechists had kept the Christians together, among them Johannes Asili and Jacob Shu, both later to be ordained. Apart from some initial trouble in Bafut, which the divisional officer persuaded the chief to settle for himself, and occasional prohibitions on the attendance of women at preachings, lest they should become impertinent, there seem to have been few collisions with chiefs. This absence of trouble can scarcely be accounted for by differences in the Mission's attitude to the question of polygamy, servitudes or pagan associations. It was as

[1] Cf. Emonts, *op. cit.*, 407, Letter from Rev. Fr. Jacobs to Rev. Fr. Emonts, 10 April, 1926; Reports on Bikom Chiefship, D.O. to Resident, 9 Nov., 1926, and Resident to D.O. 25 Nov., 1926 (Bamenda papers).

[2] *Evangelische Heidenbote*, 1921, p. 136.

strict in these matters as the Fathers. But less was heard of its difficulties because it seldom asked for the intervention of the civil authorities on behalf of its agents, who were counselled to show respect to chiefs. Possibly its easier accommodation can be ascribed to the difference in political systems in the east and west of the division, yet there were sacred monarchies or centralized chiefdoms in the west also. Part of it was perhaps the result of a far longer exposure there to the modernizing influences of plantation, school, workshop and station, which prevented the Basel Christians from claiming any special monopoly of ' new fashion '. Almost certainly the mission's pattern of evangelical settlement, its scatter of modest hedge-schools, and its eschewal of the mission quarter pattern offered less scope for political apartheid. The missionaries themselves included artisans ready to help a chief with his public buildings: and their Christians worked with them.[1]

The western districts, even if they suffered from a ten-year gap in mission schooling, had had the benefit of a Government elementary school in Bamenda since 1922 and a Native Administration school in Bali since 1923:[2] a number of Basel hedge-schools had survived the War and these were revived in 1925. In the eastern districts in 1925 there were two Roman Catholic missionary schools; in 1924, one Native Administration school had been established. From 1930 onwards an Education Officer was intermittently posted to the Division. By 1937 there were in the division one Government, six Native Administration schools, four assisted mission schools (including a Baptist school) and 76 unassisted secular mission schools: there was no secondary school in the whole province until the Mill Hill Fathers started to expand their school at Sasse in 1939. After the Nigerian Education Ordinance of May 1926 was applied, and the memoranda of the Colonial Office's Advisory Committee on Native Education in Tropical Africa had been disseminated, the way lay open in theory for closer collaboration between the divisional officers and the missionaries: it became close with the Basel Mission and with the revived Baptist Mission which first established itself in the neglected north-east of the Division. With the Roman Catholic Mission relations improved, and after 1937 became excellent.

[1] For an account of the accommodation of a Basel congregation in a small chiefdom see A. Schmidt, *Die rote Lendenschnur* (Berlin, 1955), passim.

[2] Resident Ruxton was active in promoting Native Administration Schools and the Cameroons Province pioneered them in the South.

Any rapid expansion of assisted schools was cramped by the limits on teacher-training and inspecting capacity: there were only seven local elementary teachers in training at the provincial training centre by the end of 1936.

Decentralization and its limitations

The new Southern policy explained by Buchanan-Smith to the Permanent Mandates Commission in 1932 required a far larger staff to implement it than was ever available: a plan to divide up the area into regular touring districts failed on this account.[1] The effects of breaking up the larger court areas into ' natural units ' and the organization of conciliar Native Authorities were negligible at first. In 1938 there were 18 gazetted Native Authorities, four areas in which the Native Court was the Native Authority ' pending reorganization ', and one remote directly administered area, Mbembe; there were 30 Native Courts, seven of which had limited D powers. Many of these conciliar Native Authorities, the divisional officer reported in 1937 and 1938, were ' theoretical '. Full meetings seldom occurred except when an administrative visit took place or for the distribution of quarterly salaries. Revenues were so small that there was, indeed, very little scope for the proliferation of Native Treasuries.[2] But demands for more schools, dressers and dispensaries began to be more strongly voiced and the divisional staff fostered the notion that these might be obtained if resources were pooled. In the chiefdom areas a cautious propaganda for a supporting council was made—a ' council on which all the novel elements would receive representation '.[3] In Nso, in 1932, a Native Treasury was established and much was hoped from it, but the aged ruler could not be persuaded to select an advisory financial council of progressive notables to help him consider those heads in the Native Authority estimates which could be varied, even after substantial irregularities had been discovered in his Treasury. In some other chiefdoms, where the Native Authorities were also sole, inquiries

[1] The Intelligence Reports on which Native Authority reorganizations were based demanded a period of 4–6 weeks fieldwork in a small area. (Southern Provinces Circular SP 6752/96 of 23 Feb. 1932, and a Provincial Circular of 23 Jan. 1934).
[2] In 1938 Bamenda and Nso Native Treasury revenue amounted to £6,800; £5,000 of reserves of about £6,500 were earmarked for road construction outside the division.
[3] *Annual Report, Southern Provinces* (Lagos, 1938), pp. 30–31.

were made about the composition of traditional councils, so that
' Chief-in-Council ' Native Authorities might provide the groundwork for gradual innovation.

The slowness of the conversion to more responsible and
representative local councils in Bamenda lay in part in the small
output of educated men who had completed a full primary
course. Those who had stayed the course were young men, still
considered brash boys by their seniors: educated older men who
might have entered their chiefdom's councils as hereditary office-
holders refused office on religious grounds. In fact, new ideas
were mainly channelled to the Native Authorities, as in earlier
times, by the divisional officers themselves, by court clerks,
interpreters, and Native Administration staff. In any event a
more rapid and adequately supervised conversion could not be
engineered, at the same time as the exercise of full judicial powers
by the senior divisional officer, the decentralization of Native
Courts, the oversight of Native Administration schools, and a host
of other business. The divisional officers were well aware of this.
The senior divisional officer, Dr. M. D. W. Jeffreys,[1] presented
the following table in his report for 1939:

Division	Administrative Staff 1939	Est. sq. miles per officer	Est. population[2] per officer	Tax incidence per officer (£)
Bamenda	2.3	3,014	122,156	8,223
Kumba	2.1	1,982	33,526	3,690
Mamfe	2.0	2,160	34,070	2,032
Victoria	2.4	485	19,390	3,242

The routine supervision of 30 courts, most of them away from
a motorable track, was a time-consuming business. Every Native
Court criminal case had to be read through with the prisoner
present, if there was one, and anything he said taken down.
Sentences had to be confirmed, and a warrant signed before a
prisoner could be admitted to prison. The cashbooks, receipt
books, process books, cause books and monthly returns of each
court had to be checked each month by a divisional officer before
Court revenue was paid in and salaries paid out, and to prevent
abuses in the collection of fines. At the end of 1939 eleven courts

[1] Jeffreys, Dr. M. D. W. (1890–); Brit. Col. Civ. Serv. 1915–1945: Sen.
Dist. Off. Nigeria; Asst. Ed. African Studies 1946–7; Asst. Ed. S. A. Assoc. for
Adv. Sci. J.; Sen. Lect. Anthropology, Witwatersrand 1946–56.

[2] The only reliable population figures are those of the 1953 Census which
record the total population of Bamenda (then a province with three divisions)
as 429,038.

remained to be visited and 169 reviews had piled up. In the same year a new system of direct tax collection, designed to prevent evasion and extortion, had been introduced in five areas, and of *jangali* (cattle-tax) collection in all. Revenue from direct taxation increased substantially and *jangali* by 50 per cent. This exercise was feasible because the almost insupportable burden of road works supervision had been temporarily lifted by the posting of a P.W.D. officer to supervise the completion of the long-awaited road between Bamenda and Mamfe, a one-way track but a motorable one, and other urgent works. With a more up-to-date collection system, and with the Mamfe road opening up new economic outlets—for coffee had begun to be planted—the Native Authority revenues (now 65–70 per cent of gross tax collected) might have increased enough to meet the demand for more of the simpler social services demanded. But the small divisional staff was largely diverted to war-duties—the provisioning of the Free French forces, the collection of wild rubber and palm kernels, and the organization of a local defence force. These activities at least absorbed some of the three or four thousand labourers returned to the division from the plantations. Despite staff shortages the programme of improved tax collection was pushed on with the completion of new nominal rolls for the whole division and the association of literate villagers with the issue of tax-receipts: the recorded taxable population increased by some 10,000. Before the end of the war over half the tribal boundaries had been demarcated and recorded in the Land Record Books. A third Native Treasury was set up, and others were anticipated by the keeping of separate local revenue and expenditure accounts. A good deal of time, too, was devoted to an attempt to re-establish arbitration at the village level, in order to remove a mass of petty litigation from the Native Court and the reviewing officer's desk.

Indeed, much of the administrative groundwork for a development of the 'new Southern' system of Native Administration was laid. At the end of the war divisional officers felt obliged to protest that the practice of Cameron's principles needed more staff, both political staff and technical staff. (The first Divisional Agricultural Officer arrived in 1942, the first P.W.D. Officer in 1939). With nearly three officers posted to the Division, some 350 days touring a year was feasible. This looked well in returns, but what did it mean? In a division the size of Bamenda it meant that for six consecutive months an area off the motorable road might be left unvisited. Then, an officer might travel from village to village, spending a night in each and perhaps three in a chiefdom or village-group headquarters. It was of course, easy to suppress information during such visits. In 1945, one Resident contended that the division could not be administered with less than five officers if Native Authorities were to be visited once a quarter. ' Quite apart from the uncomfortable feeling that the liberty of the subject is not safeguarded ' wrote another officer, ' it cannot be supposed that with so little support the most enlightened authorities could carry out those plans for the improvement of the area that are within reach of local resources. The progressive element in council is defeated, the reactionary prevails; there is always a case for inaction '. Most officers felt that too heavy a burden was placed on Native Administration staff. If they were inefficient it was hardly their fault. Half of them had less than a full elementary education and many worked in areas where the language was strange to them; they had little or no formal training and supervision was negligible. The proper training of head-quarters clerical staff was impossible if a divisional officer had to tour for six weeks at a time, leaving a job of work half-done. Most divisional officers would have liked to follow the advice of Resident Browne that they should live in the remoter areas for at least four months without making a single arrest or taking a penny of tax.[1] But desirable as continuous touring was, a station could not be left without a magistrate or divisional officer to deal with Native Court prisoners, petitioners who had trekked many miles to lay an urgent complaint, or messngers reporting a bitter boundary dispute that could flare up into fighting. Bamenda was regarded in Lagos as a backward division; its divisional officers contended it was backward because it was underadministered.

New politics and new men

But the impetus of the policy of decentralized Native Administration was petering out before the end of the war as divisional officers took up the developmental ideas generated in the Colonial Office between 1938 and 1940, and as the promise of metropolitan funds became firmer. In 1942 an agricultural station and demon-

[1] Resident's comments on Wum Assessment Report, 9 May, 1932 (Bamenda papers).

stration farm, and in 1944 a livestock improvement station was set up in the division. Resident Harris[1] compiled an economic survey of the province and proposals for incorporation in the Nigerian Ten-Year Plan were sent forward.[2] The new notion of mass-education presented a field in which political and departmental officers could collaborate: in 1945 a social anthropologisf arrived in Bamenda to conduct a survey of the economic rôle ot women, the subsistence-farmers, as a basis for subsequent development and adult education work. The notion that the black art of economics was irrelevant to territorial administration had gone for good.[3] But the new interventionist policies demanded closer administration, and far more direct propaganda addressed to the folk, and no means for this existed as yet. The divisional staff, moreover, was heavily engaged in the resettlement of ex-soldiers.

On the surface the division seemed calm: the first petitions to the United Nations from the division reflected pension grievances and complicated land disputes, scarcely echoing the nationalist pressures which had paved the way for the Richards Constitution in Nigeria. The Native Authorities had now been increased to 23 since remoter districts had been brought, nominally at any rate, into line: the Native Authorities Ordinance, revised in 1943, appeared to give them all the scope they could conceivably need.[4] No sooner had the network of Native Authorities been completed than the consequences of the new Nigerian constitution and the new local government policy proposed in February 1947 by the Secretary of State began to make themselves felt.

The effects of the first were the more important. The divisional meetings of Native Authorities summoned to learn of and discuss the new constitutional reforms were initially of greater value to the divisional staff in local affairs than they expected. They could now quote a body of local opinion in favour of the administrative reforms which they advocated—the break-up of the division into

[1] Harris, P. G. (1894–1945); Nig. Admin. Serv. 1929–41: A.D.O., N. Provinces 1919; Sen. Resident, N. Eastern Provinces 1938–45; H.M. Consul Gen. Duala 1940–43.

[2] Cf. Nigerian Leg. Co., *Sessional Paper No.* 24 of 1945.

[3] The annual report to the League of Nations in 1936 had stated: ' The question of the natives getting the full benefit of the trade revival is one of economics and it is difficult to see what useful measure the Administration can take to ensure it ' (p. 72).

[4] For its interpretation see *The apportionment of duties between the Government of Nigeria and the Native Administrations: Statement of Policy* (Lagos, 1947).

three and an increase in staff. The division was promoted to a province in 1949 after four years of resolute official agitation, and by 1950 three new divisions, Bamenda, Wum and Nkambe, had been created, and were staffed.

Meanwhile a Select Committee of the Eastern House of Assembly had put a vast distance between the reforms in local government projected in the Eastern Region and those immediately feasible in the new province. The report on local government reform by Brigadier E. J. Gibbons[1] upon which theirs had been based had put its finger on the fundamental weakness of decentralized native administration, based on consent as to jurisdictional areas—the assumption that it could attract the services of educated men. The current system ' had neither the scope nor the prestige to attract into its membership the really enlightened African of education and consequence in the community.'[2] The theory of inherent authority upon which it was based, was, he considered, out of place in a modern nation. He had proposed elective county councils with subordinate Native Authorities below them, responsible to a Local Government Board which would be in charge of a unified local government staff. This proposal, which might have suited the new province, was substantially modified by the Select Committee, and pressed even further in the direction of English local government practice by the Eastern House.

The new local government policy proposed in February 1947 accorded with the divisional staff's own notion of pooling, which they and Residents on their inspection tours had already disseminated. A series of local meetings were called to broach the question of federating the existing Native Authorities into agencies capable of administering local services and collaborating more effectively with development schemes. For the latter the ten-year plan funds and the profits of the Cameroons Development Corporation were available.

By 1948 agreement was reached on four amalgamations—the South-Western (Widekum) Federation with a population of 97,200,

[1] Gibbons, Brig. E. J. (1906–   ); Nig. Admin. Serv. 1929–41; Army Serv. 1941–6; Dir. Civ. Aff. S.E. Asia Command; Sec. East. Prov. Nig. 1948; Cr. Cameroons 1949–56.

[2] E. J. Gibbons, *African Local Government Reform: Kenya, Uganda and Nigeria* (Lagos, 1949); *Report of a Select Committee* (Enugu, 1948). The theory of inherent authority in its modified form had been clearly restated by Sir Bernard Bourdillon in *The apportionment of revenue and duties between the Central Government and Native Administrations* (Lagos, 1939), pp. 4–5.

the South-Eastern (Tikari) with 139,000, the North-Western (Wum Divisional) Federation with 79,660, and the North-Eastern (Nkambe Divisional) Federation with 85,000. The Bali Native Authority, with over 23,000, could not be amalgamated with its hostile Widekum neighbours. Like the Widekum and Tikari Native Authorities it was formed on an ' ethnic ' basis, as Gibbons had recommended. The two Divisional authorities were compromise structures, representing the best balance that could be achieved between viable size, communications and political considerations: the large chiefdom of Bikom and the smaller chiefdom of Bum were assigned to the north-western group.

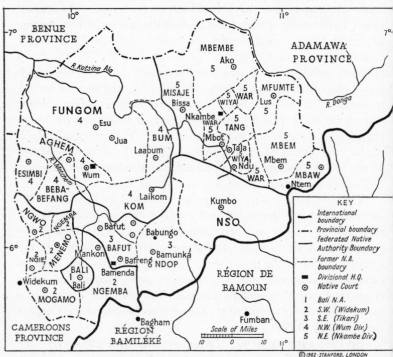

The Reorganisation of Bamenda Province 1949–50

The Native Authorities had little to suggest about changes in their membership. The divisional officers' proposals that moots of traditional councillors and village heads (terms with elastic meanings) in each of the former Native Authorities should each elect six traditional, four untitled literate and two women members was acceptable to the Tikari group at this stage. In Bali the ruler called together an electoral college of 60 ward-heads and notables to select representatives. The Widekum Native Authorities formed themselves into an electoral college of over a hundred to select representatives, who included primary teachers, traders and craftsmen. Early in 1949 the local government proposals of the Select Committee of the Eastern House were circulated to Native Authorities and explained by divisional officers orally. How far they were understood by the majority of members is uncertain. At all events they were opposed to them; the speed with which new conceptions of political authority and new procedures were being put forward, and their origin outside the province was disturbing to all but a minority. The pressure on Native Authorities to reform themselves came from all sides. The pressure to federate was accompanied by a reform of the Native Courts, which introduced literates and women to the benches, and which showed every sign of being overtaken, in turn by further changes consequent upon the Brooke Commission of Inquiry and special investigations which were expected to follow it.[1] Divisional officers believed that the new mixed appeal courts could evolve a serviceable common law on land tenure, marriage and inheritance, provided that the repugnancy clauses were applied with increasing sternness in interpreting the Native Courts Ordinance.[2]

Perhaps the most puzzling collision of doctrine arose after the report of the Africanization Commission, appointed in 1948, had been received. This made quite specific the theory that the place of the Administrative Service would be taken by ' an improved system of Native Administration and local government ' rather than by the Africanization of the provincial administration. This proposition, in a province like Bamenda, would have completely revolutionized the internal political system, based upon delegated authority influenced by a fair measure of free-spoken remonstrance, which passed through the narrow but protected channels of complaint, petition, Native Authority, resolution, a rising flow of correspondence between members of the public and divisional

[1] G.N. No. 1453 of 1950; *Report of the Native Courts (Cameroons and Bamenda Provinces)* Commission of Inquiry (Lagos, 1953). The introduction of women to the benches had been proposed much earlier, and in some cases entailed the restoration of a traditional dignity.

[2] Minutes and correspondence with Resident, 7 June, 1948, to 21 Jan., 1949, (Bamenda papers).

officers, and recourse to an increasingly professional magistrature.[1]

The gentlemen of education and consequence upon whom the Administration increasingly relied for support had formed the Cameroons National Federation early in 1949 by amalgamating delegations from the Cameroons Development Corporation's Workers' Union with a number of tribal and improvement unions including three from the Bamenda Province and one representing ' French ' Grassfielders resident in the British trust territory.[2] Its foundation had followed discussions between C.D.C.W.U. leaders and the leading men among the nearest 'Afrenchi ' political groupings: Ruben um Nyobe, secretary of the Union des Populations Camerounaises, Chief Mathias Djoumessi, leader of the Bamileke tribal union Kumsse, and members of Ngondo, the Duala tribal union. The C.N.F. had been invited to attend the Provincial Meeting called in June 1949, to discuss the Nigerian constitutional reforms in prospect: it put forward a plea for a separate regional government for the British trust territory as a prelude to eventual reunification with the French trust territory. Its views on Native Administration were then distinctly unlike those of the Eastern House: it called for the codification of native law and custom to end the ' danger of disruption of the machinery of local government as the result of growing misinterpretation, misrepresentation and falsification of Native Laws upon which local government is based ',[3] and for an end to the appointment and deposition of chiefs or natural rulers by the Government. The Federation considered that the existing Native Authority system was unsatisfactory but did not, as yet, show signs that it had absorbed the implications of financially autonomous, democratically elected local government.[4] The C.N.F. was active in promoting petitions to the U.N. Visiting Mission and among

[1] The method of handling complaints and petitions was prescribed in provincial circulars and might involve the divisional staff in prolonged inquiries, to judge by instructions issued in the 'thirties: Circular Residents' Instructions Nos. 45 and 47, 1933, and No. 67 of 1934 (Bamenda papers).

[2] For the formation and leadership of the C.D.C.W.U. see W. A. Warmington, *A West African Trade Union* (London, 1960), pp. 22–36.

[3] In 1951 an inquiry into Cameroons land tenure systems was made by the late C. W. Rowling.

Proposals for a simple cadastral survey and the codification of native law and custom as regards land tenure had been made in 1936 by divisional officers in Bamenda in answer to a circulated Governor's Minute on the subject: Memoranda by Dr. M. D. W. Jeffreys and the late F. R. Kay, 1 Oct., 1936 (Bamenda papers).

[4] Resolutions taken at the Inaugural Conference of the C.N.F., Kumba, May 14th and 15th, 1949 (roneo).

these were two from Improvement Unions in Bamenda, one of which put forward the same views on the appointment and deposition of chiefs as the C.N.F. while the other, from the Kom Improvement Union, centred in the old missionized area of Bikom, attacked illiterate and lazy councillors and pressed for a larger representation of ' the literate and enlightened '. By the end of the year a number of local associations federated in the Cameroons Federal Union, including the Bamenda Improvement Union, produced a more detailed and logically argued proposal which called for ' the purging of aged and indolent councillors ', the election of progressive youths, the federation of Native Authorities into larger groups, and ' the development of such federated group councils (which) should eventually merge with and be superseded by the proposed local government system of County Councils and Municipal Administration '.[1]

The hope of the Administration that the energies of the best men in the new associations could be devoted to community development in association with the Native Authorities, and to their democratization, was only intermittently fulfilled. The new leaders' main concern was the formation of an effective political machine at the Cameroons level, and the resolution of major policy questions—their attitude to reunification, their relations with the Northern Cameroons, and their negotiations with the politicians of the Eastern Region. The Administration, while it publicly expressed its agreement with the views of the Cameroons Federal Union, was inevitably hampered by earlier engagements to chiefs and conciliar authorities and uncertain of the strength of the new leaders' following. The indirect elections of 1951 to the Eastern House were all uncontested in the province; all seats were won by improvement union members or men associated with Dr. Endeley's[2] efforts to form an effective political party. But the lack of stir they caused gave the Administration no guidance about the speed with which it could press Native Administration reform in the direction of the Eastern Region Local Government Ordinance of 1950. Divisional officers were generally advised to remove

[1] U.N. Trusteeship Council, *Official Records*, Vol. 2, Fourth Year, 6th Session, p. 125.

[2] Endeley, Dr. E. M. L. (1916–   ); Med. Pract.; Gen. Sec. Cameroons Dev. Co-op. Work. Union, 1947–8; Gen. Pres. 1949–50; Gen. Pres. Cameroons Nat. Fed. 1950–52; Gen. Sec. Cameroons Youth League, 1940–3; Memb. Cameroons Devt. Corp., 1950–54; Cameroons Cent. Minister, 1952–4; Leader, Cameroons Delegn. to 1953–4 Conf.; Leader, Govt. Bus., S. Cam. Govt. 1954.

themselves from obtrusive rôles at the meetings of the Native Authorities at the earliest possible moment. This was impossible for the first few years of the federated Native Authorities, not only because of the mass of new and quite technical business made possible by larger revenues, but because they had to be used to disseminate information about development schemes and constitutional reforms. In the more securely established Native Authority Federations in the south of the province the withdrawal of the divisional officers from Council meetings was conscientiously carried out, and their interventions were largely limited to financial and legal explanations or the dissemination of technical information. The Native Authority Ordinance in its 1948 and subsequent revisions remained the legal basis of the new federations: consequently the province escaped the fluctuations in local government law of the Eastern Region, and the rôle of the divisional officer could be adjusted to suit the circumstances of each Native Authority.[1]

The emergence of the militant K.U.N.C. in 1951 alongside the C.N.F. placed the Divisional Officers in a difficulty: hitherto the C.N.F. had been given access to Provincial Meetings. In 1952 the K.U.N.C. asked for the same privileges and for access to Provincial and Divisional Development Committees. They were refused on the grounds that they were an association with membership on both sides of the international frontier and that representation could no longer be given to parties as such. Assemblymen were, however, given the right to address meetings of Native Authorities after their business was over.

There were stumbling blocks other than constitutional uncertainty and the difficulty of gauging the attitudes of the folk to reforms—the re-emergence, under new leadership, of old quarrels and old associations. Many of these revolved round the ancient intractable issues of tribute and suzerainty, which now became entangled with questions of new Native Authority boundaries, claims to representation in or secession from them and the delegation of tax-collecting duties by them.[2] In parts of the

---

[1] For a discussion of the vicissitudes of local government in the Eastern Region between 1950 and 1955 see L. Gray Cowan, *Local Government in West Africa* (New York, 1958), pp. 69–75, 119–135, 161–3.

[2] Some of these questions have been traced in one area in E. M. Chilver and P. M. Kaberry, ' From tribute to tax in a Tikar chiefdom ', *Africa*, xxx (1960), 1–19.

south-west of the Bamenda Division the main energies of the literates were devoted to agitation and, as it turned out, expensive and fruitless litigation in the High Court concerning land formerly occupied by them but conquered from them before the German annexation by the Bali. There were other elements in this agitation: long-standing grudges dating from the German period and earlier against the Bali overlords, the memory of expulsions which had occurred during the period of administrative breakdown in 1919–20, and the shortage of land of some of the Widekum communities. It was undeniable that the Bali had more land in relation to their numbers than communities in other parts of the province and their land was near good communications and markets. Like other land-hungry peoples, many Widekum villagers hoped to recover their lost lands from their conquerors. Local village unions were now organized by some determined men into an all-Widekum union: the effects of common historical grievance and recognition of the Widekums as a group for Native Administration were reciprocal. In 1950 one of the Widekum villages, supported by others, started a series of legal actions which resulted in an appeal to the High Court in which they claimed almost the whole of Bali land, and damages for trespass. This was dismissed with costs against the plaintiffs in February 1952, because they had not pleaded a title under the Land and Native Rights Ordinance; the judgement was hard to explain to people who had devoted more than a year to collecting funds for an appeal which they had been told they were entitled to make.[1] In March a large Widekum group descended on the Bali, looting and burning: seven persons were killed in the disturbance, which was prevented from developing into a more serious affair by the coolness of a handful of men at the moment of crisis and the subsequent posting of substantial police reinforcements. The outbreak, if it set back the reform Native Administration, provoked a re-examination of the Governor's powers under the Land and Native Rights Ordinance (which had been in doubt) and an inquiry into the economic situation of the contestants:[2] eventually land was acquired from the Bali for the resettlement of the villages

---

[1] Suits C/33/1950, C/55/1950, C/64/1950 and C/65/1950 (consolidated) in the High Court of Justice, Calabar.
[2] *Nigeria Gazette Extraordinary No. 37*, Vol. 40, 1953; U.N. Petitions T/Pet 4/82 and others.

in return for cash compensation by the government. It emerged that the Widekum chiefs who had supported the agitation could not control its excesses: their popularity now depended on their responsiveness to the programmes of the new local associations. The Assemblymen who strove to resolve the feud by negotiation also failed to prevent the outbreak. The emotions of tribal nationalism had been exploited by minor local leaders. But the explosion had not been useless. It lead to the settlement after months of delicate negotiation by provincial officers, involving over fifty meetings, of an ancient quarrel which might have remained to plague the emerging national leadership. It convinced some of these new leaders, also, of the need to channel and direct the local patriotisms which began to be expressed.

What the settlement could not do was to provide a pattern for the solution of numerous other suzerainty issues, pressing and explosive enough to be referred to the Commissioner and the Civil Secretary in 1952 and 1953. They concluded that the real solution would come with ' the introduction of local government and the effluxion of time.' The Resident was less sanguine.

In Wum Division, hauled together by the combination of disparate units, there were troubles of a different kind. The proceedings of the Wum Divisional Council reflected the unequal development of an area at the dead end of a south-facing system of communications. The first motor-car reached the divisional head-quarters in 1949 and the main centres of population were only linked by motorable roads in 1953. It was believed that some parts of the new Division had not received more than twenty administrative visits since 1917. Its backwardness was exemplified by a low rate of literacy—about 2 per cent compared with about 10 per cent for the whole southern trust territory, and a high rate of yaws infection—incidences of 60 per cent were recorded in 1950 from two areas. In two of the more important centres, Wum town and the chiefdom of Bikom, internal feuds grumbled on, preventing any effective contact between the minority of schooled men and the traditional authorities. If the new division was to catch up with its southern neighbours a large enough provincial staff to man the station continuously and tour it constantly was essential. While the main tasks of tax-collection remained in the hands of village heads and elders, it was necessary to attend to their troubles and secure their co-operation. Some, in the course of the reform of Native Courts had lost sitting fees, others, in the course of the reorganization of the Clan Councils which replaced former Native Authorities, had lost their seats. They were, for the most part, disgruntled. The Clan Councils themselves were without a legal basis or defined functions. For the first two years of its existence the Divisional Council showed few signs of life, but in its third, under the influence of a few energetic men, it pressed a demand for free junior primary education. Some Clan areas were prepared to pay an education rate. The demand, welcome as it was as a sign of vitality, presented unrealized difficulties. The education rates imposed were accompanied by a rise in general tax rates, and a rise in prices absorbed much of the new revenues. Almost half of divisional revenues were provided by the *jangali* paid by immigrant Fulani graziers whose entry had been encouraged by divisional officers looking for means of balancing the Native Authority budget. Their entry in larger numbers was accompanied by complaints of crop-damage and provoked the revival of women's regulatory societies in some areas. These difficulties were intermittently tackled but the new division was not continuously staffed, and its officers, unsupported by Cameroonian cadets, often over-extended, and too frequently transferred, were unable to arrest the growth of particular grievances. These erupted in the form of tax-collector's strikes and a women's uprising after the Southern Cameroons had achieved a large measure of local autonomy.[1]

The separation of the Southern Cameroons from the Eastern Region provided a platform which united both nationalist and traditionalist opinion in support of a new political formation, the Kamerun National Congress, which absorbed the K.U.N.C., and members of the C.N.F. and other bodies; it was created after the Southern Cameroons bloc broke with the N.C.N.C. in March 1953. The K.N.C. delegation obtained agreement in principle in 1953, subject to fiscal inquiry and the result of elections, to a separate legislature and executive, and after the resumed constitutional congress in 1954 to ' quasi-federal ' status for the Southern Cameroons as an insurance against premature inde-

[1] Wum Divisional Reports, 1957, 1958; the women's movement was canalized by local organizers into a compaign against the K.N.C., cf. R. E. Ritzenthaler, 'Anlu: a women's uprising in the Cameroons ', *African Studies*, xxix, 3 (1960).

K

pendence as a minority within Nigeria. The 1953 elections, contested by the K.N.C. and the K.P.P., allies of the N.C.N.C., were fought on this issue without any specific statements about internal government structure. In subsequent negotiations with officials the K.N.C. had agreed that the office of Resident in Bamenda, now seemingly anomalous as well as expensive, should be abolished, along with provincial status for Bamenda.[1]

The reaction of most of the Federal Native Authorities to this proposal in Bamenda was strong, and an embarrassment to the provincial staff. The arrival of a Resident was associated with many miles of new trunk road, more new primary schools and dispensaries, touring medical teams, the encouragement of coffee production and co-operatives, and the first whiffs of prosperity, at least for those near the roads. The Wum Native Authority accused the politicians of ' driving them back to bush '. The South-Eastern Federal Native Authority passed a resolution that: ' on account of the complicated traditional set-up blended with democratic modernization, prejudices arising from lack of know-how and inability to consolidate the old and the new for the purpose of political advancement, Bamenda requires a strong and competent administrative guide . . . a fatherly type of man . . . to serve as an immediate and handy adviser on all matters arising abruptly among the people '.[2] These views could not be dismissed as those of indolent councillors: they were adopted by the provincial council of the K.N.C., and a compromise, the posting of a Resident, Special Duties, was arrived at. The bigger chiefs had joined in the fray, the more violently since they believed that the Assemblymen had let them down in the matter of the House of Chiefs they were expected to press at the constitutional conference in Lagos and after. They formed themselves into an influential lobby, the Conference of Chiefs and Natural Rulers. Some European administrators (not those in Bamenda) thought that their agitation was a parochial one which would die down as soon as the hybrid Native Authorities were transformed into wholly elected bodies and direct elections called. The nationalist politicians, on the whole, did not agree: a resolution in favour of a House of Chiefs was passed at the first session of the House of Assembly, moved by

[1] Recent political developments are summarized in Edwin Ardener, ' The Political History of Cameroon ', *The World Today*, 18 (1962), 341–350.
[2] S.E.F.N.A. Memorandum, 16 September, 1954.

the future Vice-President of the reunited Cameroons, the Honourable John Ngu Foncha.[1]

For the next few years Bamenda politics remained centred on the ' traditional set-up blended with democratic modernization '. Native Authority elections were introduced, the first in the homogeneous Bali Native Authority in 1955. But despite elections the ghosts of the old chiefdom Native Authorities, now transformed into advisory local councils, refused to be laid.[2] The expatriate divisional staff removed themselves increasingly from council meetings. But as they did so, without locally-recruited divisional officers to replace them as yet, new lines of communication with authority were sought, openly or covertly, by chiefs and councillors. Local disputes with a customary flavour, formerly the divisional officer's recognized sphere of activity, increasingly attracted the intervention of national party agents, and even played some part in local elections. It could scarcely be otherwise. These matters were, after all, still a centre of political interest for the majority of villagers.

It seemed that the Resident had been right, in 1953, in thinking that elective local government would provide no means of solving problems centring on the nature of chiefly authority, and that these would always demand the intervention of the executive. For some Cameroonian ministers and opposition leaders these problems did not merely involve restoring good feeling but finding some means of harnessing an old legitimacy to a new state.

---

[1] Foncha, John Ngu (1916–); Teacher 1934–54; Member, Cameroons Ho. of Ass.; Sec. Cameroons Youth League, Bamenda 1942–5; Pres. Bamenda Cath. Teachers Un. 1942–54; Pres., N.U.T. Bamenda 1945–54; Sec. Bamenda Imp. Un. 1948–51; Organiser, Kameruns Nat. Fed., Bamenda 1948–50; Org. and Sec. K.U.N.C. Bamenda 1951–3; Sec. K.N.C. Bamenda 1953–4; Founder and Pres.-Gen. K.N.D.P. 1955; Vice-President Federal Repub. of Cameroon 1961.

[2] United Nations Visiting Mission to the Trust Territories of the Cameroons, *Report* (1956), p. 13.

GEORGE BENNETT

IMPERIAL PATERNALISM: THE REPRESENTATION OF AFRICAN INTERESTS IN THE KENYA LEGISLATIVE COUNCIL

When in 1907 the first Legislative Council met in the East Africa Protectorate, which was annexed as Kenya Colony in 1920, two views were current about its nature and function. Constitutionally it was no more than a Council established to advise the Governor on legislation and its first members, six government officials and two European settlers, were all nominated by the Governor. The Europeans, however, regarded it as an embryonic parliament and were soon demanding the right of elective representation. The Legislative Council was the body through which they expected to gain political control. During the First World War the British Government agreed that elective representation should be introduced and in June 1917 a committee of the Council recommended the election of ten Europeans (later increased to eleven for the first elections in 1920). In discussing the allotment of these seats the committee paid attention not to population but to the various ' interests ' which might be represented, such as those of commerce in Nairobi and Mombasa and of different kinds of European farming, agricultural and pastoral. Here was a new illustration of an ancient English tradition going back to the very beginnings of parliamentary history. The root-meaning of House of Commons is ' House of communes ' or communities,[1] the knights and the burgesses being summoned to represent the interests of the shires and of the towns. As new legislative bodies were established in British overseas territories during the nineteenth century the idea of the representation of interests was fundamental. Some seats were allotted to commercial interests and some to corporate bodies but increasingly the main interests for representation were considered to be those of religious or racial communities.[2] Overlooking its ancient origins in Parliament

[1] A. F. Pollard: *The Evolution of Parliament* (London, 1926), pp. 12 and 107.
[2] M. Wight: *The Development of the Legislative Council, 1606–1945* (London, 1946), pp. 85–90. This volume was the first of a series on colonial Legislative Councils edited by Miss Perham.

itself, Asian and African writers have attacked the policy as being but part of the alleged Imperial tactic of ' divide and rule '.[1]

In the multi-racial East Africa Protectorate the Legislative Council committee, while recommending that Europeans should vote, observed bluntly that since the coloured races outnumbered the whites it was ' not desirable that the franchise should be extended to Asiatics or Natives '. Instead they proposed the nomination of two Indians, the representation of the interests of the Arabs by the Resident Magistrate at Mombasa, and of those of the Natives by the Chief Native Commissioner.[2] Certainly it did not seem possible to anybody then—or for years to come— that there were any Africans who were capable of sitting on the Council and taking part in its debates.

The committee composed of officials and settlers, was endorsing the governmental view that it was the duty of administrative officials to represent the interests of Africans. In 1907 a suggestion had been made that unofficial trustees might be appointed to safeguard the proposed native reserves in the protectorate. To this Winston Churchill, then Under-Secretary of State for the Colonies, replied in the Commons that ' the government . . . in this matter, as in all others affecting the welfare of the natives, would act as their trustees '.[3] Yet in Natal unofficial trustees had long been appointed to administer and protect native land rights. In 1910, Sir Percy Girouard,[4] then Governor of the protectorate, but a man with a South African background, proposed in the controversy which arose over the second move of the Masai tribe that unofficial trustees, ' say two of the bishops and the Secretary of Native Affairs ', should be appointed specifically for the new Masai reserve. In reply the Secretary of State, Lord Crewe,[5] referred to Churchill's pronouncement and added that the Government ' could not divest itself of these responsibilities and transfer them to private persons '; even if there were suitable trustees responsi-

[1] *E.g.* K. B. Krishna: *The Problem of Minorities or Communal Representation in India* (London, 1939).

[2] Report of the Special Committee on Elective Representation, June 1917.

[3] *Off. Rep.*, H. of C., 4th Ser. Vol. 178, cc. 1165–6, 22 July, 1907.

[4] For biog. note see above p. 51.

[5] Crewe-Milnes, R. O. A., Earl, 1895, and Marquess, 1910, of Crewe (1858–1945); Viceroy of India, 1892–5, Lord Pres. of the Council, 1905–8 and 1915–6, Lord Privy Seal 1908–11 and 1912–5, Sec. St. for the Cols. 1908–10, for India 1910–15, Pres. Brd. Ed. 1916, Chairman London County Council, 1917, Ambassador in Paris, 1922–8, Sec. St. for War 1931.

bility would lie with the Government ' in the last resort ' so their appointment would only result in ' unnecessary complications '.[1]

Girouard's idea of missionaries acting on behalf of Africans was later voiced again, and then with respect to the Legislative Council. When its composition was being discussed after the war, missionaries were also concerned at the action taken by the Government to obtain labour for the settlers. Besides making specific representations on this issue,[2] they submitted that a missionary might be appointed to the Legislative Council to represent native interests.[3] Little notice was then taken since the debate over the Council was focussed on the quarrel between the Europeans and the Indians. The latter were seeking the franchise, with elections on a common roll, and this the Europeans vehemently opposed; they would yield nothing more than Indian representation by nomination. In their prolonged battle, over the constitution and over other matters, both Europeans and Indians talked of native interests and each produced in Nairobi Africans to speak against the others. In 1923 the Europeans' political organisation, the Convention of Associations, went further. Knowing the anti-Indian attitude of missionaries in Kenya, it accepted the suggestion of the Governor, Sir Robert Coryndon,[4] that the senior Church of Scotland missionary, the Rev. Dr. Arthur, should accompany its delegation to London to join in the forthcoming talks on Kenya.[5] The protests of some young African political groups in Kenya that Arthur did not represent them[6]

---

[1] *Correspondence relating to the Masai*, Cd. 5584 (1911) nos. 9, 10 and 11. The Masai had been moved in 1904 from the Rift Valley, thus freeing that area for European settlement. The tribe was thereby divided in two, part being placed on the Laikipia plateau. The division proved administratively inconvenient so that Girouard proposed to reunite the two sections in an enlarged southern reserve, but many believed that the real reason for his action sprang from pressures from European settlers desirous of obtaining the Laikipia plateau.

[2] R. Oliver: *The Missionary Factor in East Africa* (London, 1952), pp. 247f.

[3] Representative Council of the Alliance of the Missionary Societies of British East Africa, minutes of meetings, Jan. 1919 and April 1921. The Nyasaland Legislative Council had at this time a missionary as a member, though not appointed specifically to represent native interests.

[4] Coryndon, Sir R. T. (1870–1925) born in Cape Colony; private secretary to Cecil Rhodes, 1st British Resident and B.S.A. Coy's rep. with Lewanika of the Barotse, 1897, administrator N. Wern. Rhodesia 1900–7, res. cr. Swaziland 1907–16, res. cr. Basutoland 1916–7, Governor of Uganda 1917–22, of Kenya 1922–5.

[5] *East African Standard* (*E.A.S.*), 3 March, 1923.

[6] *Ibid.*, 23 and 30 June, 1923, and Arthur's papers (now in Edinburgh); see also F. B. Wellbourn: *East African Rebels* (London, 1961), p. 128.

were ignored. The Kenya Government's attitude was paternalistic, both then and in 1924, when Arthur was nominated to its Executive and Legislative Councils. These appointments followed from the decisions on the Kenya constitution in the White Paper, *Indians in Kenya*, published in July 1923. This announced, among other changes, that a missionary to advise on African matters, ' should be added to the (Legislative) Council until the time comes when the natives are fitted for direct representation '. Elective representation was conceded to the Indians (5 seats against the Europeans' 11) but from a communal electorate, not a common roll; such a system, the White Paper observed, would provide ' a framework into which native representation can be fitted in due season '.

The White Paper's declaration, that His Majesty's Government were ' unable to delegate or share ' the trust they regarded themselves as exercising on behalf of the African population, recalls Churchill's and Crewe's earlier expressions. Yet a missionary was to be appointed to the Legislative Council. In making this change from sole Government concern the White Paper insisted that this would not ' relieve the Governor and his advisers of their full responsibility for representing the native interests '.[1] The words ' to represent native interests ' occurred in the missionary's terms of appointment to the Council and were later underlined in the House of Commons by a Secretary of State, Ormsby-Gore (later Lord Harlech),[2] speaking in 1938. He insisted ' there has never been any suggestion that these . . . people represent the natives . . . [they are] representatives of native interests '.[3] This then was paternalism. In the passage of legislation affecting Africans this was the attitude of the Kenya Government which expected a similar outlook from its nominees.

Arthur indicated, however, in his first speech in the Council that they might look further. He asked about native opinion on the Bill under discussion; it was not necessary to accept it, but it should be consulted. To this the Chief Native Commissioner

[1] *Indians in Kenya*, Cmd. 1922 (1923), pp. 12–14 and 9.

[2] Harlech, 4th Baron 1938, W. G. A. Ormsby-Gore (1885–   ), M.P. 1910–38; parl. priv. sec. to Lord Milner and asst. sec. War Cabinet 1917–8. Asst. Political Officer, Palestine, 1918, Under-Sec. St. for the Colonies, 1922–4 and Nov. 1924–9, Postmaster General 1931, 1st Commissioner of Works, 1931–6, Sec. St. Colonies, 1936–8, High Commissioner for the U.K. in S. Africa, 1941–4, Chairman E. Africa Party. Commission 1924.

[3] *Off. Rep.*, H. of C., 5th Series, vol. 335, c. 693, 3 May, 1938.

replied that nothing was to be gained by such action.[1] Thus from
Arthur's first intervention different lines of development were fore-
shadowed. The missionaries would, through consultation,
develop contacts with types of African political opinion which the
Government regarded as ' unrepresentative '.[2]

At first government and missionaries regarded each other as
bringing information to the Council from different but scattered
sources, namely the administrative officials and missionaries
throughout the Colony. The views of the former could be co-
ordinated by the Chief Native Commissioner and those Senior
(later Provincial) Commissioners who were members of the
Council.[3] Behind Arthur and his successors on the Council lay the
Kenya Missionary Council. This represented all the missions,
except the Roman Catholics, though they sometimes attended
special meetings on political questions. These were discussed
mainly in the Kenya Missionary Council's executive committee,
of which Arthur was for a time chairman; this examined Bills
and occasionally instructed the missionaries on the Legislative
Council.

The selection of the Christian missionary to represent African
interests was in practice more narrowly restricted. Only members
of the two churches established in the United Kingdom were so
nominated: two from the Church of Scotland,[4] and four from the
Church of England. Of these six, five served predominantly among
the Kikuyu, either in the Kikuyu reserves or in Nairobi.[5] This

[1] 15 May, 1924, pp. 33–4 and 37. (We adopt the practice of Miss Perham's
Legislative Council series of citing debates by date and page reference only).
Perhaps the clearest expression of the Government's view came from the
Attorney-General, W. (later Sir Walter) Harragin, speaking on a Native Marketing Bill in 1935: the natives had not been consulted ' any more than a doctor
consults a patient as to whether he would like to take a dose of quinine, whether
it is good for malaria or not '. (9 July, 1935, p. 269).

[2] E.g. comments on the Kikuyu Central Association: in 1926 the Chief
Native Commissioner: ' The Association is devoid of any representative character ', 31 May, 1926, p. 197; see also the Acting Chief Native Commissioner,
14 November, 1938, p. 310.

[3] In fact the Senior, and Provincial, Commissioners contributed little to the
debates, so that in 1934 a European suggested in his election manifesto that
they should speak for the natives instead of being just ' cogs ' in the ' Steam
Roller ' of the official majority. (E.A.S. 3 Mar. 1934). The later speeches of
S. H. Fazan, Provincial Commissioner Nyanza (1936–42), appeared as a new
departure.

[4] Besides Arthur the other was the Rev. R. G. M. Calderwood (Kenya
Official Gazette, 2 May, 1939, p. 446) but he never sat.

[5] The one exception was Canon J. Britton. A missionary in Nyanza, he
became Secretary of the Church Missionary Society in Feb. 1926 and thus lived
in Nairobi, being able to sit on the Council in 1926 and 1927. (E. Richards:
Fifty Years in Nyanza, 1906–56 (Nairobi, 1956), pp. 19 and 75).

was, perhaps, a little ironic when the Government was protesting that because of tribal differences an African could not represent the African peoples of Kenya. The Kikuyu specialisation was largely necessitated by the impossibility otherwise of having a missionary within easy reach of Nairobi and able to attend the Council. More oddly, a family connection linked half of the appointees: Canon H. Leakey, his brother-in-law Canon (later Archdeacon) G. Burns, and Archdeacon (later Bishop and Archbishop) L. J. Beecher, son-in-law of Canon Leakey. The Anglican Church Missionary Society freed these men from its normal discipline with regard to speech on political matters, a freedom extended also to the most outspoken missionary critic in Kenya, Archdeacon Owen of Kavirondo (Nyanza).[1] Never appointed to the Council and believing that ' every missionary ought to be a politician ',[2] he could be an embarrassment not only to the Government but sometimes to the missionaries on the Legislative Council through his outspoken remarks.[3]

The missionaries there knew that they were in a difficult situation where they had to tread warily.. The Council was dominated by European settlers who hoped eventually to obtain self-government on Southern African lines; already their influence had gone, as the Hilton Young Commission reported in 1929, far beyond ' the strictly constitutional position '.[4] Speaking on the important Native Lands Trust Bill in June 1928, Leakey appealed ' as a settler ' to the Europeans to support the Bill, although he could not have done his cause much good by referring in the same speech to books by Dr. Norman Leys and by W. McGregor Ross as ' by friends of mine '.[5] Already Leakey had been in touch with secretaries of ' Native Political Associations ' on the Bill,[6] though he was later to confess: ' I did not mix up with politics at all until I was forced to '.[7] The line he was taking produced a marked

[1] Owen, reported in *East Africa*, 9 July, 1931, p. 1306. Owen, Ven. W. E. (1879–1945), missionary in Uganda 1904–18, Archdeacon of Kavirondo 1918–45 Founder and first president of the Kavirondo Taxpayers' Welfare Association, 1923.

[2] *Ibid.*, 13 December, 1934, p. 291.

[3] See Arthur's comments in K.M.C. exec. cttee., mins. of meeting, 15–16 May, 1928.

[4] *Report of the Commission on Closer Union of the Dependencies in Eastern and Central Africa*, Cmd. 3234 (1929), p. 89.

[5] 14 June, 1928, p. 324. The reference is to N. Leys: *Kenya* (London, 1924; 3rd ed. 1926) and to W. M. Ross: *Kenya from Within* (London, 1927).

[6] Letter to *E.A.S.*, 14 Apr., 1928, p. 36.

[7] Evidence to the Parliamentary Joint Select Cttee. (*J.S.C.*), 1931, Vol. II, p. 243.

reaction in October 1929 from Scott,[1] the Director of Education:

' I should like to say here and now, Sir, that I do take exception on my own part—not perhaps on the part of the Government—to the hon. Member claiming the right to speak for the Africans whom he represents. I think every one of us on this side of the House has a perfect claim that we speak for the Africans (hear, hear).'

Scott then added:

' It is a most dangerous thing to say that we have to do this because Africans are yearning for it.'

Leakey found it necessary to apologise if his zeal had led him astray.[2] While Scott was only restating the Government's position, the European leader, Conway Harvey,[3] later obtained a wider acknowledgement with his remark:

' The hon. reverend gentleman announced that he was the only representative of native interests. We all take exception to that, Sir, as we do and always have regarded ourselves as representatives of the interests of the natives.'

Canon Leakey: ' On a point of explanation, I beg to apologise. I never meant that at all. I am here merely as a representative of the natives and there is no other reason why I am on this Council; because there is no native yet ready I have been chosen. I absolutely agree with the hon. Member; I have said it over and over again. I know there are many amongst the unofficial Members who do have a great interest in the natives and wish them as well as I do.'[4]

Indeed, Leakey referred before the Parliamentary Joint Select Committee on East Africa in 1931 to an earlier elected European, MacLellan Wilson, as being ' very interested in natives ' and as having ' represented native interests ' before a missionary was appointed.[5]

Both in his memorandum and in his evidence to the Joint

[1] Scott, Sir Herbert Septimus (1873–1952) Inspector of Schools, Transvaal 1902, Sec. Transvaal Education Dept. 1911, Director of Education Transvaal 1924, Director of Education Kenya 1928–35, Member of Colonial Office Advisory Cttee. on Education in the Colonies, 1948.

[2] 23 October, 1929, pp. 546 and 552.

[3] Conway Harvey (1880–1943), farmer settler East Africa from South Africa, 1910, member Kenya Legislative Council 1921–38.

[4] 11 Apr., 1930, pp. 188–9.

[5] J.S.C., vol. II, p. 243. Wilson had been a missionary before becoming a coffee-farmer in Kiambu. He was a nominated member of the Council from 1916 to 1920 and elected from 1923 to 1927.

Select Committee Leakey explained the difficulty of his position on the Council, making particular reference to the powerful and important Select Committee on the Estimates.[1] There, said Maxwell,[2] the Chief Native Commissioner, who supported Leakey in these representations, the unofficial Europeans 'take complete charge of the Budget' for, as Leakey wrote in his memorandum:

'Of the official side of the Legislative Council there sit only the Colonial Secretary and the Treasurer. Not even the Chief Native Commissioner is present except when his own department's estimates are being considered. This means that there are 11 persons pledged to vote in the interests of European constituencies and one person specially appointed to lift up his voice on behalf of all the Africans in the Colony.'

Leakey and Maxwell both urged the establishment of a separate budget for the natives,[3] but the idea was never accepted.

Missionary opinion wanted also an increase in the number of representatives of African interests on the Legislative Council. The Kenya Missionary Council suggested to the Hilton Young Commission that there should be eight, of which at least three should be administrative officers and three missionaries.[4] Three African political associations also submitted memoranda to the Commission. The Kavirondo Taxpayers' Welfare Association and the Kikuyu Association, bodies with missionary links, wanted representation by a mixture of officials, missionaries and Africans but the Kikuyu Central Association, which protested in a separate letter to the Government that Europeans did not have 'true sympathy' or 'thorough contact' with Africans, asked for direct representation by twelve Africans of whom three should be Kikuyu.[5]

The Hilton Young commissioners, having heard African witnesses from these organisations, concluded that it would be long before suitable Africans could be found for the Council, both

---

[1] For which see G. Bennett: 'Early Procedural Developments in the Kenya Legislative Council—II' *Parliamentary Affairs*, X (1957), 469–472.

[2] Maxwell, G. V. (1877–) colonial civil servant: Fiji 1898–1921 (chairman Native Lands Commission, 1912–21), Chief Native Commissioner, Kenya 1921–31, where he was known as 'Fijive'. The difference of opinion between him and the Governor, Sir Edward Grigg, led to part of his evidence to the Parliamentary Joint Select Committee being given *in camera*.

[3] *J.S.C.*, vol. II, p. 380, and vol. III, pp. 23 and 64.

[4] Evidence to the Hilton Young Commission, vol. I: Evidence taken in Kenya part I, p. 513 (Colonial Office Library).

[5] *E.A.S.*, 24 and 31 Dec., 1927, 14 Jan. and 4 Feb., 1928.

through lack of education and also because ' it would be impossible to find any single man who could represent, or command the confidence of, more than a section of the people '. The commissioners discussed at some length possible Europeans. They considered that ' only in exceptional cases ' would a missionary have ' the leisure to obtain that general knowledge and mastery of the problems of native administration which would enable him to represent native interests effectively '. They cast doubts on the suggestion of Sir Edward Grigg,[1] the Governor, that there were settlers with the necessary knowledge. Instead they produced an idea important for the future: that recently retired officials might be appointed, and they suggested four such ' in addition to the missionary already appointed '. Besides this, they wanted provision for informal councils to consult native opinion on legislation affecting native interests, the representatives of native interests being associated in such consultation.[2]

The Hilton Young Commission's Report, in January 1929, proved so controversial—among other things raising once again the idea of the common roll—that it produced no action. The representation of native interests accordingly remained for the Joint Select Committee to consider in 1931. Its members recorded how impressed they had been by the African witnesses. While the Committee accepted, for the Hilton Young commissioners' reasons, that the time had not yet come for direct African representation, they recommended, as the only change they would allow for the Kenya Legislative Council, an increase of nominated representation. They suggested also that the Governor might include among such nominated members ' persons of African descent, when he considers suitable representatives are available '. Such names might be obtained through ' the machinery of the native councils ' whose development would provide training for ' a wider political life '.[3] As the Committee did not give any figure for the increased representation it suggested, this remained for the

[1] Altrincham, 1st baron, 1945, Sir Edward W. M. Grigg (1879–1955); journalist (editorial staff *Times*, 1903 and 1908–13), military sec. to the Prince of Wales, 1919, priv. sec. to Lloyd George, 1921–2, M.P. (L) Oldham, 1922–5, Governor of Kenya, 1925–31, M.P. (Nat. C.) Altrincham 1933–45, parl. sec. Min. Info. 1939–40, finl. sec. War Office, Jt. Parl. Under-Sec. St. for War 1940–2, Minister Res. in the Middle East 1944–5, publications include *Kenya's Opportunity* (1955).
[2] Cmd. 3234 (1929), pp. 185–8.
[3] *J.S.C.*, vol. I, pp. 42–3.

despatch of commentary from the Kenya Governor, Sir Joseph Byrne[1]: he put the minimal figure of one. He accepted that the door should be kept open for an African but ' the time for such an innovation ' had ' not been reached '; further, the restriction to a Christian missionary might be removed. All these points the Secretary of State accepted but since, he said, the increase had to be considered in relation to other suggestions affecting the Council[2] no changes were made until new Royal Instructions were issued in 1934.

Until then Leakey and his successor, Burns, who had acted during Leakey's absence in England, continued in the lone position. An Australian, choleric and apoplectic, Burns was involved in tiffs with the European members from the first. When he refused, in January 1931, to support a motion for financial aid to the European maize farmers Conway Harvey expressed himself as ' absolutely amazed ' and the Director of Agriculture ' profoundly deplored ' his remarks.[3] During 1931 Burns was away on a final leave before retirement in Kenya; thus he was strictly no longer ' a missionary ' but the Kenya Government did not think this debarred him from appointment, as a narrow interpretation of the Royal Instructions might have done. Almost immediately Burns took up a matter which became a regular theme with him: the abuse of power by headmen. He wanted particularly an end of their exaction of compulsory labour.[4] Here was a change from Leakey who had refrained from introducing a motion on compulsory communal labour as he did not wish to embarrass the Government whom he regarded as making an honest endeavour to prevent abuses in such matters.[5] Burns pressed his attacks in subsequent debates, finally obtaining in 1936 a commission of enquiry into the methods of collection of the Hut and Poll Tax. Although its Report[6] revealed little, the fact that the officials were compelled to submit to an enquiry did not

---

[1] Byrne, Brig.-Gen. Sir J. A. (1874–1942) Inspector-Gen. Royal Irish Constabulary 1916–20, Governor: Seychelles 1922–7, Sierra Leone 1927–31, Kenya, 1931–7.
[2] *Correspondence* (1931–1932) *arising from the Report of the Joint Select Committee on Closer Union in East Africa*, Cmd. 4141 (1932), pp. 30 and 55.
[3] 17 Jan., 1931, pp. 1229–48.
[4] 17 Dec., 1932, pp. 428 and 443.
[5] *J.S.C.*, vol. II, pp. 244–5.
[6] *Report of the Commission to Inquire into Allegations of Abuse and Hardship in the Collection of Non-Native Graduated Poll Tax and of the Native Hut and Poll Tax* (1936).

increase their affection for Burns or for the Church Missionary Society missionaries who had produced the initial ammunition for his attacks.

In 1933 the Kenya Missionary Council established a Race Relations Committee which attempted, among other activities, to bring Burns into contact with African opinion. In March 1934 it arranged for him to meet representatives of the Kikuyu political associations. There had been complaints, Burns acknowledged, that ' he had not been to them to find out their views for representation in the Legislative Council ' but he ' thought it was rather their duty to come and see him '. In the following months Burns held ' regular consultations ' with Kikuyu leaders,[1] while the committee attempted, during the next two years, to brief him on Bills and motions before the Council. Burns could thus tell the Council, in August 1935, that he had ' gone to a considerable amount of trouble ' to question natives with regard to a Native Marketing Bill.[2]

There were, however, matters on which missionary and native views did not coincide. This was especially so over the independent schools which were being set up, more particularly among the Kikuyu in consequence of a break with the Church of Scotland over female circumcision in 1929.[3] In 1936 the secretary of the Kikuyu Independent Schools Association complained that Burns was a ' representative for Missionary Interests ' and that he was not supporting them in their application for grants.[4] Outside the Legislative Council there was a rising demand among Africans for direct African representation. A missionary, however sympathetic and knowledgeable, could not fully meet their needs. They were beginning to want more than the apologetic tone with which Burns felt compelled on occasion to plead their cause in the hostile atmosphere of the Council. There Burns, as the lone representative of African interests, could on occasion only move motions by seeking support from the Indian members. Their return to the Council, in 1933 after a long period of non-co-operation, enabled him to find a seconder for a motion on problems in

---

[1] Race Relations Committee minutes, 16 March, 1934, and E. E. Biss (Secretary) to Archdeacon Owen, 13 June, 1934 (R.R.C. files).
[2] 3 Aug., 1935, p. 627, cf. W. Harragin *supra*, p. 145.
[3] For which see F. B. Welbourn, *op. cit.*, chaps. 7 and 8, and *Historical Survey of the Origins and Growth of Mau Mau*, Cmnd. 1030 (1960), pp. 172 f.
[4] Letter in *E.A.S.*, 19 June, 1936, p. 31.

the Kakamega gold-mining area. However, the Indian who agreed to do this could only remark that he was seconding ' as it is very important ' and then conclude that he had nothing else to say but that he entirely agreed with Burns's remarks.[1]

Seeking allies from the Indians did not increase Burns's popularity either with the officials or with the elected Europeans. With the latter a dramatic clash occurred in the lengthy debate, in October 1934, on the report of the Morris Carter Commission on land.[2] Burns neglected the points put to him by Kikuyu political leaders at the Race Relations Committee—their views only found expression through the Indians—and concentrated on the proposed move of the Samburu tribe. His remarks produced a vigorous reply from the European leader, Major (later Sir) Ferdinand Cavendish-Bentinck.[3] He accused Burns of ' employing the tactics of a publicity agent ' and put words, ' the valley of desolation and death '[4] into Burns's mouth, words he was not quick enough to deny as having used about the Samburu's proposed destination. The Europeans were touchy because they wanted the Samburu land on the Laikipia plateau. After this debate a clear rift developed between them and Burns. Since his relations with the Government remained poor as a result of his attacks on their headmen, Burns had reason to say, in August 1936, of his task of representing native interests:

> ' I try to, but it is not always easy when I am up against certain elements in this House.'[5]

A Provincial Commissioner, S. H. La Fontaine, described Burns in 1937 as:

> 'A Don Quixote in these debates affecting natives, with commendable chivalry but with a rather sketchy acquaintance with the facts.'[6]

This was the civil service view and hostilities continued until Burns's retirement from the Council in 1938.

[1] 9 May, 1933, p. 393.   [2] Cmd. 4556 (1934).
[3] Cavendish-Bentinck, Major Sir Ferdinand, K.B.E., 1956 (1889–), priv. sec. Governor of Uganda 1925–7, then in Kenya as hon. sec. Convention of Associations, 1930, M.L.C., 1934–60, Member for Agriculture and Natural Resources, 1945–55, Speaker Legislative Council 1955–60, Chairman Agricultural Production and Settlement Board, 1939–45, Member East African Civil Defence and Supply Council, 1940–5, leader the Kenya Coalition 1960.
[4] 25 Oct., 1934, pp. 701–3.
[5] 2 Aug., 1936, p. 572. I have been told that Burns would come home from the Council and weep for the hardness of heart of the Government and of the European elected members.
[6] 9 Mar., 1937, p. 182.

Then, in the typically British fashion, amends were made after the battle. The Governor, Sir Robert Brooke-Popham,[1] paid tribute to a gallant fighter in words unusually warm for such occasions. After referring to Burns's arrival 39 years before in Kenya, he said:

> ' Ever since then he has devoted his whole time and energy with complete unselfishness to the welfare of the African. In him we had an experienced and strenuous advocate of the true interests of the natives.'[2]

Earlier the *East African Standard* had defended Burns against ' a petulant Chief Native Commissioner ' and commented that he did his ' plain duty ' in a way which showed that the representation of African interests was ' a responsibility which has a tangible meaning.[3] A final tribute from Africans may perhaps be recorded. The area of the Church Missionary Society's former headquarters in Nairobi, where the new Parliamentary building has been erected, is known in Swahili as ' *Kwa Burns* ' (' Burns's corner ' or ' *chez* Burns '). It is fitting that Kenya's Parliament should meet in a place known as the home of one of the Legislative Council's most valiant, if sometimes choleric, speakers.

Early in 1934 the Secretary of State, Sir Philip Cunliffe-Lister (later Lord Swinton),[4] visited Kenya to discuss, *inter alia*, possible changes in the Legislative Council. In December 1933, the *East African Standard* had acknowledged that it was ' an impossible task ' for one man to represent African interests and recounted that Africans came to the paper's office because they did not meet their representative in the reserves.[5] The Race Relations Committee produced a memorandum for Cunliffe-Lister. They wanted a ' team ' of three members on the Council: occasions might arise when it was difficult to get a seconder to a motion, whilst in debate, if the member spoke early he could not

[1] Popham, Air Chief Marshal Sir Robert Brooke- (1878–1953), retired from R.A.F. after being A.O.C. in C., Middle East 1935–6, Governor of Kenya 1937–9, C.-in-C. Far East 1940–1.

[2] 8 Apr., 1938, p. 4. Burns died in Sept. 1944.

[3] Leading article, 6 Dec., 1935.

[4] Swinton, 1st Viscount, 1935, Earl of, 1955, Philip Cunliffe-Lister (1884–), M.P. 1918–35, parl. sec. Board of Trade, 1920–1, Pres. Brd. Trade 1922–3, 1924–9, and 1931, Sec. St. for the Colonies 1931–5, Sec. St. for Air 1935–8, Cabinet Minister Resident in West Africa 1942–4, Minister for Civil Aviation 1944–5, Chancellor of the Duchy of Lancaster and Minister of Materials 1951–2, Sec. St. for Commonwealth Relations 1952–5, Deputy Leader, House of Lords, 1951–5.

[5] Leading article, 6 Dec. 1933.

L

counter the arguments of others, and if he waited until later others might have committed themselves to definite positions; further, native interests needed stronger representation on committees, especially that on the annual estimates, than one man could give.[1]

As a result of the Royal Instructions of 1934 Burns received a colleague in the new Council of that year: R. W. Hemsted, who, like Burns, had come to East Africa in 1899. He was a civil servant until 1930, postponing his retirement to deal with the re-organisation of the Northern Frontier Province,[2] and was a member of the Morris Carter Commission before joining the Council. There he could make a new and valuable contribution for he had special knowledge of the pastoral tribes on whom the missionaries were particularly weak. He was soon saying of the Masai, the Samburu and the Kipsigis that he ' must accuse the Government of never having had any definite policy among them '.[3] Not unnaturally he took little part in the debate on the Carter Commission Report: whilst he confessed that he had had little opportunity of hearing native views on it, he thought that they had been ably represented by Burns.[4] Two months later he not only left Burns to find an Indian seconder for an amendment to stop the employment of Africans as barmen but opposed this as ' grandmotherly legislation '.[5] It was good to have an official astringent to deal with a missionary teetotal fad! While Hemsted was occasionally prepared to criticise the Government he did not do so with Burns's vigour nor did he ever show proof of a knowledge of African views. The dictum of a European elected member that nobody was more suitable to represent the natives than a retired Provincial Commissioner[6] would seem open to question. Hemsted's advantage was that he might be able to obtain action when others failed: the settler editor of the *Kenya Weekly News* of Nakuru believed that he was ' easily the most influential member in the Legislative Council ' and that the Government ' ate out of his hand '.[7]

In some situations moderation may be more effective than

---

[1] *E.A.S.*, 10 Mar., 1934, p. 47.   [2] 9 Nov., 1928, p. 692.
[3] 30 July, 1934, p. 386. Hemsted had worked among the Masai from an early date. G. R. Sandford's *Administrative and Political History of the Masai Reserve* (London, 1919) is said to be based on Hemsted's notes (Letter from C. E. V. Buxton in *E.A.S.*, 28 Mar., 1952, commenting on Hemsted's death).
[4] 23 Oct., 1934, p. 635.   [5] 21 Dec., 1934, p. 1178.
[6] Major Riddell, 4 Dec., 1935, p. 878.
[7] *K.W.N.*, 28 Dec., 1934.

vigour. If Hemsted's career on the Council suggests this, further illustration may be found from that of his successor, Dr. C. J. (' Dan ') Wilson. A member of the Colonial Medical Service in East Africa from 1911 to 1929, he retired as Director of Medical Services in Malaya and Singapore in 1933 and settled in Kenya. In June 1935 he acted as a substitute for Hemsted, replacing him later in the year when Hemsted was compelled to resign because of ill health.[1] Wilson explained that he did not admit that the interests of the settlers and the natives were opposed for otherwise he would not be on the Council.[2] Like Hemsted he found himself unable always to support Burns: he believed that it was necessary for African development to keep native taxation at the existing rate and opposed Burns's demand for an enquiry into the methods of Hut and Poll Tax collection.[3] However, he later agreed that two representatives of native interests were not sufficient.[4] When, early on, he crossed swords with the elected Europeans they spoke of him ' as an echo of Government opinion'.[5] Thus his later criticisms are the more telling. By January 1937 he had decided that the natives were heavily taxed. After referring to the Reports of Lord Moyne and Sir Alan Pim as saying that the Europeans were ' lightly taxed ', he concluded: ' the natives have been paying more than their fair share '. He then enunciated a theory novel in the Kenya Legislative Council:

> ' The only sound principle is to spend money where it is most needed regardless of race. The natives are the poorest and most backward section of the community.'[6]

Speaking on the budget that year, he called for a reduction of direct native taxation and also described the opinions of two European elected members, Majors Cavendish-Bentinck and Riddell, on Labour Officers as ' reactionary ', a word he withdrew in face of European protests.[7]

---

[1] 20 Nov., 1935, p. 661.
[2] 28 Nov., 1935, p. 761.
[3] Ibid., p. 758 and 9 Jan. 1936, pp. 1168–70.
[4] 8 Aug., 1938, p. 50.
[5] Major Riddell, 22 May, 1936, p. 188, also Lord Francis Scott, 5 Dec., 1935, p. 930.
[6] 5 Jan., 1937, pp. 1048–9. Lord Moyne had reported (Cmd. 4093 (1932) as the Financial Commissioner called for by the Parliamentary Joint Select Committee in 1931. In view of Kenya's continuing difficulties Sir Alan Pim was sent out to Report . . . on the Financial Position and System of Taxation of Kenya, Col. 116 (1936).
[7] 19 Nov. 1937, pp. 494–7.

Despite some vigorous criticisms,[1] Wilson's thinking never departed from the basic paternalistic principle under which he was appointed. Indeed a vein of paternalism towards, and pessimism about, Africans ran through his speeches and writings. He believed 'African history is a record of tyranny, injustice and cruelty '[2] and that while:

'African characteristics may change with the passing of time . . . the point for emphasis is that it is useless and in no way virtuous, to assume any significant change to lie within the range of practical politics.'[3]

Although he constantly pressed for an alleviation of the African tax burden, and called for a greater expenditure on African medical needs and for a provident fund for African civil servants, Wilson could not come close to the people whose interests he represented.

In 1937 Wilson was absent for a few months. His substitute, Colonel T. O. Fitzgerald, was even more remote from African opinion. On his second day in the Council he referred to the one event, which in the eyes of a more sensitive government, would have debarred him from all consideration for such an appointment: he had commanded the military called out in aid of the civil power in Nairobi in the Harry Thuku riots in 1922.[4] His comment to the Council illuminated his attitude to African affairs:

' Having spent some forty years of my life in the military forces of the Crown, I am of opinion that any form of discipline is good discipline.'

After his brief speech two Indian members had reason to ask what connection his reminiscences had with the Trade Union Bill under discussion.[5]

In 1938 the Government seemed determined to underline the paternalism inherent in its appointments. On Burns's departure it nominated H. R. Montgomery, the recently retired Chief Native Commissioner and a brother of the later Field Marshal,

---

[1] Miss Perham's judgment of Wilson was that he was ' rather exceptional. He does what must be an extremely unpleasant duty for a European settler bravely and well.' (Letter to E. Huxley, 25 Mar., 1943, in *Race and Politics in Kenya* (London, 1944), p. 133).

[2] 9 Jan., 1936, pp. 1168–9.

[3] C. J. Wilson: *One African Colony* (London, 1945), p. 5.

[4] *Papers Relating to Native Disturbances in Kenya (March* 1922) Cmd. 1691 (1922) in which a report signed by Col. Fitzgerald appears.

[5] 26 July, 1937, p. 56.

to join Wilson. This appointment provoked wide criticism, both in England and in Kenya.[1] The *East African Standard* considered it ' open to grave objections ' as Montgomery would have to represent the views of Africans on policies he had helped to formulate; moreover, he would be an embarrassment to his successor and other administrative officers. The *Standard* also voiced a new conception of the post which, it acknowledged, Burns had carried out. There was ' no ready made organisation ' for the consultation of African views and:

' The missionary is peculiarly fitted to arrive at an understanding (so far as this is possible to any European) of what the African's reaction is to actual or proposed Government policy.'[2]

The *Standard* did not let the matter drop. In January 1939 it suggested the appointment of Archdeacon Owen, the outspoken critic in Nyanza of the Government. Increasingly he had found it necessary to appeal to British opinion, writing frequently for the *Manchester Guardian*. This the *Standard* described as fighting for the right things in the wrong places. It suggested Owen's knowledge, experience and fighting ability should be canalised into the Legislative Council for:

' It cannot be argued that the African's interest is best represented in the higher councils of Government by two ex-civil servants in whose selection they have had no choice.'[3]

Certainly Africans turned increasingly at this time to Indians to voice their grievances. One, in particular, Isher Dass,[4] was long a spokesman for the Kikuyu Central Association. In 1929 he accompanied its general secretary, Johnston (later Jomo) Kenyatta, on a visit to Britain, introducing him to left-wing political circles in London.[5] Dass more than once read into the Kenya Hansard ex-

---

[1] *East Africa and Rhodesia* 12 May, 1938, p. 1044, and in the House of Commons where the criticisms provoked Ormsby-Gore's definition quoted earlier (*supra* p. 144).
[2] Leading article, 8 Apr., 1938.   [3] *Ibid.*, 27 Jan., 1939.
[4] Isher Dass (1901–42), born in India, he came to Kenya in 1927 as private secretary to A. M. Jeevanjee, ' the Grand Old Man ' of Indian politics in Kenya and quickly became the leader of the non-co-operating wing in the East African Indian National Congress of which he was elected secretary in 1930. In 1940 he supported the war effort becoming Secretary of the Indian Manpower Committee and, in 1942, Deputy Director of Indian Manpower; his activities in this position led to his murder in the same year.
[5] G. Delf: *Jomo Kenyatta* (London, 1961), p. 69, and 19 Oct., 1934, p. 582, Dass: ' In that year (1929) I took the initiative on my own of taking a member of the K.C.A. to England to represent their cause.' Kenyatta presented a petition

tracts from memoranda of the K.C.A. and of the Kavirondo Taxpayers' Welfare Association, but the most striking example of his activity occurred in July 1938, when 1,500 of the Kamba a tribe noted for loyalty to the Government, marched on Nairobi in protest against the Government's policy of culling their cattle. Dass acted as a go-between, bringing the Kamba leaders to Government officials. He denied that he had instigated the march but compared it to a ' hunger march ' in England. He asked that the Governor should see the people, quoting the *Kenya Weekly News's* regret that this had been refused, and finished by asking the Governor to hold a *baraza* in the Kamba country. Montgomery could only note that no official headmen had taken part in the action and thought it was:

> ' quite inconceivable that Your Excellency should see a band of malcontents every time they want to obstruct the passage of the law.'

The Chief Native Commissioner agreed more with Dass than with Montgomery and concluded by announcing that the Governor would go to Machakos to hold a *baraza*. The whole incident provided a striking comment on the representation of Africans in the Council.[1]

Although the Government did, in 1939, consider other appointments, including that of an African,[2] no change was then made. Montgomery's ' official ' view became notorious, causing adverse comment even from officials in the Council. When the Colonial Office insisted on a change in legal administration against the wishes of Kenya officials, the Chief Native Commissioner was able to express his gratitude to Montgomery for putting the administration's case. Then he added:

' But I do not think the native aspect has been stressed very strongly.'[3] On a budget debate, the Nyanza Provincial Commissioner, S. H. Fazan, asked, of the matter Montgomery had raised, whether:

(14 Feb., 1929) to the Secretary of State asking for direct elections of 3 African and 2 European representatives as an initial step to represent Native interests, though ' ultimately the number of African representatives in the Legislative Council should predominate '. *Correspondence between the Kikuyu Central Association and the Colonial Office*, 1929–30 (London, 1930), p. 8.

[1] 17 Aug., 1938, pp. 230–41, 255–7 and 271–81.
[2] Unpublished material, Nairobi Secretariat.
[3] 16 Nov., 1939, p. 122.

' natives, if speaking in their own interests, would single out that particular point for mention.'[1]

The situation became more and more anomalous. Outside, Africans were increasingly demanding that there should be an African on the Council.[2] Then in 1942, the independently minded and outspoken elected European, S. V. Cooke,[3] himself a former administrative officer, launched a number of attacks in the Council on the members appointed to represent African interests. He suggested that as the members concerned had, when appointed, only recently left Government service:

> ' They were naturally—if I may say so—not perhaps *persona grata* with the native people.'[4]

He later argued for an increase in representation, as the Hilton Young Commission had urged, and added:

> ' I think two of these members should be missionaries of the militant type. It is no use having in this Council missionaries or others who are unable or unwilling to present the African point of view as strongly as possible.'[5]

This was said in moving a motion for a progressive native policy. Two days later, in replying to the debate, Cooke noted that neither of the members concerned was present and suggested Wilson had ' deserted the Africans for pyrethrum ',[6] a subject on which as a grower and member of the Pyrethrum Board Wilson spoke more than once. Amid these attacks Montgomery agreed that the native representation was not entirely satisfactory; whilst the time

---

[1] 14 Dec., 1939, pp. 406–7.
[2] Meeting of Central Province Local Native Council representatives, Nyeri, 9 Sept., 1941, and Memorandum from Central Kavirondo L.N.C., Mar. 1942.
[3] S. V. Cooke became an Asst. Dist. Cr. in the E.A.P. in 1917. In 1925 he obtained a judicial enquiry after settler attacks on his actions over labour (W. M. Ross, *op. cit.*, pp. 113–4). Promoted Dist. Cr. in 1928, he was transferred in 1931 to Tanganyika as a Dist. Offr. but there the Govt. decided to retire him compulsorily at the end of 20 years' service, though the matter was taken up by D. N. Pritt in the Commons (*Off. Rep.*, vol. 324, cc. 1087–93, 2 June, 1937). After six months' retirement in his native Ireland he returned to Mombasa ' to try his hand in politics and deep sea fishing ' (*East Africa and Rhodesia*, 19 Aug., 1937, p. 1554). In the following March he defeated the sitting member for the Coast, an old established European political figure, Major (later Col.) E. S. Grogan. Cooke held the seat until it was abolished in the new 1960 constitution. He was the only European founder member of the Kenya National Party in 1960 and his outspokenness on the African behalf received recognition by the Kenya African National Union nominating him for a National seat in the Leg. Co. in 1961, though he was not elected. He wrote much for the *Kenya Weekly News* in the forties, acting as editor on occasion.
[4] 21 Apr., 1942, p. 98.
[5] 15 Sept., 1942, p. 380.　　　　　　[6] 17 Sept., 1942, p. 507.

had not arrived for direct African representation he said he would welcome it and that he would have no objection to names of suggested representatives going before the African local government bodies, the Local Native Councils, for approval.[1]

During 1942 and the early months of 1943 a Committee on Post-War Employment was sitting. Its sub-committee on the employment of Africans had as members both Montgomery and Cooke, and they followed a pattern typical of committees in Kenya by going beyond their terms of reference. The sub-committee reported that ' many witnesses, European and African ', had spoken of ' the need to provide the returning soldier, no less than the man who has remained at his civil job, with an outlook for his political aspirations ' lest feelings of frustration develop. They considered that they would be lacking in duty if they did not draw the Government's attention to something on which ' many thinking Africans feel strongly '. Dissatisfied with their representation on the Legislative Council, Africans ' would welcome some Europeans as representatives provided they had a say in the selection ' but felt there should also be Africans and that there would be ' no quarrel as to the tribes they were taken from provided they were trustworthy men '. The sub-committee recalled the Hilton Young Commission's recommendation of five representatives of African interests but would not express an opinion as to the number or the method of ' their selection or election ', thinking, without being able ' to make a recommendation ', that an 'African General Council ' of delegates from local provincial councils and local native councils should be established with power to submit names of possible representatives to the Governor.[2] This was clearly a compromise between Cooke and Montgomery but it had a quick effect on the Kenya Government which treated it as the culmination of other representations. When Wilson resigned on account of ill health it was decided to appoint, in August 1943, a missionary, the Rev. L. J. Beecher, in his place.

Beecher had come to Kenya in 1927 as a member of the Church Missionary Society to teach at the Alliance High School, the leading Protestant school for Africans. He later undertook teacher training and pastoral work in the Fort Hall district where he

---

[1] 22 Apr., 1942, p. 115 and 15 Sept., 1942, pp. 398–9.
[2] *Report of the Sub-Committee on the Post-War Employment of Africans* (1943), p. 22.

incurred the disfavour of the Government by supplying much of the information on which Burns's allegations of tax collection abuses were based.[1] His very appointment had thus the quality of a dramatic change, something Beecher marked the more by telling the press that he had tried to avoid any form of ' manifesto '. This was a revolutionary word for a representative of African interests, but Beecher also announced that he had already said that he looked forward to the day when Africans would sit alongside the European nominated members and even replace them.[2]

With Beecher's nomination African interest in the Legislative Council quickened. Letters from Africans appeared in the press: one welcomed him as the first representative to seek openly through the press for African views.[3] An interesting sign of the appreciation of Beecher's efforts came from James Gichuru,[4] a committee member of the Kenya African Union at its formation in October 1944. Initially he had refused to join other Africans in congratulating Beecher on his appointment, since ' no European could possibly represent African opinion ', but he welcomed his reappointment to the new Council in 1944 since he was:

' unique as a European representative of our interests, for most of the others have been of a " quiet " nature.'[5]

Beecher had revealed himself as a ' militant missionary '. An early occasion for plain speaking was a Trespass Bill:

' It seems to me sheer hypocrisy to pretend that this Bill is non-racial. . . . It is patent that it is designed solely to operate against the African.'[6]

Such expressions encouraged Africans to write to Beecher, still more when he acknowledged correspondents' help in preparing a case for the Council. Before he finally resigned he could talk of his

[1] *Report of the Commsision to Inquire into . . . the Native Hut and Poll Tax* (1936), pp. 12–3.

[2] *E.A.S.*, 13 Aug., 1943 Suppt. (a). Three months later the *E.A.S.* suggested that one of the two Europeans might be replaced by an African who would thus have an opportunity to learn from a European colleague (leading article, 26 Nov., 1943).

[3] *Ibid.*, 20 Aug., 1943, p. 9.

[4] Gichuru, J. S. (1914–   ), educated Alliance High School and Makerere College, teacher at Alliance High School 1935–40, and headmaster Church of Scotland Mission School, Kikuyu, 1940–50, helped form K.A.U. 1944 and became its second president, 1945–7, chief of Dagoretti Location, Nairobi, 1950–2, restricted 1955–60 but taught in teachers' training college, ag. pres. KANU 1960–1, M.L.C. for Kiambu 1961–   , Minister of Finance 1962–.

[5] *Ibid.* Suppt. (a) and 13 Oct., 1944, p. 7.

[6] 9 Dec., 1943, pp. 667–8.

'enormous mailbag', but explain also how the multiplicity of committees and the general pressure of work made it:

> 'quite beyond the capacity of two people, irrespective of their race, to represent the African community, particularly at this stage of their development.'

He confessed that he was no longer able to attend Local Native Council meetings and *barazas*, official and unofficial.[1]

He had done this in 1943 and 1944 so that then for the first time Africans had a member who went into the countryside to meet them. Among the Kikuyu he was with friends. At Kiambu 'Chief Philip expressed delight of Government's choice of a man who knew the Kikuyu tongue so well and who had an accurate knowledge of the tribe'.[2] In Fort Hall's Local Native Council he was greeted as 'an old resident of the District and a friend of the members'; the meeting broke off for an hour's informal discussion when one member, James Beuttah (later prominent among those detained in connection with Mau Mau), said that they would prefer to talk to him.[3] Elsewhere things were not so easy. Beecher found it difficult to go to Nyanza and when he did meet the Kipsigis there could not be the same informality.[4] At least he did try to meet the pastoral tribes. For a missionary representative he broke new ground with the Masai, more than once giving special attention to their needs. He related how he had attended a Masai *baraza* and found 'the real old men' concerned over both the 'lamentable' veterinary position and 'the sparse opportunities for education' in the tribe. Except for the Northern Frontier, the Masai District was 'the most backward and neglected area of the country'.[5]

Throughout Beecher was jealous of his position, refusing to countenance any suggestion that anybody except the properly appointed members could speak on behalf of African interests. He was soon insisting in a letter to the *East African Standard* that the Rev. R. W. Sorensen (a Labour M.P. and frequent critic of colonial affairs) had raised a question in the House of Commons about his views without any reference to him;[6] he could not allow an impression to grow that he was conducting his battles through

[1] 20 Nov., 1946, pp. 230–1.
[2] Minutes of the Kiambu L.N.C., 16–17 Sept., 1943.
[3] Minutes, Fort Hall L.N.C., 28 Feb., 1944.
[4] Minutes, Kipsigis L.N.C., 30 Mar. to 1 Apr., 1944, and minutes, Central Kavirondo L.N.C., 4–6 May, 1944.
[5] 20 Nov., 1946, p. 232.   [6] *E.A.S.*, 17 Dec., 1943, Suppt. (a)

others, and especially not outside Kenya. In the Council he rebuffed the Indians: he reported that he had:

' been asked to say by Africans that so far as they and their friends were concerned, no authority has been conveyed to the hon. Indian members of this Council to voice opposition on their behalf.'

In the same speech he regretted that the Director of Agriculture should have felt ' any justification ' in referring to African opinion before he or his colleague had spoken.[1] When an elected European, Mrs. Olga Watkins, moved a motion on native policy, he expressed ' very considerable regret that this had been done without reference to the members for African interests ', commenting that if he or his colleague had introduced a motion on European policy without consulting other members of the Council they would have been strongly criticised by Mrs. Watkins.[2]

Earlier representatives of African interests might have apologised for vigorous speech; not so Beecher. He carried the attack into the European camp. On the Land Control Bill concerning the White Highlands, in April 1944, he argued that if the Europeans rightly demanded to be associated in African development they should allow for ' a measure of reciprocity '; this brought Montgomery to intervene since he found the idea of African representation on the Land Control Board ' strange '.[3] Then, too, Beecher provoked—and not for the only time—Cavendish-Bentinck, Burns's old enemy of 1934. But there was a difference: Beecher compelled respect. Mrs. Watkins said that his efforts were ' not so much a representation as dedication ' and Vincent,[4] the European leader, remarked that:

' his great desire, and earnestness to represent the whole of the natives of the country and not one particular clique of them almost becomes an obsession with him.'[5]

[1] 20 July, 1945, p. 108.
[2] 26 Nov. 1945, p. 258. Mrs. Watkins was of Austrian background (v. her *Tales from the Tyrol*). She came to Kenya in 1914 and married Col. O. F. Watkins, Sen. Cr. and Ag. C.N.C. during the twenties. She became the European elected member for Kiambu in 1941, being supported by the small coffee farmers, and held the seat until her death in 1947, but had a reputation for ' liberal ' views respecting Indians and Africans.
[3] 12 and 13 Apr., 1944, pp. 32 and 62.
[4] Vincent, Sir Alfred, Kt. 1946 (1891–   ), in Kenya Member Exec. Co., 1944–8, M.L.C. 1942–8 and 1957–60, Member East African Civil Defence and Supply Council, 1942–5, Member Kenya Devt. and Reconstruction Authority, 1945–53, Member East African Central Legislative Assembly, 1948–.
[5] 23 Oct., 1947, p. 144, and 24 July, 1945, p. 177.

Yet Beecher would not simply report the views, requests and ideas of Africans; there was also his position as it had been defined by Ormsby-Gore. Beecher exposed the fulness of the obligation as he saw it in two speeches:

' I regard the terms of my appointment as imposing upon me a double duty. I have unquestionably to represent, where necessary, certain individual African views, whether those are of the majority or not, and whether they conform with my own interpretation of the situation or not. But I cannot regard that as my sole, nor necessarily my most important, duty. I feel obliged to consult African opinion as freely and as conscientiously as I can. . . . It is the second part of that double duty . . . that I should endeavour to the best of my ability to present in what I say in this Council a synthesis of those views, in a manner best calculated for the advancement of the African people as a whole in particular, and of the country as a whole in general.'

And again:

' Insofar as I am called upon to represent interests and not only persons, I feel that I am entitled to express a personal view.'[1]

Beecher repeatedly pressed for the addition of African members : for their ' valuable contribution ' and as a means to ' inspire very much greater confidence '.[2] In November 1946 he suggested that in the new year there should be at least six representatives of African interests and also gave a hint of his forthcoming resignation.[3] Already Sir Philip Mitchell,[4] the Governor, had acknowledged that Beecher's position was an ' embarrassment ' to him, but there were, he urged, ' very strong reasons ' why he should continue.[5] Beecher refused to accept one of the Government's reasons, namely that there should be no change of a constitutional type during the life of a Council, but he did agree to withhold his resignation until March 1947.

---

[1] 20 July, 1945, pp. 104–5 and 20 Nov., 1946, p. 221.
[2] 20 July, 1945, p. 112.   [3] 20 Nov., 1946, p. 81.
[4] Mitchell, Maj.-Gen. Sir P. E. (1890-) Asst. Res. Nyasaland, 1912, officer K.A.R. 1915–9, Asst. Pol. Offr. Tanganyika 1919, Chief Secretary, 1934–5, Governor of Uganda, 1935–40, Deputy Chairman, Conference of East African Governors, 1940, Political Adviser to General Sir A. Wavell 1941, British Plenipotentiary to Ethiopia and Chief Political Offr. on staff of G.O.C. in C., East Africa 1942, Governor of Fiji and High Commissioner for the Western Pacific 1942–4, Governor of Kenya 1944–52, pubn: *African Afterthoughts* (1954).   [5] 4 July, 1946, p. 81.

From the formation of the new Council in October 1944, Beecher had an African, E. W. Mathu,[1] as his colleague. Thus Kenya's was the first Legislative Council in East Africa with an African member. The son of a Kikuyu medicine man, Mathu had spent a year at Balliol College, Oxford, marking thus strikingly the pace of change in this part of Africa during the twentieth century. Mathu soon showed his considerable ability in the Council. His maiden speech, on the budget in November 1944, was graced by quotations from Addision and Shaw, but there was more: he showed a real debater's command, picking up and answering points made earlier in the morning by Vincent, the European leader.[2] He fully warranted E.A. (later Sir Ernest) Vasey's[3] expressed respect for him and ' his fine brain '.[4]

Mathu's approach was that of a moderate, as was seen in the controversy in 1947 over the *kipande*. Africans had been demanding, at least since 1921, the abolition of this ' pass ', compulsory for Africans to carry outside the reserves. In their wish to retain it the Government intended to end the sense of discrimination by introducing a general system of registration for all races. In the end this proved popular with none, although a Bill to set up such a system was passed in July 1947. The Chief Native Commissioner then described it as ' a personal triumph ' for Mathu for he had been prepared to defend this compromise to African audiences.[5]

Certainly there was a marked contrast between Mathu and F. W. Odede[6] who was a temporary member in 1946. In Odede's first speech, again on a budget, he immediately put what the

[1] E. W. Mathu (1910–) was one of the first pupils at the Alliance High School, 1926–9, then a teacher before continuing his education: at Fort Hare, South Africa, 1933–4, Exeter University College, 1938–9, and Balliol Coll., Oxford, 1939–40, a year under special arrangements made by Miss Perham; principal of a Kikuyu Karing'a school 1943; Member Kenya Leg. Co.19 44–57, and Ex. Co. 1952–7, Member Central Legis. Assy. East Africa 1957–59, and then deputy exec. sec. United Nations Economic Cn. for Africa, being apptd. U Thant's special rep. in Katanga, July, 1962.
[2] 22 Nov., 1944, pp. 107–117.
[3] Vasey, Sir E. A. (1901–) Mayor of Nairobi, 1941–2 and 1944–6, M.L.C. for Nairobi North, 1945–50, Member for Education, Health and Local Govt. 1950, Member for Finance 1951, Minister for Finance and Devt. 1954–9, and in Tanganyika: Minister for Finance and Economics 1959–60, for Finance 1960–2.
[4] *E.A.S.*, 25 Jan., 1946, p. 10.
[5] 24 July, 1947, p. 137.
[6] F. W. Odede (1921–   ), Asst. Veterinary Officer 1940, M.L.C. 1946 and 1952–3, Ag. Pres. K.A.U. 1952–3, arrested and detained 1953–60, National M.L.C. 1961.

Acting Director of Education called a ' staggering proposal ', that there should be universal compulsory education for Africans.[1] Odede refused to be bound by any hesitations of speech, though he was a junior government official. In a debate on the future status of Tanganyika, in July, he rose, despite the Governor's warning that it was ' inappropriate ' that officials should speak or vote on the subject: ' on behalf of the African community ' he opposed the European leader's motion. Beecher followed: while acknowledging that Odede felt it necessary to speak in that way he added that only 24 hours' notice had been given of the debate so that neither of them had been given the opportunity to consult African opinion effectively.[2]

The difference of opinion between Beecher and Odede in that debate arose partly from their different premises regarding their function. Moreover, although the Africans may have learned something of parliamentary techniques from Beecher, theirs could not be an easy relationship; this was perhaps more particularly so with Mathu who had earlier been Beecher's pupil at the Alliance High School. Yet they were ' colleagues '—Beecher's constant word—if not always a team. Mathu acknowledged in his speech on the 1945 budget that they did not always find it easy to divide up the various subjects between them.[3] He then gave a perfect example of the difference between the two minds: he poured out African fears and grievances on a series of issues, while Beecher's usual approach tended to a rationalisation of them. Besides, Beecher was still a missionary. A small example of this had been seen in July 1945, when Beecher put a question about illicit liquor traffic among Africans, but Mathu, in a supplementary, pressed for the ending of racial discrimination, so that Africans might be allowed to drink European beer.[4]

Perhaps James Gichuru's first opinion was right. With all his virtues Beecher, as a European, could not fully represent Africans, something he himself fully admitted. While African criticisms of Beecher developed particularly after the Beecher report on education in 1949,[5] there were some signs earlier. After he had resigned from the Council, Beecher was a member of the Plewman

[1] 10 Jan., 1946, pp. 722 and 727.
[2] 18 July, 1946, pp. 126 and 157.
[3] 14 Nov., 1945, p. 147.
[4] 17 July, 1945, p. 3.
[5] *African Education in Kenya* (1949).

committee on taxation.[1] When its report was debated Mathu attacked it strongly, seeing a racial aspect in it arising from ' the exclusion of African membership ' from the committee. The Chief Native Commissioner detected an attack on Beecher. Agreeing first with much that Mathu had said, he commented that Beecher had the African interests at heart and had the ability to put the African ' point of view far better than I can and certainly far better than any African can '.[2] The first part of this acknowledgement was a striking contrast with the earlier position taken by civil servants on missionary representation but the second raised a deeper issue.

Such views about Beecher have frequently been expressed by Europeans in Kenya. That they had some substance may be seen by comparing Beecher's and Mathu's budget speeches in both November 1945 and November 1946. Yet while Beecher spoke forcibly and ably for Africans and while he was appreciated by them, as we have seen, a comment of Bernard Shaw is not inapposite:

' Like Democracy, national self-government is not for the good of the people: it is for the satisfaction of the people. One Antonine emperor, one St. Louis, one Richelieu may be worth ten democracies in point of what is called good government; but there is no satisfaction for the people in them.'[3]

A first faltering step towards democracy through an elected African membership of the Kenya legislature was taken in 1944: for Mathu's appointment the Local Native Councils were consulted.[4] Then Mathu played a prominent part in the formation of the Kenya African Union,[5] intending it to serve to strengthen his hand in the Legislative Council. However, the essential weakness of the first Africans on the Council remained: they were only nominees. When, in 1946, Jomo Kenyatta returned from his long

[1] Report of the Taxation Enquiry Committee, Kenya (1947).
[2] 21 and 22 Oct., 1947, pp. 66 and 91.
[3] Preface to John Bull's Other Island (London, 1930 ed. collected works) vol. XI, p. 42.
[4] During the war Peter Mbiyu Koinange canvassed for signatures for a petition that he should be the first nominated African (8 Nov., 1943, pp. 443 and 474). In his The People of Kenya Speak for Themselves (Detroit, 1958), pp. 8–9, he claims that the L.N.C.s voted for him rather than for Mathu but such records of L.N.Cs as I have examined raise doubts about his account.
[5] Formed as the Kenya African Union in October 1944, it changed its name a month later, under Kenya Government pressure, to the Kenya African Study Union, but reverted to the original name at the second Annual Delegates' Conference in Feb. 1946.

absence in England he hoped, as the aspiring nationalist leader, to be appointed but this the Government refused.[1] There was thus a certain delicacy of relationship between the nominated African members on the one side, and Kenyatta and those others who obtained control of the Kenya African Union. The Union refused to regard government nominees as true African representatives although they were allowed to attend the Union's executive committee.[2] Mathu knew well that in the post-war rise of African feeling there was a danger of its taking to extra-parliamentary and violent forms. Early in 1948, in words perhaps more intelligible in the light of later knowledge, he spoke of secret meetings taking place behind locked doors, in caves and ' in the depths of banana groves '.[3] The last months of the first Legislative Council with African members were those of the beginnings of Mau Mau among the Kikuyu.

The new Council, formed in 1948, had an unofficial majority for the first time. In this there were four Africans, still nominated although on the basis of consultation with the Local Native Councils. The new members remained, throughout the new Council, ' representatives of the interests of the African community ', their title being changed to 'African Representative Members ' only in 1952. Yet 1948 was the real end of the old system. As Africans by themselves, they could now become a parliamentary group, the African Unofficial Members' Organization under Mathu's leadership. There lay the beginnings of African parliamentary action in Kenya. The day of European paternalism, at least in this respect, was over but not that of ' interests ' as the basis for representation.

When directly elected seats for Africans were to be introduced, Africans themselves saw that the idea of ' interests ' had some value. They, in their turn, paralleled the arguments of the Europeans in 1917. In the preliminary discussions of 1955 before the first direct African elections of 1957, Africans asked that in the allotment of seats regard should be paid to the administrative districts. The districts are related often to tribal ' interests '. In the divisions of Kenya it was seen that the weighting of seats in favour of the smaller tribes could be a useful protective device.[4]

[1] Sir P. Mitchell: *African Afterthoughts* (London, 1954), p. 259.
[2] African Unofficial Members' Organization files.
[3] 9 Jan., 1948, 759.
[4] G. Bennett and C. G. Rosberg: *The Kenyatta Election* (London, 1961), pp. 47–8.

The modern British practice of relating seats proportionately to population, a change which occurred gradually in the nineteenth century from the original pattern of the ' House of Communes ', may work well only in a homogeneous society.

M

MICHAEL McWILLIAM

ECONOMIC POLICY AND THE KENYA SETTLERS
1945—1948

By 1945 the European community in Kenya enjoyed great political influence, as a result of successive modifications to the conventions of Crown Colony government, and at a time when the lines of post-war economic development were being worked out. Of the other two racial communities the Asians, although very articulate and directly represented in Legislative Council and on Executive Council, had rather little influence even on matters which closely concerned their community if these were at all contentious. The Africans were largely outside the political system and their presumed interests were interpreted by indirect means through the colonial administration and through nominated representatives in Legislative Council. On certain matters this arrangement was highly effective. However there was no doubt but that the Europeans were still the most influential racial community in the early post-war period. This was perhaps especially true in connexion with economic questions for, on the one hand, Asian and African spokesmen tended to show less interest in, or speak with less authority on such matters; while on the other hand, just because these topics often had little overt racial content, the colonial officials were more amenable to forceful expressions of unofficial opinion, even if they came mostly from one quarter. An assessment of the detailed reactions of the government officials in Nairobi and of the Colonial Office in London to this sectional pressure must await the opening of the public archives, but in the outspoken conditions of Kenya politics a considerable amount of evidence is already available which makes possible at least a preliminary appraisal of the impact of ' settler '[1] thinking on the main economic issues of the day. We shall first

---

[1] Although the settler label is obviously derived from the European agricultural landowners, it would be quite wrong to limit its political application only to this section of the European community. Settler politicians represented the views of the European community in Kenya and this included professional and businessmen, and even civil servants off-duty.

consider the various avenues of influence that were open to the settlers at the end of the war and then try to determine how far their views were reflected in government policies.

I

At the end of the war the influential position of the settlers was buttressed in five main ways. First, the Governor's Executive Council contained two European elected members. Second, it was an established practice to consult the European leaders on all important matters affecting the community. Third, there was an unofficial majority on the Standing Finance Committee in Legislative Council. Fourth, most of the important economic controls affecting distribution and production, which had been set up during the war, were directed by leading figures in the European community and not by officials. Fifth, the character of Kenya society was favourable to settler influence. These avenues of influence will be considered in turn.

Membership of Executive Council did not of itself carry with it executive responsibility for Government policy, as far as the unofficial members were concerned. It was a body advisory to the Governor and it is very probable that many important questions were settled without any reference to Executive Council, particularly in view of its mixed membership. Nevertheless it was an important forum for pressing the views of the European community, as well as for consultation with its leaders when this was desired. A significant pointer to the absence of true cabinet status was the way the European members of Executive Council were not restrained from pressing their criticisms of Government policy publicly in Legislative Council and elsewhere; indeed such behaviour was politically necessary.

However, the constitutional adjustments[1] introduced by Sir Philip Mitchell[2] in 1945 soon after his arrival had the effect of greatly increasing the authority of the settlers in the Government. Two quasi-ministerial posts in Executive Council were designated as the Member for Agriculture, Animal Husbandry and Natural Resources and the Member for Health and Local Government. The latter post was filled by the same nominated member who had

---

[1] *Proposals for the Reorganisation of the Government of Kenya.* Sessional Paper No. 3 of 1945, Nairobi, 1945.
[2] For biog. note see above p. 164

been in charge of Local Government affairs, the uncontentious Mortimer.[1] But the post of Member for Agriculture was offered to a leading European elected member, Cavendish-Bentinck.[2] The Agricultural and Veterinary Departments had not previously enjoyed representation in Executive Council, so their elevation was all the more dramatic, particularly as there was general agreement at the time that agrarian policy was the most important post-war issue facing the Government. At the same time as Cavendish-Bentinck became Member for Agriculture, a powerful Board of Agriculture was created, manned by the European farming community, to advise the Member of policy and legislation. The other main emphasis of Mitchell's reforms was to strengthen the machinery for dealing with post-war development and reconstruction problems. To this end he created a special agency—the Development and Reconstruction Authority—to implement the Government's plans. Its chairman was the Chief Secretary and its two other members were the General Manager of the Kenya-Uganda Railway (a public official) and Vincent,[3] who was leader of the European elected members and already a member of Executive Council. Thus another leading settler acquired a direct responsibility in a major area of government policy.

It was the Government's aim always to introduce agreed legislation where important interests were at stake, at least as regards the European community.[4] It was rare therefore for a bill to be contested by the settlers' leaders when it came to Legislative Council. Indeed, two important pieces of legislation on economic matters were actually introduced from the unofficial benches. The Pig Industry Bill of 1945 was introduced by Cavendish-Bentinck while still an unofficial member. Again, Vasey[5] introduced the Hotel Industry Bill of 1948, presumably because he had been

[1] Mortimer, Sir C. E. (1886–   ); Methodist Minister 1910–16; Land Dept., Kenya, 1917–27; Land Sec. 1928–30; Commissioner, Lands and Settlements 1938–39; Commissioner, Local Govt., Lands and Settlement, 1939–46; Member for Health and Local Govt., 1946–50 and 1952–54.

[2] For biog. note see above p. 152.

[3] For biog. note see above p. 163.

[4] The phrase ' government by agreement ' had been coined by Delamere in 1925 (25 August, 1925, p. 770), but the concept had undergone many vicissitudes sincet hen, according to the temperament of succeeding Governors and the temperature of local politics. It was strongly in the ascendant during the war and in the period under review.

[5] For biog. note see above p. 165.

chairman of the Hotel Control and was regarded as the person best calculated to carry this somewhat unpopular measure. From the protests made from time to time by spokesmen of the Asian and African communities, it was evident that consultation there was less successful. Consultation also took place on major policy issues. Perhaps the biggest set piece of this kind took place in connexion with framing a 10 year development programme for the colony at the end of the war. Not merely did the Development Committee which was appointed in 1945 have influential unofficial member-ship,[1] but this body in turn set up a series of sub-committees to draw up detailed sector proposals which drew heavily on unofficial membership. Another example was provided by the Govern-ment's decision to de-ration a group of essential foodstuffs in 1948. Action was delayed for some time until Legislative Council met again in order to demonstrate through a debate there that it had the approval of unofficial, and especially settler, opinion.[2] An example of a different kind is provided by the Government's approach to the report of the Woods Fiscal Survey[3] in 1946, which was unpopular with the settlers.

In introducing a motion agreeing with the conclusions of the Report, the Government announced that it would be withdrawn if it became evident that there was strong opposition to the Report. Not surprisingly this provoked an attack from the European members which successfully achieved this end.[4]

The passage of the annual estimates involved a far more elaborate consultation than is usually implied by a Crown Colony budget debate, since the motion before the Council was to refer the Estimates to the Standing Finance Committee, which had an unofficial majority. This was no empty formality. The limitation of government expenditure was regarded as a real responsibility and the Committee could, and did, amend the Estimates up or down, including the introduction of new financial proposals,

[1] The unofficial members of the Development Committee were: Lord Francis Scott (a former member of Legco and leader of the European elected members); F. H. De V. Joyce (elected member for Ukamba and member of Executive Council); H. B. Hamilton (a leading businessman); R. B. Pandya (a leading Asian businessman).

[2] This was emphasised in the speech by the Secretary for Commerce and Industry. 9 June, 1948, p. 32.

[3] Report on a Fiscal Survey of Kenya, Uganda and Tanganyika, by Sir Wilfred Woods, K.C.M.G., K.B.E., Nairobi, 1946.

[4] 24 September, 1946. Vol. XXV, Pt. 1, p. 19, et seq.

provided the Government members of the Committee could be persuaded to agree to them. For example, the surplus presented by the Financial Secretary in his budget speech on the 1945 Estimates was reduced from £73,000 to £6,000 by the Standing Finance Committee; on the 1948 Estimates the Committee turned the proposed deficit of £130,000 into a surplus of £77,000, which involved writing up expenditure by £380,000 and revenue accordingly. In this connection, one of the main duties of the Standing Finance Committee was to examine the feasibility of the many recommendations made by members during the course of the budget debate, for which purpose departmental officials could be cross-examined. Thus the unofficial members were given considerable opportunities for initiative on financial matters, as well as for persuasive influence. The many amendments made to the Draft Estimates each year—while not all stemming from unofficial suggestions—show that these opportunities were not neglected. One might say that the role of the Standing Finance Committee in this period is more reminiscent of a Committee of the United States Congress than of British parliamentary practice.[1]

At the outbreak of war the Government machine was both unprepared and incapable of running alone the extra administrative apparatus which was made necessary by war conditions, ranging from import controls to commodity rationing, to an agricultural production drive. The missing expertise was largely provided by the European business and farming community. Men like Vincent, Cavendish-Bentinck, Vasey and many others in and out of politics wielded great power in Government's name and acquired practical experience of directing many aspects of the country's economic life. Even had the controls all lapsed at the end of the war—which was far from being the case—this sharing of Government's executive responsibilities over several years would have provided a strong case for analogous devolution in the post-war period. And so when it was decided to preserve the machinery which had organised the great production drive in the Highlands, and to lay special emphasis on agrarian matters in the

[1] The reforms of 1948 restored financial initiative to the Crown and brought procedures more into line with the British tradition; since however an unofficial majority was introduced into Legislative Council that year, there was no marked weakening of settler influence. In the budget debate at the end of the year several reductions in the Estimates were forced on the Government, e.g. on the price control department. 21 January, 1949, p. 1241.

post-war development plans under a new member of Executive Council charged with these responsibilities, who better was there for the job than the main architect of the wartime achievement— Cavendish-Bentinck?

The character of Kenya 'society' greatly reinforced the influence of the settlers. The white community was very small. Social life in it was active. It has already been seen that wartime exigencies brought officials and unofficials into working partnership as never before. Virtually all important people would be known to each other, if not directly then at least by close repute. Such conditions naturally gave numerous opportunities for personal influence and attunement of ideas, quite apart from established avenues of consultation or authority. The special position of the settlers was, of course, all the more marked by contrast with the Africans and Asians where, generally speaking, none of these conditions applied. An added factor of importance in such a small society was a curious convention whereby the settlers maintained a constant barrage of public criticism of the conduct of government, which could on occasion be very sharp, whereas colonial service officials by and large held their silence. It meant that if the normal channels of consultation and influence were not yielding the desired results, the European leaders would not hesitate to put on the pressure through the press and at meetings.

It will be seen therefore that by the end of the war the European community was accustomed to being consulted on policy formulation and to playing a leading part in the execution of many wartime policies. At the same time the leaders were free, in a way not possible for official members of the Government, to criticise government actions in private and in public. Such a position greatly increases the influence of determined men. Vincent, especially, was an expert in the curious art of brotherly enmity, capable of attacking the Government strongly in public without sacrificing his personal influence or regard. It was one of the crucial tests for a successful European leader. It might have been expected that a situation like this would deteriorate easily into one of irresponsible power in favour of sectional interests. Several factors militated against this however. First, the colonial officials were not mere puppets. Kenya had some notable public servants in this period: Mitchell, Rennie,[1] Troughton,[2] Foster Sutton,[3] Wyn Harris,[4] Thornley,[5] and—particularly where African interests were directly at issue—they were notably hard to move, for instance on matters connected with labour policy and land tenure. The presence in Britain of an alert group of colonial affairs experts, in and out of Parliament, was no doubt an important factor in strengthening their position. Second, the settler leaders in this period had generally a wide view of their responsibilities; there was a very genuine concern over the agrarian problems of the country at the end of the war, for example. Nevertheless, because of the weakness of African (and to a lesser extent Asian) influence it could well happen that important matters went by default. Third, the very fact that the Government openly shared responsibility with unofficials was in itself a safeguard since, given the existence of a vigorous and ambitious European community, the alternatives were backstage pressure and partisan demands without any of the checks which follow from openly assumed responsibilities. In short, the imperial Government was making its customary adaptation to a colonial pressure group, only this time it was composed of white settlers.

II

There were two large issues of fiscal policy in the early post-war period: taxation and the rate of public sector development. On the first, the European elected members had firm views to press on the Government and they won considerable successes. On the second issue, opinion was divided and somewhat confused

[1] Rennie, Sir Gilbert (1895–); Ceylon Civil Service, 1920–37; Fin. Sec. Gold Coast, 1937–9; Ch. Sec. Kenya, 1939–47; Gov. N. Rhod., 1948–54; High Cr. in U.K. for Federation of Rhod. and Nyasaland, 1954–61.

[2] Troughton, J. F. G. (1902–); Admin. Service Kenya, 1926–44; Econ. Secy., 1944; Fin. Secy. Member for Finance, 1946–49; Fin. Controller, Overseas Food Cor., 1949–50.

[3] Foster Sutton, Sir Stafford (1897–); Sol. Gen. Jamaica, 1936; Att. Gen. Cyprus, 1940; Member for Law and Order Kenya, 1944–8; A. G. Malaya, 1948–50; C. J. Malaya, 1951; Pres. W. A. Court of Appeal, 1951–5; C. J. Fed. of Nigeria, 1955–58; Pres. Pensions Appeals Trib. Eng. and Wales, 1958.

[4] Wyn Harris, Sir Percy (1903–); Admin. Service Kenya, 1926–44; Labour Cr. 1944–6; Ch. Native Cr. and Member for Afr. Affairs Kenya, 1947–9; Gov. Gambia, 1949–58; Member Devlin Comm. on Disturbances in Nyasaland, 1959; Mt. Everest Expeditions, 1933 and 1936.

[5] Thornley, Sir Colin (1907–); Admin. Ser. Tanganyika, 1930–39; Col. Off., 1939–45; Admin. Sec. Kenya, 1945–7; Dep. Ch. Sec. Kenya, 1947–52; Ch. Sec. Uganda, 1955; Gov. Br. Honduras, 1955–62.

and the Government was able to resolve the issue in its own favour without great difficulty.

Income tax was a sore point with the European community. It had at last been accepted with ill grace in 1937 and there was strong feeling that the whole subject should be reviewed *ab initio* as soon as the war ended. The debate was coloured by two powerful cross-currents of feeling. On the one hand it was felt that income tax was unfair in its application because of widespread tax avoidance by the Asian community which the understaffed Income Tax Department was incapable of getting the better of. This view was strengthened by the habit of lumping together European companies and individuals in the racial analysis of income tax statistics, which fostered the smug conclusion that Europeans paid 90 per cent of the income tax collected.[1] Since also it was generally held that the Asian community—largely traders—was very wealthy, there was an irresistible suspicion of enormous tax evasion. The second cross-current was directed at Africans. There was a feeling that the Africans were not paying their fair share of the cost of government services and that the shortfall was being made up by the long suffering European taxpayer.

The Government's first reaction was to commission a fiscal survey (which was later extended to cover Uganda and Tanganyika as well).[2] Sir Wilfred Woods did not fall in with the views of the European community on any of the contentious income tax issues; he played down the significance of tax evasion; he did not consider that the overall burden of income tax—as increased during the war—was too high; he did not think there was any scope for increased African taxation. The Government motion in Legislative Council to accept the report was strongly opposed and, as we have seen, was withdrawn. When the Budget which followed soon after made no provision for retrospective tax relief or for a reduction in tax rates, but merely followed the Woods recommendations of larger depreciation allowances and improved personal allowances, the European members took the extreme step of voting against the Budget. Shrewdly, they also called for another, locally based, taxation committee. The Government was alarmed at this open rupture in the conventions of government by agreement and a committee was quickly appointed, with a chair-

---

[1] See for example the way income tax statistics were used by the Plewman Committee: *Kenya—Report of the Taxation Enquiry Committee*, Nairobi, 1947.
[2] Woods Report, *op. cit.*

man and secretary from South Africa, but an otherwise local membership. The Plewman Report[1] reasoned that wartime levels of taxation should be adjusted when normal conditions returned and held it as self-evident from the economic statistics then available that they were too high for economic health in 1947. Moreover, it considered that a tax rebate should be granted as well. Away from the passions of the time the arguments and figures appear much less compelling, and indeed they were effectively demolished by the Commissioner of Income Tax during the debate on the Report. But the prime need was to restore confidence between the Government and the settlers and the Report provided the means. The Government decided accordingly to accept the recommendations regarding a tax rebate as well as the recommendation for a reduction in rates of tax, on the announced grounds of helping those affected by the rising cost of living, to provide a stimulus for development and because its finances were buoyant. Needless to say, it was a major victory for the campaign of the European leaders, as Vasey unkindly rubbed home: ' If you go through the budget speeches of last year you will find that the honourable members on this side said time and again almost exactly what has been said in most cases by the Committee.'[2]

The problem of development policy provides an interesting contrast to the tax campaign, particularly as the two issues were contemporaneous. Kenya approached the end of the war with buoyant revenue and reserves. At the same time colonial development was much under discussion, stimulated by the prospect of greatly increased disbursements under Britain's Colonial Development and Welfare legislation. Colonial Governments were requested to draw up 10 year development programmes in connexion with applications for funds under the Colonial Development and Welfare Vote and, in Kenya, elaborate departmental planning got under way in 1944.[3] A Development Committee, with strong unofficial membership, was appointed in January 1945 with the task of converting the departmental exercises into an overall plan. The Committee also conducted extensive investigations on its own account and reported in July 1946.[4] Meanwhile,

[1] Op. cit.   [2] 22 October, 1947, p. 118.
[3] The procedure was laid down in Secretariat Circular Letter No. 44 of 29 April, 1944. The document was laid in Legco in June 1944.
[4] Report of the Development Committee. Nairobi, 1946.

as we have seen, a Development and Reconstruction Authority was constituted in August 1945, ready to take over the executive direction of the development programme. However, to set against all this activity, there were lively fears, which Government spokesmen acknowledged, of a severe slump shortly after the end of the war. In particular it was argued that Kenya had enjoyed an artificial prosperity during the war which made an unsound basis for estimates of peace-time economic activity. Had Kenya moved decisively away from the 1939 level of economic activity, or should that year be taken as the norm? The Woods Report in 1946 reflected and in some ways reinforced these fears; it saw no prospect of increased taxable capacity for a decade and recommended an almost static budget to match this view.

The defensive reaction to these conflicting arguments was to call for a delay in launching the development programme and in any expansion of government services, in spite of the buoyant revenue position, until it became clearer what the post-war word was going to be like. Couldrey[1] championed this line, but the elected members were not united on the issue as there were too many things they badly wanted done to be able to support such an austere policy of its conclusion. Since the Government for its part was convinced of the necessity of starting straight away with its development schemes, and was confident that the main revenue heads would not fall back to pre-war levels, it was able to tip the scales decisively in favour of expanding recurrent services and a large development programme. Yet the legacy of this debate was not altogether happy. There remained a guilty feeling among the settlers that government expenditure was far too high and the cramping habit persisted for several years of harking back to pre-war economic conditions, instead of assessing the contemporary capacity of the country to pay for increased services. Its effects were most serious in delaying the build up of services for Africans, notably education.

III

The appointment of the outstanding European politician to the most important post created by the reconstruction of the Government in 1945 was rightly hailed as a major advance in

[1] Couldrey, J. G., D.S.C. (died 1948); European elected member for Nyanza; Editor, *Kenya Weekly News.*

power for the European community. The most obvious result of Cavendish-Bentinck's appointment as Member for Agriculture, Animal Husbandry and Natural Resources was that the system of agricultural self-government in the Highlands that had been developed so successfully during the war was to continue afterwards, backed by the full authority of the Government. The network of production committees and sub-committees which covered the Highlands had proved itself in the wartime drive for greater food production. Since staff shortages severely restricted the expansion of government services for several years after the war, the existence of this tested instrument for implementing production policy, land control measures and the selection of credit-worthy farmers for development loans, enabled the Highlands to make a quick getaway in postwar development. Like farmers everywhere, those in the Kenya Highlands favoured controlled marketing for their products—and they achieved outstanding success. Building on the wartime measures, producer-controlled statutory marketing became the characteristic of postwar agricultural organisation in the European farming areas.

Although some of the measures to extend control over agricultural activities produced lively debate on occasion, as for example the Coffee Industry Bill of 1945 which set up a single marketing organisation for the coffee industry, the substantial identity of viewpoint between ' the government ' and the settlers over the principles of postwar agricultural policy in the Highlands was eloquent testimony to the succeses of the settlers' takeover bid of this sector of government. Furthermore, the very distinction had become blurred as a result of the many producer-controlled activities that had been set up. The real focus of debate in agricultural policy was in the African reserves. Intensive cash crop production (mainly maize) without the benefit of scientific knowledge; growing herds and dwindling pastures; more people endeavouring to carry out traditional expansive farming within fixed tribal boundaries; all had combined to exhaust the land in many areas, as well as to produce disturbing evidence of soil erosion, especially in Machakos where the position had been aggravated by drought. Although by the end of the war this situation was widely deplored within and without the Government, the settlers felt keenly that the Government was doing too little to tackle the problem. This was clearly one of Cavendish-Bentinck's main preoccupations when he became Member for Agriculture.

If the land in the native reserves became exhausted and incapable of supporting a growing population, then the Highlands themselves would become more vulnerable to African claims for land there. As Cavendish-Bentinck remarked bitterly at the end of 1944, the Carter Commission of 1933 had been supposed to solve the African land problem ' at any rate within our lifetime.' 'And in our foolishness we really thought that these native land problems were more or less reasonably settled for quite a long time to come.'[1] The settlers felt that they had been let down, particularly by the negative attitude of the Administration towards reforms in native land tenure and cattle ownership practices. The policies which emerged under Cavendish-Bentinck's leadership were accordingly wide ranging. The first, defensive, task was conservation measures to arrest the progress of soil erosion. The second was to open up new areas for native settlement in order to relieve the worst affected districts. And the third was to bring about new concepts of land and stock use amongst Africans so that the cycle would not have to be repeated all over again. This last entailed a considerable research progeramme. But the idea of the reserves as a productive economic asset was largely absent from settler and official thinking; indeed there was a certain revulsion against the very idea of African cash crop farmng at all, as this was held to have been greatly responsible for the deterioration of the land in the past.[2] It was not until the nineteen fifties that the Agricultural Department had built up sufficient research knowledge and experience to initiate a decisive reversal of this attitude by showing that under appropriate conditions intensive cash crop farming on peasant holdings was compatible with maintained, even increased, land fertility.

Settler concern at the deterioration of the land in the reserves at the end of the war undoubtedly gave considerable impetus

[1] 30 November, 1944. p. 328.
[2] See for example Joyce in Legislative Council in July 1945, (18 July 1945, p. 61), and also the following passage from the statement of policy issued by Cavendish-Bentinck soon after he took office as Member for Agriculture: There is little doubt that a great deal of the prevalent erosion and soil deterioration can be traced to the premature pressure of cash cropping upon agricultural systems which had evolved for the limited purpose of providing the peasant and his family with no more than the food they themselves consumed, with perhaps a small margin for dues to the Chief, festivals and other incidents of primitive society. *Land Utilisation and Settlement*. Sessional Paper No. 8 of 1945. Nairobi 1945.

to the measures that were taken to combat it and to the high priority given to this task. At the same time the very closeness of this interest, mingled as it still was with traditional feelings about the reserves as a source of labour and the dangers of African coffee growing, not to mention the open derision of tribal tradition, brought its own complications. For it made it all too easy for Africans to suspect that their land was somehow in peril from the settlers. The close association of prominent settlers with the Government on agrarian policy only made it more difficult for the Government to gain African confidence on matters connected with the land. The contrasting approaches to the question of agricultural settlement according to whether it took place in the Highlands or the reserves, provides a interesting example of how settler thinking coloured official policy.

Agricultural settlement was a major topic of policy after the war, both for the Highlands and the reserves, but it was animated by quite different considerations in the two cases. In the Highlands, further settlement connoted a major contribution to economic development; in the reserves it was part of the rescue operation to save the land. The contrast underlines the extent to which it had become axiomatic to see economic development in terms of European activity. The settlers had traditionally attached great importance to closer settlement of the Highlands under Government sponsorship. The war had prevented the proper implementation of the 1939 settlement scheme of assisted land purchase;[1] but at the beginning of 1944 Cavendish-Bentinck—as chairman of the Agricultural Production and Settlement Board—appointed a committee to make recommendations on post war-settlement, having particular regard to the needs of ex-servicemen. Detailed proposals were made by the committee by the end of the year,[2] with the result that when post-war development plans were being considered, this was one of the few fully worked out projects ready to hand and it immediately gained top priority under Cavendish-Bentinck's advocacy. Settlement was included in his portfolio in 1945 and the full amount requested by the Committee —£1.6 million for up to 500 new settlers—was allocated. By early 1948 these funds had been largely committed and there were 121 tenant farmers on Crown land with another 140 to

---

[1] *Settlement Committee Report.* Nairobi, 1939.
[2] *Report of Settlement Schemes Committee,* 1944. Nairobi, 1944.

come, and 16 assisted owners with another 14 to come.[1] They had nearly all been given special training at the newly opened Egerton School of Agriculture. When seeking the approval of Legislative Council to put the arrangements onto a statutory basis in 1948, the Government claimed that the settlement scheme represented ' the greatest hope of an immediate increase in our national income.'[2]

While the undeveloped estate of the Highlands was being tackled in this fashion by new immigrants aided by revolving loan funds, settlement in new areas and resettlement on reconditioned land was regarded as one of the main specifics for remedying the serious agricultural condition of the reserves. Within a few months of taking office Cavendish-Bentinck had decided to establish a special organisation to deal with the subject, the African Land Utilisation and Settlement Organisation. No less than 39 per cent of the 10 year Development Plan allocation for agricultural and veterinary services was made available directly to the A.L.U.S. Board and kept separate from general agricultural and soil conservation expenditure.[3] One of the great attractions of this approach was the opportunity it seemed to offer of making a new beginning by creating strictly controlled agricultural regimes away from the cramping influences of tribal custom and of hesitant administration in the main reserves. The Kenya political scene being what it was, the most obvious empty land of good quality in the Highlands or in other tribal areas (e.g. Masai) was not available for settlement schemes and a costly search was instituted to open up new areas from the tsetse fly and to develop water supplies for them. Not surprisingly, and especially in view of the early postwar shortages of men and materials, these African schemes were very slow in getting under way and they failed in their declared purpose of providing immediate and substantial relief to the over crowded districts in the reserves. On the largest and most important of these schemes at Makueni only 445 families had been settled by the end of 1951.[4] The relief to the reserves, such as it was, came more from the growth of employment

[1] 15 March, 1948, p. 68.
[2] 15 March, 1948, p. 70. There was also, of course, a considerable influx of self-financed settlers from Britain and from India after independence.
[3] *Report of the Development Committee*, pp. 22–3.
[4] Department of Agriculture *Annual Report*, 1951, Vol. 1, p. 36, Nairobi, 1952.

opportunities elsewhere in the country as economic expansion there got under way.

On a longer view, it can be seen that the effort that went into African settlement schemes was, at its lowest, an escapist solution, and at its best a temporary safety valve. It took nearly a decade for it to become apparent that the traditional agricultural systems could be successfully reformed to the extent that the demographic problem lost its menace and a prospect was opened up of rising rural living standards. In the late nineteen forties, however, there remained an unfortunate contrast between stagnating African reserves and growing prosperity in the Highlands and towns which may have been significant ingredients in the explosion in Central Province in 1952.

IV

When it came to determining a post-war industrial and commercial policy for Kenya, the settlers rightly apprehended that considerable modifications were required in the Government's arrangements for dealing with these matters. By mid-1948 they had been largely successful in securing the desired reforms. However, this achievement turned out to be far less momentous than might have been expected owing to the fact that the European leaders had scarcely anything in the way of policy to urge on the Government. Having fashioned a potent instrument for gaining acceptance of their views, one finds neither any consensus of opinion on commercial and industrial matters, nor any disposition to accept the views of the one member of Legislative Council, Vasey, who spoke with some authority. In the absence of a spur from unofficial opinion, and subject to negative pressures from other members of the East African customs union, the Government was slow to develop firm policies of its own.

Businessmen had occupied influential positions in the government machine through their association with the many economic controls that were instituted during the war. Once gained, it was only to be expected that ways would be sought to perpetuate such influence in peacetime conditions, especially in view of the recognition in general terms of the need for greater industrial development in the country. The successful arrangement for exerting influence on agricultural policy provided the obvious starting point, and it was not surprising to find, for example,

N

Cavendish-Bentinck in November 1944 advocating a board for
dealing with trade matters analagous to the forum which the
farmers had, i.e. a predominantly unofficial body that would effectively determine commercial policy.[1] As the colonial service officials
at the time were rightly held to be largely ignorant of such matters
and as there was virtually no departmental experience to call on,
the European members in the same budget debate pressed the
Government to appoint an adviser to assist it in laying down
policy in the post-war period. Both these lines of thought were
acceptable to Mitchell, the new Governor, who agreed to establish
a Trade Advisory Committee and to recruit an Economic and
Commercial Advisor. In practice neither of these creations
proved very effective in themselves, nor did they put the business
community on a par with the agricultural community in the 1945
reorganisation of the machinery of government. The farmers had
the powerful figure of Cavendish-Bentinck sitting in Executive
Council and in charge of the departments dealing with agricultural
matters, whereas the arrangements on the commercial side were
diffuse. Vincent, a leading businessman, also sat in Executive
Council, but he had no direct departmental responsibilities.[2]
The new Economic and Commercial Advisor, Hope-Jones,[3] was
chairman of the Trade Advisory Committee, but neither had
much authority. Moreover no less than four senior officials
had direct responsibilities for commercial and industrial subjects:
the Chief Secretary, the Financial Secretary, the Chief Native
Commissioner (trading in native areas), and the Member for
Health and Local Government (trading in municipalities). It
was small wonder that, with the quickening of commercial activity
on the one hand and the continuance of controls over many
aspects of commercial life on the other, dissatisfaction grew during
1946 and 1947 at the absence of any real leadership in this field.
As was to be expected, the constructive side of these complaints
took the form of a demand for a Member for Commerce and
Industry. Their champion was Vasey and eventually, in January

---

[1] 30 November, 1944, p. 324.

[2] Vincent's membership of the Development and Reconstruction Authority
would have given him a say in the execution of the Development Programme,
but not on industrial and commercial policy.

[3] Hope Jones, Arthur (1911–); Fellow Christ's College, Cambridge,
1937–45; Miny. of Food, 1940–44; Econ. Adv. Anglo Iranian Oil Co., 1944–6;
Econ. Adv. Kenya 1946–8; Member 1948–54 and Minister 1954–60 for Commerce and Industry Kenya.

1948, he felt impelled to bring the issue to a head with a formal motion in Legislative Council.[1]

The Government's failure to adapt its organisation to meet the criticisms of the commercial community was not due to any fundamental difference of opinion over the suggestion for a grouping of departmental responsibilities under a Member for Commerce and Industry, so much as that it was playing for a bigger fish, namely that commercial and industrial matters should become an East African subject under the proposed East African High Commission. Well aware of the fears in Uganda and Tanganyika of Kenya domination, the Government had adopted the weak strategy of playing down its own involvement in the fostering of commercial and industrial development in Kenya. Business opinion of course supported the Government's objective, but became increasingly impatient at the chosen method of approach. When the 1945 proposals of Colonial 191[2] were replaced in 1947 by those of Colonial 210[3], and it became apparent that there was not going to be a uniform commercial policy on an East African regional basis, the European leaders concluded that progress in Kenya should no longer be held back by inter-territorial considerations and decided to force the Government's hand.

The tactic was a great success. The Government, while announcing that it would make a final effort to establish a ministry on an East African basis, meanwhile agreed immediately to set in train administrative improvements for dealing with commercial subjects and to increase the responsibilities of the Economic Commercial Advisor. Within a few weeks he was redesignated as Secretary for Commerce and Industry.[4] By July the Government was ready to take a motion in Legislative Council for the appointment of a Board of Commerce and Industry in place of the Trade Advisory Committee, with responsibilities for reviewing legislation and advising on industry development policy.[5] Short of one of their number actually being appointed to the post of

---

[1] 14 January, 1948, p. 818.

[2] *Inter-Territorial Organisation in East Africa.* Colonial No. 191 H.M.S.O., 1945.

[3] *Inter-Territorial Organisation in East Africa, Revised Proposals.* Colonial No. 210, H.M.S.O., 1947.

[4] Hope-Jones was not appointed Member for Commerce and Industry until 1949.

[5] 15 July, 1948, p. 91.

Secretary for Commerce and Industry it seemed that the business community could at last achieve parity of influence with the farmers.

Parallel with the attempts to improve the Government's handling of commercial subjects and to increase the formal influence of the European business community, efforts were being made to formulate a policy for post-war industrial development in Kenya. But compared with the clearcut and authoritative ideas on the future development of the Highlands, thinking on the future industrial development of the country was notably vague and confused, perhaps because there was no tradition of businessmen from the leading firms going into politics. Vasey was the only member with direct experience of the industrial problems of an important company. The top executives of the expatriate companies have nearly always been kept away from public affairs in Kenya, with the result that the field has been left clear largely to farmers and the professions. To begin with there was a widespread tendency to discuss industrialisation not in terms of commercial opportunities, suitable raw materials, potential markets and the like, but for pessimistic reasons: a fear that the land could not support a growing population engaged in agriculture, so that alternative pursuits must be found in ' secondary industry '. This approach was particularly noticeable in the debates on reabsorbing African soldiers after demobilisation although, apart from the establishment of an artisans training centre at Kabete, there was very little follow through. A Legco debate in May 1945[1] again dwelt on the importance of economic diversification, but it was mainly notable for the enthusiasm of Couldrey and Vincent for cheap power as a means to industrialisation. Perhaps fortunately for Kenya, the outstanding hydroelectric opportunity was recognised to be at Jinja, and it was left to Uganda to discover the cost of the cheap power fallacy. However, the debate led the Government to appoint a special sub-committee of the Development Committee, to which the General Manager of the East Africa Power and Lighting Corporation was appointed, to examine the problem of industrial development. In the event it had nothing more concrete to suggest than the establishment of a Government Finance Corporation ' although we had no evidence that there is at present any shortage of capital for industrial

[1] 2 May, 1945, p. 18, *et seq.*

development,'[1] and also a technical institute. On the other hand it was all for controls to prevent cut-throat competition, monopoly, dumping and to determine industrial location.

It might have been anticipated that one wartime initiative of the Government's would have had a more decisive impact on policy after the war. £200,000 had been provided to establish secondary industries, often relying on the fortunate presence of Italian prisoners of war to provide the required technical skills. Pottery, caustic soda, sulphuric acid, edible fat, fibre board, fire bricks and pyrethrum extraction, these ' war babies '[2] were administered on an inter-territorial basis by an East African Industrial Management Board under the direction of the East African Council. Although the successful ventures were sold off without difficulty to private interests after the war, the experience did not generate any great enthusiasm for the possibilities of direct Government participation in, or stimulation of, industrial development, and the East African Industrial Management Board languished until as late as 1954 before being converted into the present Industrial Development Corporation. During the period of acute shortage of building materials immediately after the war, the idea was mooted that the Development and Reconstruction Authority should establish publicly owned brick and tile works[3], but nothing came of it. Had there been a member of the Government with clear responsibility for industrial development at the end of the war, the precedent of the wartime ventures and the immediate reconstruction needs of the country might well have led to fresh schemes. Their absence is eloquent testimony to the void in policy at that time.

The only important legacy of the wartime industrial ventures which had been established under Defence Regulations, making them monopoly industries, was a singular policy which eventually, came to the statute book in 1948 as Industrial Licensing Acts in all three territories of the common market. With the strong support of organised commerce, the Government decided at the end of the war that the principal measure to encourage and promote industrial development in East Africa should be statutory control

---

[1] *Report of the Sub-Committee on Industrial Development*, printed in *Report of the Development Committee*, Vol. II, p. 184.

[2] The phrase is Elspeth Huxley's in *The Sorcerer's Apprentice, A Journey Through East Africa*, London, 1948, p. 62.

[3] *Report of the Development Committee*, p. 25.

of new entrants into any particular industry. The procedure
envisaged was that an industry considered ripe for development
would be scheduled under the Act, after which the East African
Industrial Council would select a suitable manufacturer according
to a stated procedure. The collapse of hopes for a strong East
Africa High Commission, especially in the commercial field, made
this plan highly vulnerable, because Uganda and Tanganyika
were primarily interested in it as a device for ' apportioning '
industrial development equally between the territories. The four
years' delay in bringing the scheme to the statute books only
revealed the more clearly the superior industrial attractions of
Kenya and the negative opportunities it gave to the other Governments. By 1948 disillusionment with the proposed policy was
already fairly pronounced in Kenya. When the first schedule
list came to Legislative Council for approval in July 1948 and
only contained three items: cotton textiles, woollen textiles and
glazed pottery, even the Secretary for Commerce and Industry
was moved to express his public disappointment at such a meagre
result, ' I am disappointed the schedule is so short, that it is so
widely divergent from the real needs of these territories as I see
them.'[1]

It has already been seen that Vasey played the leading part
in the campaign to reform government machinery for dealing with
the affairs of commerce and industry. He alone of the unofficials
had a consistent view on industrialisation, that the Government
should give tariff assistance to new industries. But he failed to
secure sufficient support for this view from his colleagues to
make it a major question of policy. Kenya's post-war industrial
development has consequently been achieved with very little
direct political assistance from the settlers.

V

We began by considering what might be called the institutional
means whereby the settlers were able to exert an influence on
economic policy in Kenya. In the light of the succeeding discussion
we may conclude by reflecting on the effectiveness of settler
exertions in the early post-war period. Bearing in mind the
original qualifications about the difficulties of precision on this

[1] 14 July, 1948, p. 67.

subject, it seems possible to distinguish three gradations of influence.

First, there were the clearcut occasions when there was direct settler initiative. As one would expect they are most apparent where their economic interests are strongly involved. The campaign for tax relief at the end of the war was sharp and successful. The case for more intensive settlement of the Highlands under official auspices proved as acceptable in 1945 as in 1939. Of much greater long term significance for the economy was the system of agricultural self-government that was achieved in the Highlands, or producer controlled production and marketing in more familiar language. Other pieces of initiative stemmed from a somewhat wider vision. The campaign to strengthen the Government's handling of commercial and industrial matters was well founded, even though the follow through was fumbled. The settlers were also the main driving force for the development of a local capital market, leading to the Local Loans Ordinance of 1945 and a borrowing amendment to the Muncipalities Ordinance in 1948. Couldrey and later Vasey were the outstanding figures here. The success of these direct campaigns depended very often on the absence of organised opposition as well as on their objective merits. A reminder that the settlers could not carry all before them is provided from the employment front. Serious labour shortages persisted after the war and the settlers repeated their traditional argument that the Government should ' organise ' the labour market, even to providing a Labour Corps. Although this idea was apparently seriously considered by the Government during 1947[1], there was never much likelihood of it being adopted and the settlers were left to fulminate at the influence of ignorant critics overseas.

Next we may notice the occasions where settler and official thinking showed a substantial identity of viewpoint. The priority given in post-war thinking to tackling the agrarian problem is one example. The genuineness of settler concern on this topic led, as we have seen, to the Government charging one of their leaders with the main responsibility for measures to save the land. The introduction of the membership system was again very much in accord with settler thinking on how the Government should progressively share its authority. They were the only racial group

[1] 27 November, 1947, p. 499.

in Legislative Council to welcome it and the only one whose participation was invited. Perhaps the outstanding factor was the similarity in their approach to economic problems shown by the Governor
and the settlers. It would be wrong headed to suggest that a
man of Mitchell's authority and experience was dominated by
the settlers, but it remains that his understanding appraisal of
their importance to the country's development led to mutually
acceptable economic policies on many occasions.

Lastly we come to an even more intangible factor, and yet
one that indubitably marks off Kenya from other African colonies,
namely the influence of the settlers on the general climate of
opinion on economic matters, as distinct from their contribution
to individual policies. Three examples seem significant. First,
there was the belief in the settlers as the main agent of economic
growth in Kenya. This was a contingent truth rather than a
necessary one, but the vigour of the settler community virtually
suceeded in blurring the distinction. As a corollary to this view
there was the general acceptance of the White Highlands as the
country's main economic dynamo. We have seen how this
produced what almost amounted to a blind spot over the economic
possibilities of the reserves. Finally, one may note the settlers'
tendency to encourage strong government intervention in economic
matters, whether it be to regulate agricultural production, control
marketing, determine industrial location, or organise the labour
supply. Kenya became a highly controlled economy in the post-
war period and much was expected of the Government in its
economic performance. It produced over the years an outstanding
government machine and a habit of state initiative in economic
matters.

BRYAN KEITH LUCAS

THE DILEMMA OF LOCAL GOVERNMENT IN AFRICA

In 1947 Mr. Creech Jones, as Secretary of State for the Colonies, issued his famous dispatch to all governors of African territories, calling for the rapid development of local government. In doing so, he was careful to contend that he was introducing no new policy, but only giving added emphasis to long accepted principles.

A century before, Earl Grey had enunciated a similar policy; writing of the people of British Guiana he said:

' I conceive that gradually to prepare them for a more popular system of government ought to be one of the principal objects of the policy adopted towards them, and it is one of which I never lost sight. It was more particularly with this view that I endeavoured whenever practicable to create a system of municipal organisation, entertaining a strong conviction that the exercise of the power usually entrusted to municipal bodies is the best training that a population can have for the right usage of a larger measure of political power.'[1]

So also in 1865 Sir Benjamin Pine, recommending self government for all the West Coast, said that he would proceed by gradually accustoming the people to manage their own affairs; ' he would begin by giving them municipal institutions, by making them drain their own towns and take care of their local affairs '.[2]

Lord Ripon had followed a similar course in India, and for the same reasons; in his Resolution on Local Self Government of 1882, he laid down the policy to be followed, and explained that ' it is not primarily with a view to improvement in administration that this measure is put forward and supported. It is chiefly designed as an instrument of political and popular education.'[3]

With these precedents, it is surprising that so little was done

[1] Grey, *The Colonial Policy of Lord John Russell's Administration*, Vol. I, p. 32.
[2] Evidence before Select Committee on British Establishments on the West Coast of Africa, 1865, p. 130.
[3] *Resolution on Local Self-Government*, 18 May, 1882, para. 5.

to develop similar modern forms of local government in Africa before the second war. There were municipal councils in a number of towns, copied in painful detail from their English counterparts, but in general no comparable bodies in the rest of the country.

No doubt the difference was due in great part to a difference in aim; Durham in Canada, Grey in the Caribbean, and Ripon in India stressed the importance of local government, not so much for its own sake as for its value in educating people who would in due course take over political responsibility for the government of their countries. In Africa, there was before the war less sense of haste. The leading authorities were 'unanimous that the era of complete independence is not as yet visible on the horizon of time.'[1] The objective was a different one, and not necessarily inferior. The aim was not so much to prepare the people for self government in the future as to give them good government in the present; not so much to give them the advantages of European ideas and methods, as to give them the security and opportunity to develop their own. The system of Indirect Rule was in many ways in conflict with the conception of developing municipal institutions and Local Government;[2] in Lugard's view such methods of government were appropriate only to the towns and the educated Africans, and should be kept separate and isolated from the Native Authorities of the rest of the country.[3]

These conceptions were being modified in the 1930's, but, with the second war the whole picture changed; independence was now clearly visible on the horizon. First in the Gold Coast and Southern Nigeria, and later in other territories, the demand for self-government grew clamant and urgent; it became apparent that much more could be done by government action to accelerate economic and social development, even in the remotest areas; the British Government came to recognise the part that rural as well as urban local government might play in the changes that were inevitably coming. Moreover, the old conception of developing indigenous forms of government was fading; instead there was growing up after the war an implicit assumption that, though

---

[1] Lugard, *The Dual Mandate*, p. 198.
[2] The conflict between the conception of Indirect Rule and the development of parliamentary institutions on a European model was stressed by Lord Hailey, *An African Survey*, 1st Edition 1938, p. 134–5.
[3] Lugard, *The Dual Mandate*, pp. 570–574.

self-government was the ultimate goal, it must be self-government based on a parliamentary democracy; that Britain could not hand over control except to rulers who accepted British rather than African methods of government. Such a principle was, however, as Hailey had already pointed out, in conflict with the philosophy of Indirect Rule. The development of local government, however, offered the possibility of building a foundation of local democracy, on which the structure of parliamentary government could be based. And, unlike the earlier experiments in India, the stress in Africa was on rural rather than urban government. The problems of adaptation were accordingly much greater.

Mr. Creech Jones's dispatch emphasised two main reasons for the rapid development of an ' efficient and democratic system of local government '. First was the part that local authorities could play in economic development; second was the need for political education of the people in countries which were moving rapidly towards responsible government at the centre. Closely linked with this conception of political development was that of the local authorities acting as electoral colleges for provincial, regional and central councils or assemblies; ' local Government must at once provide the people with their political education and the channel for the expression of their opinions '.

The rather vague phrases of this dispatch were spelt out in detail in the report of the Summer School on African Administration held at Cambridge in 1947, which Mr. Creech Jones summoned to discuss the topics he had raised in his dispatch. Here the same basic principles were accepted; the importance of local authorities serving as electoral colleges was reaffirmed, and emphasis was given to the desirability of copying the general principles of local government, as it exists in England, without, apparently, very much discussion of the different patterns that are to be found in the United States, France, and other countries.

After this there came a surge of activity at the top; in the Colonial Office the African Studies Branch was established and started publication of the *Journal of African Administration*; an Advisory Panel on Local Government in Africa was appointed to make men with English local government experience available to advise on the problems of Africa. In the African territories, a large number of commissions and advisers prepared reports on the problems of local government, its finance, elections and administration in the respective countries.[1] It is characteristic of these reports that they thought of the problem as one of adapting English local government to the circumstances of each African territory, rather than of evolving new forms based on the traditions of the country, or of selection of the best features of the various systems which are to be found in Europe and America. Moreover, surprisingly little attention was paid to the experience of India, where British administrators had also wrestled with the problems involved in introducing local government in an alien soil. Though traditional authorities were not ignored, they were in general regarded as factors to be fitted into the pattern of English local government rather than as the basis on which the new structure should be built; in Northern Nigeria, Nyasaland, parts of Uganda, and elsewhere, however, this pattern obviously would not serve; the new system had to be based on the traditional authorities, adapted to meet changing ideas of government.

But in the 1950's the whole nature of African government was changing. The picture was no longer one of British administrators preparing Africans for eventual self-government. The initiative was passing from the white man to the black, and all aspects of government came to be seen in a different light—the light of their rôle in relation to the coming of national independence. The arguments that had been used in favour of local government on the English model lost some of their force, or came to have somewhat different meanings. The emphasis changed in many ways.

The conception of 'local authorities' serving as electoral colleges did not survive long. It was tried in Uganda in 1950, in Western Nigeria in 1951, and in Kenya in 1952, but public opinion

[1] e.g. Gold Coast: *Report of the Committee on Constitutional Reform* (Chairman, Mr. Justice Coussey) 1949; *Reports of Select Committees on Local Government in the Colony, and in Ashanti*, 1950; *Report of Committee on Local Government in the Northern Territories*, 1950.

Uganda: *Report of an Inquiry into African Local Government in the Protectorate of Uganda*, C.A.G. Wallis, 1953.

Tanganyika: *Report of the Special Commissioner appointed to examine matters arising out of the Report of the Committee on Constitutional Development*, W. J. M. Mackenzie, 1952.

Sierra Leone: *Report on the Functions and Finances of District Councils*, H. W. Davidson, 1953.

Nigeria: *Report on Local Government in the Northern Provinces of Nigeria*, K. P. Maddocks and D. A. Pott, 1950. *East African Local Government Reform, Kenya, Uganda and Eastern Nigeria*, Brig. E. J. Gibbons, C.B.E., 1949. *Report of the Committee on the Future Administration of Urban Areas* (Chairman, D. A. Pott), 1953.

Sudan: *Report on Local Government in the Sudan*, Dr. A. H. Marshall, 1949.

was strongly against it; people wanted to play a direct, not an indirect, part in choosing their representatives; the new political parties saw it as a hindrance to their progress; outside advisers regarded it as a danger to the integrity of the local authorities.[1] So the argument for local government based on the conception of indirect elections lost its force.

Another principal argument for the policy that was being pursued was the value of local authorities in educating the people in the ideas and the working of democracy. Mr. Creech Jones had declared in his Dispatch that ' an efficient and democratic system of local government is in fact essential to the healthy political development of the African Territories; it is the foundation on which their political progress must be built '. Furthermore, he envisaged the local authorities as providing a stream of members to the central legislature, who would act as a counterweight to the urban professional politicians, out of touch with the people in the countryside, who, he feared, would otherwise dominate the political scene.

Only to a very limited extent has this in fact occurred. Events moved too quickly, and the new political parties of West Africa— C.P.P., Action Group and N.C.N.C.—took control of events. It was the urban, educated professional politicians who won power, not the councillors from the local authorities. The process by which it was hoped that men would graduate from the district council to the Legislative Assembly never really had a chance when Nkrumah, Awolowo and Zik were setting the pace.

But political education was not envisaged as being necessary only for the members of a council or an assembly. The ordinary man and woman would, it was argued, learn the ideas of democracy, and the significance of the ballot box. Bit by bit a whole people would become imbued with democratic principles. Even though at first they might not be able to grasp the issues in a national election, local government would serve as an introduction to the system, and an introduction which they could understand, in terms of familiar problems and candidates whom they knew personally. How far this has proved to be the case is hard to say, but probably it is true that local government has served a valuable purpose in this way. Perhaps the gulf between local and national

[1] *Report on Local Government in the Sudan*, 1949; *Report of the Electoral Reform Commission*, Sierra Leone, 1954.

problems has not been so great as one thought; the considerations which have influenced voters in both local and central elections are hard to define;[1] tribal loyalties and rivalries, allegiance to national parties, obedience to secret societies or tribal rulers, hopes of self-government and more personal motives have all played their part. But none the less, the local councils have done much to help the local people understand what elections and ballots mean.

A third aspect of this educational approach to local government was the idea that, by copying the English model, a large number of Africans would come to understand the British attitudes to government; how minorities should work with majorities; how officials should remain non-partisan and aloof; how majority decisions should be accepted, and how voluntary service was its own reward, without seeking personal profit or advantage. But in the social and economic environment of modern Africa such ideas have not been easily assimilated by local councillors. Some of them cut across his traditions and habits. The custom of reaching decisions by the sense of the meeting, and the sense of loyalty and obligation to one's tribe and family, are difficult to reconcile with the system of counting votes, and the condemnation, of nepotism. In fact the system has not worked, in general, as it was meant to. It has not been easy to reproduce the English town clerk in Africa, nor to persuade the councillors to accept his position as they do in England. Political parties are very different things in Africa and England. So the process of teaching the basis of democracy through the working of local councils has been a difficult one. The initial failure of the system in practically all the larger towns of West Africa[2] showed that the stresses and pressures can be too strong for the structure, and it can, and does, too easily collapse. But yet, step by step, progress has been made, and municipal councils, overcoming their early difficulties, have in many cases become effective and well organised units of local administration.[3]

[1] See, e.g., Lucy Mair, ' Representative Local Government as a Problem of Social Change ', *Journal of African Administration*, Vol. X, No. 1, pp. 11–24, and W. J. M. Mackenzie and K. E. Robinson, *Five Elections in Africa*, passim.
[2] *Vide, e.g., Report of the Commission of Inquiry into the Administration of the Lagos Town Council*, 1953, by Bernard Storey, and *Report of the Commission of Inquiry into the Administration of the Ibadan District Council*, 1956, by E. W. J. Nicholson.
[3] See U. K. Hicks, *Development from Below*, Chapter 20.

Perhaps the fault here was that the English system was adopted too completely. The Colonial Office Advisory Panel repeatedly advised those concerned to avoid too close an imitation of the system, but their advice was not always taken.[1] The English system was not only known, in its bare outline at least, to the administrators, but it was also demanded by the Africans. It was possible to send African officials and councillors to see it in action in English towns. Moreover, in the general need for hurry, there was not time to work out a completely new system. In some cases conscious efforts were made to adapt the system to the needs of the country,[2] but in others (most outstandingly Eastern Nigeria), the English pattern was adopted, and too often it proved too delicate a structure to withstand the buffetings of political winds. This weakness arose partly from the fact that the two corner stones of the structure were very weak—the town clerk and the supervision of the central Ministries. It was not possible at short notice to reproduce either of these essential parts of the system. In England, town clerks take years of training and preparation; in Africa they had to be produced at once. In England, the system of central control is a peculiar and rather complex set of relationships between civil servants and local government officers, rather than a legal code. This also was impossible to reproduce in Africa. Even in England, in a town with centuries of experience and tradition, local government would probably break down if there were neither of these two ingredients—the town clerk and the central supervision. It is therefore not surprising that there were some failures in Africa, where these were so often lacking. In many cases the District Commissioners managed to prop up the District Councils by carrying much of the weight on their own shoulders. In the towns this was more difficult, and failures were more common. More recently, however, as the staff have become more experienced, the system has worked with increasing ease, and new patterns of relations with the central ministries have been evolved, more suited to the social and administrative background. The common feature of these has been the existence of an agent

[1] See A. H. Marshall, ' The Adaptation of English Local Government to Colonial Territories ', *Public Administration*, Winter 1949, pp. 264–268.

[2] *e.g.* Uganda—*Report of an Inquiry into African Local Government in the Protectorate of Uganda*, C. A. G. Wallis, 1953.

Tanganyika—*Report of the Special Commissioner Appointed to Examine matters Arising out of the Report of the Committee on Constitutional Development*, W. J. M. Mackenzie, 1952.

of the central government in each area, acting rather as the ears and eyes of the Minister of Local Government than as an administrative officer exercising his own authority. The details vary; in Ghana and, more recently, in Sierra Leone and Tanganyika, the senior man in the field has been a party politician rather than a civil servant.[1]

There was a belief too that a democratic local government system would act as a protection against extremist politicians, and as a solid foundation of stability in the nation. Mr. James Griffiths, when he was Secretary of State for the Colonies in 1951, proclaimed that ' Local Government is in the first place the field of activity to which Africans can first look for political training. Equally important, local government can protect a country against unbalanced political development. As we have found in our long experience in this country, strong local government has been the safeguard against the exercise of excessive and even dictatorial power at the centre '.[2] English history is in fact ambiguous in this respect; it is probably only to the record of a few municipalities in resisting the power of James II that one can point with certainty as examples of such heroic corporations; too many have been venal and subservient, and even outright corrupt. So too in Africa, there is little evidence as yet of municipal authorities defying the aggressive encroachments of central power. Neither in the Sudan, nor in Ghana, nor in Rhodesia, can one fairly claim that local government has served to defend the people's liberties. Had it existed longer, and had its structure grown more solid, it might have had the strength to do so.

In his dispatch of 1947 Mr. Creech Jones had put first in his list of reasons for the establishment of local authorities the part they could play in developing the economic resources of the countries.[3] The Colonial Development and Welfare Act of 1940 had marked an important change in British policy, which recognised that governments must play a substantial and growing part in development of natural resources and social services in the

[1] The system of Regional Commissioners and Government Agents in Ghana has been reorganised in 1962.

[2] Opening address to the Cambridge Conference on African Administration, 1951.

[3] For the development of this economic argument, see Hailey, *An African Survey*, revised, 1956, pp. 202–203, 1325–1343, Colonial Development and Welfare Act, 1940, and *Statement of Policy on Colonial Development and Welfare*, Cmd. 6175, 1940.

colonies. Mr. Creech Jones saw the local councils as a link between the central government, with its Ten Year Development Programme, and the people in the villages, who must carry out the plans. For such purposes it was essential that local authorities should be not only efficient, but also large enough in area and resources to be able to play an effective part in economic development. But at the same time other considerations were dictating that the unit of local government should be small, and working on a scale which the ordinary villager could understand. So the areas and revenues have often been too small, and the staff too inexperienced, for the councils to be able to make any effective contribution to the economic development of the nation. Such a task might have been successfully undertaken by local authorities which had already established themselves and learnt the arts of government. But the inexperienced councillors and officers of new councils, still floundering in the mire of Standing Orders, Internal Audit and Electoral Rules and Orders, were not suitable bodies for such a purpose. In general, they failed. In many parts of Africa the contribution of Local Authorities to national economic development has been very slight, though in the field of social services—schools and clinics, water supply and drainage—they have been more successful. The achievements of the District Councils of Kenya and Uganda, for example, in such matters are impressive.

The conception of local authorities working as the agents of the central government in large projects was in fact in some ways in conflict with the emphasis which was, at the same time, being placed on the democratic aspects of local government, and its value as a school of self-government. Economic considerations pointed to large authorities; the conception of ' grass roots ' democracy demanded small authorities. Economic planning needed co-ordination and central control, but political experience could only be gained if councils were free to make mistakes.

The question of how much liberty should be given to the new councils has always been a difficult one. There have been these conflicting pressures for more, and less, central control. There has been the influence of the English model, in which very little ministerial authority is to be found in the statutes, but yet central control is there, exercised in more subtle, hidden ways. There has been the controversy about the function of the District Commissioner in a system of local government. So the position

o

has varied from country to country and from year to year. At first, in many cases, the English pattern was too closely copied, and hopes were set too high. Local Authorities were allowed a degree of independence which sometimes proved disastrous. Then sterner control became necessary, as in the Local Government Ordinance of 1955 in Eastern Nigeria, which re-established the power of the central authority,[1] though in a different form.

So also the relation between local councils and traditional authorities has varied from territory to territory and from time to time. At first there was, in many cases, a tendency to copy the English model of excluding all ex-officio members. Some gesture was made to the chiefs, first in Uganda, by allowing them to act as ceremonial heads of elected councils; the same system was recommended by the Coussey Committee[2] in the Gold Coast in 1949, and adopted in Western Nigeria in 1952. Generally, however, there was in the early days a tendency to regard the chiefs as a relic of the past, to be politely put on the shelf.

By 1956 or 1957, however, the pendulum was beginning to swing back in many parts of Africa. The first enthusiasm for political development on the European model was being modified by a growing desire to be African first. Institutions which were essentially African came to have a new virtue in people's eyes, as did African clothes and African literature. In 1956, the Cambridge Conference reported that ' what we choose to call " tribal particularism " is however very rarely decreasing in importance, is sometimes static, and more generally growing. By "tribal particularism " we mean the cleaving together of persons for one reason or another according to their tribal affinities, and if then it is accepted that tribal feeling is strong and likely to continue to be strong and can be used as a basis for local government purposes, then it will obviously be so used.' To-day, whatever may be the case elsewhere, this tendency to accentuate tribalism is clearly a major influence in Kenya and Uganda.

There were, however, two strong and conflicting influences at work. On the one hand, this African Renaissance, laying stress on the inherent value of African tradition, led to a demand for more recognition of traditional authorities, and their integration

[1] See *Policy for Local Government*, Eastern Region Sessional Paper, No. 2, of 1956.
[2] Gold Coast (Report to H.E. the Governor by the Committee on Constitutional Reform), 1949. Colonial No. 248.

into the system of local government. On the other hand the growth of nationalism pointed in the opposite direction. The new nation-states demand a loyalty to the state, rather than to the tribe, and in some cases, such as Ghana, a conflict arose between the two; the traditional authorities began to lose their status in local government, and were elbowed out. Elsewhere, however, they have been retained, for a time at least, on the ground that they give a degree of stability to the system; and this may be closely linked to the knowledge that the chiefs, as in Sierra Leone and Uganda, are bound by custom or discretion to the government of the day. In Uganda the predilection for hereditary rulers and ceremonial figures is so considerable that districts without such traditional rulers have created ceremonial heads, like the Kyabazinga in Buroga (1940) and the Won Nyaci in Lango (1960).[1] Thus nationalism pulls in one direction, tribalism in another.

If one were to attempt to summarise the achievements of the whole movement to develop local government in African territories over the past twelve years, one would inevitably be forced to speak in wide and dangerous generalisations. But yet some general tendencies may perhaps be observed in the continent as a whole. The conception of local government as a part of a pyramid of indirect election with a legislative assembly at the top has been abandoned. As a part of a great movement for political education, it has achieved something, but not as much as was hoped at first, because the pace of political development, and the growth of political parties, have outstripped it. National politicians have in general not worked their way up the ladder from District Councils, but have sprung fully armed from the ground of the educated minorities in the cities. As a part of the machine for social and economic development, local government has not been as successful as was once hoped, partly because the process of creating efficient local authorities, able to take on such functions, has been slow; hampered by difficulties of staff, finance and organisation. As a stabilising element in politics, local government has not really been put to the test, except perhaps in Ghana, where it has been submerged in the nationalist flood.

At first sight this seems a gloomy catalogue of failure. But yet the movement as a whole should not be judged by the standards of the highest hopes of idealists in those post-war years. Local

[1] *Report of the Uganda Relationships Committee* (The Munster Report), 1961, p. 54.

Government on the English model has not proved a cornucopia of blessings which transform the nations. But on the other hand it has served a very useful purpose. So also in England, Mr. Gladstone thought in 1893 that parish councils would transform the English countryside, and bring in a golden age of equality, cooperation and liberty. The fact that his hopes were so high does not mean that parish councils have failed. They have in fact done much useful, if not spectacular, work.

Similarly in Africa, the local councils have done much good. They have brought tens of thousands of Africans into the process of governing themselves; they have filled a gap created by the shrinking of the powers of District Commissioners; they have in many areas provided roads and bridges, schools and hospitals. There have been failures and disappointments, but yet, on this practical level, much has been achieved.

Looking back on the history of these last fourteen years, one can see some of the mistakes that were made; the over-large areas, the creation of too many tiers of local authorities, the failure to start training courses soon enough, and, in some respects, the too careful imitation of English methods. At the same time one can see much that showed remarkable foresight in Mr. Creech Jones and his advisers. They were right when they forecast the rapid development of representative government at the centre; they correctly assumed the need for speed if local government was to make a contribution to the new democracies. They foresaw the decline of the power of the District Commissioner, and the growing demand for economic and social development. Moreover, seeing these things, they took immediate and appropriate action to anticipate them. They created a machinery to provide for the situation which they saw developing. They may have been too optimistic in some respects, they may have made some miscalculations, but the creation of elected local authorities has certainly done much to help prepare these peoples for independence.

Now, however, the days of preparation for independence are over, or coming to an end. Independence has arrived, and the question, therefore, arises of the rôle of local government in the new era. Do the old arguments still hold good? Is the conception of more or less independent local authorities compatible with the demands of nationalism?

The claim that local government is needed as a form of education, so that the people may learn the arts of government and the meaning of democracy sounds rather impertinent when referring to an independent nation. Such an argument was used in England by Mr. Gladstone, when the mass of the population had not yet got the right to vote; but now, in an age of universal adult suffrage, it would probably be resented by people who do not admit that they are in need of any further political education of this sort. So the argument is no longer heard today in England, nor, generally in Africa. It is out of date.

How far local authorities will continue to be used as a means of economic and social development is uncertain. The new leaders are inclined to be impatient of the delays and variations of local authority action. New services are needed, and needed quickly—schools and hospitals, roads and dams. In many cases local authorities have shown their capacity to provide these services; elsewhere the councils have not achieved enough to prove their ability to do so. There is a natural tendency to turn instead to direct action by the central ministries, or to government corporations set up for the purpose, unhampered by municipal boundaries, and more closely controlled by the ministries.

Politically the future rôle of local government is not easy to assess. There are several possible lines of development. The new rulers may feel that local authorities with any substantial degree of independence are potentially a threat to the unity of the state. How to build a united nation out of a number of tribes and races is the prime problem of these countries. The forces of disintegration are strong, and loyalties to a tribe and a tribal ruler may be more powerful than loyalty to a new-founded state. If local authorities are geographically and politically based on tribal units, they may become a force working against national unity.

On the other hand it may be only by giving to such local authorities a great degree of independence that a nation can be held together at all. Federation may be the only way in which such nations as Canada and Nigeria can exist as single states. The independence guaranteed to the provinces or regions makes cooperation at the national level possible. So too, if the units be smaller, a generous degree of local autonomy may be a necessary condition of national unity. In Uganda, for example, the Munster

Commission[1] has apparently seen this as the basis on which a united independent country should be built.

There are here two conflicting views—that strong local authorities may become centres of separatist feeling and so a threat to the unity of the nation, and that strong local authorities are essential as an outlet for separatist feeling, if the unity of the nation is to be maintained. Both, no doubt, are wrong in some circumstances, right in others. It may be that a wise ruler would tend to make such concessions to tribal feeling, and a cautious one to avoid this danger of disruption.

In the early years of independence, there is likely to be what most Englishmen would regard as an undue insistence on uniformity. The unity of the nation becomes supremely important. There is little room for variations of aim and purpose—the new state must be organised, its industries developed, its communications improved. There is bound therefore to be a certain impatience with opposition groups, and with minorities. Small tribes that want to do things their own way, political groups that see things differently, are apt to be regarded as nuisances, and as barriers to the progress of the nation. It is significant that, of the twelve new states of West Africa, only Nigeria and Ghana have Opposition members in their Parliaments.

The British Government in writing Bills of Rights into the constitutions of the new states and entrenching them in constitutional safeguards, tries to reach out a hand into the future, and control to some degree the way in which the newly won liberties will be used. But it may be that the new rulers will not have the same tenderness for minorities as many Englishmen have; that they will be less willing to delay the whole progress of the nation for the sake of dissident groups. In such a case, the Bill of Rights can not defend the minorities for ever, but can only make arbitrary acts more difficult and more public. Whether the local authorities can play a part in this defence of liberty is doubtful. Mr. Griffiths' hopes may have been too high when he spoke of local councils acting as a safeguard against the exercise of excessive or even dictatorial powers. What looks to one man like the defence of local liberties often looks to another like disruptive particularism, and the governments of the new countries may not be prepared to allow the local authorities to play such a part. The central

[1] *Report of the Uganda Relationships Commission*, 1961.

governments are unlikely to appreciate the value of local democracy if it results in opposition and resistance to the government's policy.[1]

Experience shows that newly enfranchised countries do not, as a rule, take the same pride in local independence as more established countries do. There is too much to be done, and too little time, for Ministers to want to spend their time arguing with recalcitrant councillors, or trying to convince uncooperative authorities. Although in India much has been done to give new life to the panchayats, yet in Pakistan, for example, the Basic Democracies are in effect controlled by the civil service; in the Sudan the system of elections in local government has been abandoned, and real power has passed to the Provincial Authority, composed of the Military Governor and other Government officials.[2] In Ghana the structure of democracy remains, but the political control appears to be such that constitutional control is not needed. The all-powerful C.P.P. seems to have reached down into the District Councils and made them into local branches of its organisation. Inevitably one wonders what will happen in the other newly independent countries and in those which will reach independence in the next few months or years. Will they too find that the need for national unity and the need for co-ordinated effort in the public service leaves little room for local self-government, for local variations and independence? Or will they find that local self-government is a necessary corollary to a united national government at the centre?

A secondary question that will arise if elected local councils are to survive is the form that they will take. The arguments for following the English pattern in the first instance were very strong. But now they are losing some of their force. There has been time to consider alterations and modifications, and to learn some lesson from experience. It is apparent, for example, that community development and local government should not have been allowed to grow up as two separate and sometimes unsympathetic systems. The Committee System, with its subtle problems of the relation of officer and councillor, is not easy to import. The

---

[1] See G. Langrod, ' Local Government and Democracy ', *Public Administration*, Spring 1953, pp. 25–34, and K. Panter-Brick, 'A Rejoinder ', *Public Administration*, Winter 1953, pp. 344–348.

[2] *Report of the Commission on Co-ordination between the Central and Local Government*, 1960.

English conception of a mayor or chairman bereft of all power is difficult for many people to understand. The lack of clearly defined fields of responsibility is confusing. The relation of local councils to traditional authorities needs further study. In all these and other ways the pattern may need to be altered. According to the role that local government is to play in the community, it may be necessary to strengthen the executive part of the machine, or to give more emphasis to the deliberative function of the council; to look perhaps at other local government systems, in America, Asia or Europe, and see what lessons can be learnt from them.

MARY HOLDSWORTH

THE APPLICATION OF SOVIET NATIONALITY THEORY TO AFRICA IN SOVIET WRITING

The emergence of new states in Asia and Africa whose political institutions, at any rate initially, follow western models have revived old echoes as well as bringing some new problems before soviet ideologists and political leaders. Africa and Asia provide no exception to the well-worn theme that in soviet policies ideology and pragmatism cannot be divorced. Relations with these new states, which have acquired a decisive potential in world affairs, pose a practical problem. To meet it, soviet leaders devise policies towards African leaders, decide on economic relations with one state rather than another, sell arms or encourage subversive activities. All such decisions are strongly influenced if not determined, by pragmatic considerations. But a discussion of ideas, including politico-social ideologies and the interpretation of historical processes, forms the infrastructure to such decisions and in its turn is influenced by them. This ideological discussion is peculiarly important because to-day's African leaders are themselves concerned with ideologies. Several among them manipulate with ease those Marxist conceptions and terms with which soviet discussion are concerned. Because without exception the African leaders look at such conceptions through the prism of their own needs and aspirations they provoke the soviet writers, who have somewhat brashly entered this field, to re-examine their own doctrinal positions. This essay surveys the restatement of soviet nationality theory and the recent additions to it in the new context of Africa by those soviet scholars and journalists who specialise in African affairs. It will discuss where relevant the controversies and political decisions which have gone to make the soviet multi-national state, since it is from this corpus of ideas and conditioned by this experience that soviet writers look outwards to Africa. It concludes with some general observations on the Soviet-African encounter.

Soviet Africanists, when speaking as a group, see their task as the analysis in Marxist-Leninist terms both of nation-building

and of the break up of imperialism, and the application of historical
materialism to the history of the African continent. What equipment do they bring to qualify them for such studies? Obviously
they are far behind their western fellow-experts in intimate local
knowledge, or in detailed study over a long period of time. Their
training and intellectual tradition has been linguistic and ethnographic, rather than in political science or in law. Close attention
to language and to descriptions of material culture, which were
general practice in 19th century ethnography and anthropology,
has characterised Russian studies of peoples well into the contemporary period, although this approach has been largely superseded
in Europe and America by studies of social cohesion and organisation. The old approach, however, has a certain utility in this
specific instance. Russian readers could find out little about
Africa from Russian books. Nineteenth century contacts and
travels in Africa, apart from Ethiopia, were minimal. (A journey
in 1847–48 to Egypt, Sudan and Abyssinia by Evgraf Kovalevsky
was an exception).[1] So when in the mid-20th century a knowledge
of African affairs became necessary, even if only as a sequel to
the status of the U.S.S.R. in the United Nations, a descriptive
presentation of the African continent met this new need in a
familiar way. Incidentally, this type of approach also lends itself
readily to popularisation, and Benin bronzes, Ife terracottas and
Baluba carvings became familiar to Russian readers in schools and
evening classes through cheap paper backs only a very few years
after any similar awareness extended beyond specialist groups in
Britain.[2] Another characteristic of their approach is that soviet
Africanists do not concern themselves with the history of particular
European powers in Africa. They thus step directly into the
modern trend in African scholarship by including the whole of
the continent in their terms of reference particularly for the
pre-colonial period, and by regarding the peoples of Africa rather
than imperial administration as their object of study. Finally,

[1] *Kovalevsky, Ev. P.*, 1811–68. Educated as a mining engineer. Served in
Perovsky's Khiva expedition of 1839. Travels in Egypt, Nubia, Sudan, Abys-
sinia as gold prospector, 1847–8. Served on Pekin mission and negotiated
Kuldzha agreement on Russian trade with China, 1849. Head of Asian depart-
ment in foreign ministry, 1896–61. Historian of siege of Sebastopol. Fellow of
Royal Geographical Society. *Puteshestviye v Afriku*, vol. 1 and 2, St. P., 1849
(Journey into Africa).

[2] Ol'derogge, D. A., *Isskustvo Narodov Afriki v museyakh S.S.S.R.*, M.,
1958, (The art of the peoples of Africa in museums in the U.S.S.R.) Orlova,
A. S., *Afrikanskiye Narody*, M., 1958. Illustrated article on African art in
Ogonek, 1961, May 27.

soviet historians and sociologists bring Marxist tools to the study of African societies. In recent years this has included both a rigid application of Marx's historical materialism and of Engel's universally applicable pattern of social evolution as well as more flexible studies of society with socio-economic criteria primarily in mind. Soviet scholars themselves regard Marxism as their most decisive methodological contribution to African studies.[1]

At the linguistic and ethnographic level soviet scholars have carried over into the African context the conception of ' a people ' (*narodnost*'), and have built up most of their sociological and polemical writing round it. The concept is still widely used within the Soviet Union itself, both in discussing the welding together of the soviet community of peoples and in such practical matters as census returns. A people emerges from tribes which have affinities of language and of material culture; the latter is subject to change through the penetration of modern standards, but language is developed by literacy and the growth of a cultured élite. This stage represents a half-way house between isolated, self-enclosed tribes and a modern nation. In political and socio-logical organisation it can span the transition from the break-up of the extended family to the emergence of political authority and of a market economy. It is thus a concept which has a place in the modern world, and ' people ' and ' people's ' has an acceptable contemporary connotation, which ' tribe ' and ' tribal ' has not. Both the concept and the word itself have had a strong emotive force in Slav history, literature and polemical writing.

To those concerned with the Russian, the Austro-Hungarian and the Turkish empires definitions of ' people ' and ' nation ' were pressing and challenging problems. But as the early social democrat groups in Russia and the reformist and radical groups before them found, the concept of ' people ' is extremely difficult either to define or to fit into a political or economic doctrine. This applies both to *narodnost*' with its linguistic and ethnic definition, and more particularly to *narod*, with its imprecise, subjective and strongly emotional flavour. Herzen argued that the Slavophils used the words as a screen to avoid hard thought on fundamental problems of political rights.[2] To all reform groups

[1] Potekhin, I. I., *Etudes africaines en Union Soviétique* in *Des Africanistes russes parlent de l'Afrique*, Pres. Afr., Paris, 1960.
[2] Venturi, F., *The Roots of Revolution*, London, 1960, for discussion of *narodnost*' and of Russian radical thought of the 19th century.

the ' people ' meant both the oppressed and illiterate Russian
people itself and any minority peoples who were subjected to
similar indignities by an oppressive government, Russian or other.
The dilemma with which Herzen (and the Decembrists before and
Populists after him) grappled was that in the Russian empire the
oppression of the latter was carried on in the name of the former.
In both radical and liberal groups, at any rate in Russia itself,
political and social reform, therefore, became more often than not
the priority issue, with the explanation that the rights and aspirations of national minorities could best be satisfied by the working
of a juster and more politically educated society. The controversies on national questions in the bolshevik party, and later in
the Comintern, were by no means new, and Lenin when he
developed his nationality theory was perfectly aware both of the
emotional strength and of the contradictions in the concepts
involved. Lenin, as a Marxist, was much more decisive in his
views than the earlier Russian radicals [for example the *Narodnoye
Delo* (People's Cause)] that revolution must take absolute prece-
dence over the national question. But he understood the strength
of national feelings and particularly their almost limitless potential
as a revolutionary force in existing Russian conditions. Hence the
duality which lies at the very heart of his nationality doctrine: the
right to ethnic self-determination up to and including secession,
but the overriding right of the bearers of revolution to decide
whether and when such self-determination furthers, or on the
contrary hinders, the revolution's course. Stalin defined more
narrowly who decides on self-determination and ruled that it was
the lower or working strata of a people with whom this decision
rested. He held that ethnic and linguistic features were the outward forms in which autonomy manifested itself. Its content
must be the class revolution. Finally, he launched the slogan
' socialist in content, national in form ', at the XVIth Party
Congress in 1931 in ideological controversy with the Ukrainians.[1]

Just as the early bolsheviks had to move on from polemics on
nationality to the series of political and administrative decisions

---

[1] XVIth Congress of All-Union C. P. (b), Moscow, 1931. Stalin's definition
of a nation as ' . . . a historically evolved stable community of people, based on
community of language, territory, economic life and psychological make-up
manifested in a community of culture ' is still adhered to by soviet political
writers. Stalin, J., *Marxism and the National Colonial Question*, London, 1936,
p. 8.

through which they built up the soviet multi-national state, so soviet Africanists have at a given point to move on from ethnic analysis and discuss political criteria. Although most of them, like Dr. I. Potekhin, repeat constantly that the forms and structures which African states will eventually adopt are matters for their people's own decision, they nevertheless use their own standards by which to assess such choices. Whatever might have been the application of the bolshevik nationalities policy had Lenin lived (and there is little in the events of 1918–1922 to suggest any possibility of national revolutions being allowed to go their own way), the multi-national U.S.S.R. is a Stalinist creation, welded together by Stalinist methods. This fact was fully appreciated by the older generation of African nationalists who saw it at close quarters (notably George Padmore).[1] What was (and is) probably less appreciated is that political and cultural ferment among the national minorities in the U.S.S.R. persisted until it was crushed by force in the middle of the nineteen thirties. Leaders of such movements were not satisfied with mere ethnic and linguistic trappings but wanted the substance of political and cultural decision. Two of the most interesting of these movements have considerable relevance to the contemporary African problems in which Soviet writers are immersed.

The first of these, associated with the name of Sultan Galiev, was an intellectual movement which sought to devise an ideology for Muslim socialism. Sultan Galiev was concerned with three main problems: first, how to adapt Marxism to the Muslim world, since Muslim society had not yet developed antagonistic classes; secondly, what was Islam's special role in a socialist world; and thirdly, how to assess the rôle of the colonial countries in the strategy of world revolution. He and his followers held that it was unrealistic in Muslim colonial societies to struggle simultaneously both for a national *and* for a proletarian or social revolution and that, in the existing circumstances, the latter effort only endangered the former. He therefore gave absolute priority to the national revolution. He considered it sheer nonsense to pretend that the Muslims in Turkestan had developed a proletariat. Neither the indigenous working class nor the indigenous peasantry could possibly, he contended, provide a ready-made élite for the national revolution; at such an early stage a social revolution as well would

---

[1] Padmore, G., *Pan-Africanism or Communism?* London, 1956.

only inundate the country with Russian leaders. It was more sensible to entrust the national revolution to the only national élite capable of carrying it through, i.e. to the national intellectuals, the progressive clergy and the rising bourgeoisie. This whole corpus of ideas was contested by Stalin, Rykov and the other rigid ideologists, and at the 1923 *Congress with the Responsible Workers of the East*, Sultan Galiev was expelled from the party. Accused of complicity with the recurrent popular risings in Central Asia, he was executed in 1929.[1]

The controversies about the Ukrainian problem (of immense complexity in itself and further complicated by large Jewish and Russian minorities in the Ukraine) concerned efforts to find effective forms for the de-centralisation of power. Ukrainian social revolutionaries and bolsheviks struggled stubbornly until 1923 to establish a national bolshevik party, which would be affiliated with, but not form part of, the Moscow party. For the state organs, all the Ukrainian bolsheviks wanted a confederal or federal structure, with wide and entrenched powers for the constituent republics: in fact they wanted to preserve in the projected constitution of 1924, the treaty relationships of 1920. Both the Ukrainian bolshevik, Skrypnyk, and the Pole, Rakovsky, challenged every step in the organisation and definition of executive functions and budgetary arrangements in order to preserve some effective rights for the republics. All such decentralising views were contested by Stalin. The discussions of 1922 and 1923 between the federalists and the centralists about minority ' safeguards ' and similar devices within the all-Union constitution are akin to those over the ' constitutions by arithmetic ' for the multiracial territories of British Africa, about which the soviet commentators are so scornful to-day. The final upshot of the minorities controversies, on which the 1936 Stalin constitution set its seal, established the clear primacy of the socialist revolution, the principle of working class hegemony, and stripped ethnic and linguistic groups of any rights of political decision.

The first exceedingly superficial articles by soviet Africanists reflected the rigid Stalinist doctrine that nothing but a proletarian revolution could set the emergent African nations on their way. It was not until the year of change, between Bandung in April,

---

[1] Bennigsen, A., *Islam et Nationalisme en Union Soviétique, Centre de Recherche du Bien Politique*, Paris, 1961.

1955, and the Twentieth Congress in Jan.-Feb., 1956, which began the public break-up of Stalinism, that these rigid attitudes were shaken, and soviet writing on emergent countries became more relevant to the new world with which it was dealing. Three doctrinal adjustments were then made. First, the validity of a ' national ' revolution was acknowledged, that is to say of a revolution which is largely the work of a national bourgeoisie and a national educated class. Secondly, it was admitted that the achievement of political independence and status is in itself an all-important milestone in a country's progress on the road to the socialist revolution and it came gradually to be suggested that a fairly long pause before the next step might legitimately be made there. Thirdly, it became legitimate to think that armed conflict might not be essential to a national liberation movement. Within these, to western eyes not very startling, ideological concessions (though it should not be forgotten that these very ideas were forbidden to the Georgians, Ukrainians, Uzbeks and others in their time), soviet Africanists vary between those who are obviously happiest as near as possible to the old familiar ideas, and others who give considerable space to the serious study of African nationalist parties and political slogans, and who admit the possibility of an African interpretation of socialism. Dr. Potekhin, who is the most powerful and influential of soviet African specialists, stays nearest to the old traditions in his attitudes and conclusions, but even he became a good deal more objective in his appreciation of African intellectual élites after his first long stay in Legon, and his *Ghana Diary* (October–December, 1957) contained what is virtually the only acknowledgement by a soviet author of the missionary contribution to education in Africa.[1] In a recent booklet called *Africa looks into the future*, which was quickly sold out and widely quoted, Dr. Potekhin examined Pan-Africanism, the idea of an African personality or *Négritude*, and looked briefly at concepts of African socialism (including President Senghor's *Congrès Constitutif du P.F.A.*, M. Mamadou Dia's *Nations Africaines et Solidarité Mondiale*, President Nkrumah's programme of social reconstruction, and President Nasser's Arab

---

[1] Potekhin, I. I., *Afrika smotrit v budushcheye*, M., 1960, *Gana Segodniya, Dnevnik, 1957*, M., 1959 (Ghana to-day: a diary), *Nekotorye problemy Afrikanistiki v svete reshenyi XXII s'ezda C.P.S.S.* in *Narody Azii i Afriki*, 1962, 1 (Some problems of African studies in the light of the decisions of the XXII Congress of the C.P.S.U.). All these are available in English translation.

socialism). In a chapter on Patterns of Marxism in Africa he described fairly dispassionately, using like many western commentators the word ' eclectic ', alternative patterns of socialism which are in vogue among African leaders, but stated unequivocally that, compared with scientific socialism as exhibited in the U.S.S.R., the half-socialisms he had examined appeared amateurish. He argued that insofar as ideologies of African socialism deny the existence of class in African society, they rest on a false analysis and they cannot therefore have a firm theoretical structure. Although in his view it was conceivable that systems of land tenure in certain parts of Africa could be changed into genuine socialism, this could only happen if a Marxist party of the proletariat formed the government. He conceded, nonetheless, that in states it is possible for the all-purpose anti-imperial national government to grow into a government dedicated to re-building society on theoretically correct socialist lines. Dr. Potekhin does not discuss the Christian basis of M. Senghor's socialism, nor the Muslim basis of President Nasser's, nor the fundamental points on which M. Sekou Touré's ideology differs from atheist Marxism/Leninism. If he has modified his scorn for the doctrines of non-violence adopted by the original African National Congress and by modern Pan Africanism, he himself has nevertheless invariably inclined towards the more violent alternative when commenting on discussions at the successive conferences of African states at which such a choice has arisen. His unrelenting anti-imperialism makes him assess all political leadership in Africa solely by the criterion of the attitudes it adopts towards the former metropolitan country. In articles during the first half of 1962 Dr. Potekhin reiterates the need to study meticulously the ideologies of contemporary Africa and to analyse the social structures from which they stem. He says that for this purpose researchers and propagandists well grounded in Marxism are essential and that these are now forthcoming in increasing numbers among local Marxist groups.

A specialist on Nigeria, Dr. L. Pribythovskiy, devotes about half his short study of Nigeria's road to independence[1] to the formation and programmes of the N.C.N.C., Action Group, and

---

[1] Pribytkovskiy, L. N., *Nigeria v bor'be za nezavisimost'*, M., 1961. (Nigeria's struggle for independence).

the Northern People's Congress, and to discussions of the successive constitutions. He handles fairly objectively the fundamentals of political institutions: where does power lie? what type of society did indirect rule tend to perpetuate? He makes no secret of his distrust of regionalism, and of his own preference for a centralist party. The first part of his book is a socio-economic analysis of postwar Nigeria and here he places immense emphasis on the contribution of the ' working class ' to the independence movement. His contribution to soviet African studies on the occasion of Nigeria's independence was a study of the labour disputes at Enugu in 1948 which ended in tragic loss of life. He used this as a text to show that even in an African country an organised working class plays its heroic part in the vanguard of the national liberation movement.

Most discussions in the west and in Africa of the relevance of soviet experience to the new states emphasise the rôle of the single party in creating a unitary community out of a multinational empire. This emphasis was prominent, for instance, in President Nkrumah's speeches on the occasion of his visit to the Soviet Union in July and August, 1961. Before leaving the political content of soviet ideologies in regard to the new states, it is important to examine this point. Soviet ideology, it must be remembered, does not prescribe single party government simply as a means of ensuring political stability or for any similar reason. It prescribes specifically the Communist Party, and not any other, for example a nationalist or a religious one. The Communist party alone is the depositor and generator of all political wisdom and the essential ingredient in and overseer of every facet of human life. Dr. Potekhin represents this clear cut attitude: Marxist groups are not a militant Communist party, and nationalist parties as they stand at present in Africa cannot achieve a communist revolution, though they may be effective in creating and holding together a multi-national state.

Sociological analyses of African societies from Marxist standpoints by soviet writers have so far been somewhat piecemeal. They reflect the interests and predilections of individual scholars to an extent not very usual in the general run of soviet social studies. Monographs represent both the rigid and the more liberal attitudes and several recent papers show a greater concern with following up clues suggested by the material than with

P

pushing the material into the preordained categories.[1] Rigid
Marxist interpretation prevails among several of the prominent
figures, notably Professor E. Zhukov, Secretary of the Academy
of Science Institute of History (who, however, wrote one of the
more open articles on the possibilities of different interpretations
of socialism in the new countries), and no-one strays far from it.
Nor do any of the soviet Africanists question in print the universally
applicable pattern of social evolution, though some make it rather
elastic. This is one reason why most soviet writers describe all
precolonial African societies as feudal, and why every type of
social stratification, however diverse in origin, is seen in terms of
economic classes based on production. Marx's pattern of history
was evolved in terms of Western Europe, where an economic and
social order based on land was replaced by an economic and social
order based on capital. This social order is scheduled in turn to
break up and be replaced by a society where society itself owns the
means of production, i.e. by socialism. In nearly all modern
Russian writing the term ' feudalism ' is not limited to western
European classical feudalism, and the conception is not confined
to rights and obligations attached to a fixed parcel of land. The
term covers all rights and obligations which involve the transfer
of goods or the performance of services which are determined by
customary law and not by a cash purchase-and-sale or work-and-
wage agreement. This makes it possible to group under a general
heading of ' servile institutions ' all socio-economic transactions
in which the key words are ' right ', ' obligation ', ' usage ', and
not ' purchase ' and ' sale ' whether of land, goods or services.
The historians and sociologists (with two notable exceptions) who
seek to interpret to African students the history and internal
development of their own societies use this analysis to prove that
the economic rather than the charismatic basis is central to the
institution of chieftainship. They regard chieftainship as pertaining to the feudal period, and point out that it must disappear as
an outworn form unless it is artificially preserved when, in transition to capitalist society, it outlives its economic usefulness.
Finally, writers in the party or the mass circulation journals
propound the universal historical pattern at its simplest and say

[1] Orlova, A. S., *O meste i roli traditsionnykh vlastey Afrikanskogo obshchestva
v proshlom i nastoyashchem*, in Sov. Etnogr., 1960, 6 (The place and function of
traditional authorities in African society in the past and to-day). Further papers
on the same subject in Sov. Etnogr., 1961, 6 and 1962, 1.

that African societies, like everyone else's, go through the feudal period, throw up antagonistic classes, and will move on to communism by the inexorable laws of history.

These then are the ways in which soviet writers apply to Africa soviet ideologies and soviet experience relevant to the building of nations and to internal sociological change. But one still has to look at their doctrines concerning the processes by which peoples disentangle themselves from outside control and emerge as states, that is to say concerning the break-up of imperialism. Here it is clear that current soviet writing has moved very little, if at all, from the basic attitudes of Lenin and Hobson. Neither Dr. Potekhin, nor Dr. Pribytkovskiy, nor a legal and constitutional writer, Dr. Yudin, is willing to move away from the stereotype of a crafty and grasping imperialist power fighting a stubborn rearguard action over every phase of the national-liberation movement. Soviet writers never entertain the idea of the transfer of power and hold that imperialism is disappearing in the death throes of capitalism, precipitated by the rivalries of imperial powers which caused the 1914 war. The October revolution is regarded as the decisive turning point, and the growing power of the Warsaw Pact countries as the guarantee to-day for the emergence of free nations from the shadow of imperial exploitation. In the manifest changes in the map of the world between 1915 and 1962 the part played by ' the party of Lenin ' is given far greater prominence than the whole evolution of the British empire into the Commonwealth. In the recent years of Africa's accelerated move into independence soviet journals dealing with international affairs have launched the doctrine of economic colonialism. This teaches that political independence without economic independence is in the long run illusory and that the latter in erstwhile colonial and weakly developed countries can only be obtained through a strong state sector in the economy and in the swift or gradual elimination of foreign companies and financial interests. Some of the younger economists dealing with emergent countries have opened up considerably since about 1958 and are ready to discuss the advantages and disadvantages of mixed economies rather than of wholly state-managed ones, but soviet advice to new countries on economic policies is nearly always to sever at any rate financial links with the old metropolitan country, to curtail the activities of foreign-controlled concerns, and try out new trading patterns. In urging these courses an anti-imperialist, i.e. political, argument is used, and it is the political writers who have remained fanatic in their attitudes to imperial action. The lie that Mau Mau was an invention of the British administration to excuse armed suppression of the nationalist movement has never yet been contradicted by soviet writers.[1] To it Dr. Pribytkovskiy in his book referred to above adds the further lie that the Enugu shooting was deliberately provoked by the British. In every situation where the British government has been or is engaged in complex negotiations for the transfer of power soviet commentators question Britain's good faith and suggest motives of greed or tactics of divide and rule. Dr. Yablochkov took this line on the federal issue in his study of British Central Africa in 1958. Britain's part at the Kenya constitutional conference in March, 1962, was described in such terms, not only in the daily press but in journals published under the auspices of the Academy of Sciences. The freezing of ideas on the imperial issue at around 1915 explains in large measure the uncomprehending and baffled bewilderment of soviet researchers and politicians concerning relations between the new African states and the former metropolitan powers.

Soviet Africanists have not extended to British or French imperialism the revised approach which soviet historians have adopted to Russian 19th century imperialism. Instead of regarding all imperialism as an evil, Russian imperialism is considered as a partial good, and even an absolute good in so far as it put the peoples of the backward societies into contact with the progressive thought of left wing and social democrat (Marxist) groups in Russia. Even when considered in terms of culture contact rather than in those of government action (at which level czarist imperialism too is criticised by its historians, though not as vehemently as it was in the twenties), western imperialism is wholly rejected as an affront to personality and is not considered as being in any sense an enriching experience. In the majority of cases soviet writers almost wholly ignore the evidence of technical progress, such as contour farming, locust control, or the gradual elimination of some endemic diseases, though all such factors are taken into account when drawing up the balance sheet of Russian expansion

---

[1] Ismagilova, R., *Narody Kenii v usloviyakh kolonial'nogo rezhima*, in *Afrikanskiy Etnograficheskiy Sbornik*, I., M., 1956. (The peoples of Kenya under colonial rule).

into Asia. But what answer do soviet writers give to the pertinent question on soviet imperialism or, in other words, what do they mean when they assert that ' the solution of the national question is the greatest triumph of socialism '? Have they given thought to the fact that the one area where the world political map has hardly changed at all (with the exception of Finland) is the home of the October revolution itself? Their answer is contained in the premise that exploitation of man by man and hence of nation by nation is the product of a class society and that once a classless society is established, national enmity and imperialist aggression will disappear.[1] By definition ' socialism ' and ' imperialism ' are incompatible. Once the former is established, the ' voluntary coming together of nations ' of which Lenin spoke, will become a reality. Soviet Africanists claim to speak as experts, who come from a society which has achieved this transformation in the relationship between the imperial centre and its former dependencies. From this pedestal they misconceive and consequently misrepresent the really fundamental transformations of the other imperialisms. The self-enclosed, theoretical argument becomes to them the reality, while the presence of Nigeria and the absence of Uzbekistan or Georgia in the councils of the nations becomes the illusion.

This paper began by suggesting that the emergence of the new Asian and African states had both confronted soviet political ideology with new problems and had resurrected some which had seemingly been disposed of in the breakneck and ruthless speed of building communism. It is not easy to disentangle the influences that contemporary soviet political thinkers are likely to exert on leaders in the new states from those which they themselves are experiencing from the contact, and this provides a good reason for speculating on the soviet African encounter. Looking at it from the soviet side first, it seems now that contact with the new states and the soviet desire and need to stand well

[1] Cf. *Comintern* discussions between 1919 and 1924 on the relation of national revolution to world communist revolution. Resolution at Fourth Congress, Nov., 1922, reads: ' Taking full cognizance of the fact that those who represent the national will to state independence may, because of the variety of historical circumstances, be themselves of the most varied kind, the Communist International supports every national revolutionary movement against imperialism. At the same time it does not forget that only a consistent revolutionary policy, designed to draw the broadest masses into active struggle, and a complete break with all adherents of reconciliation with imperialism for the sake of their own class domination, can lead the oppressed masses to victory.'

with them has made soviet leaders realise that national self-assertion at a particular point in history is a force that cannot easily be relegated to second place. It also seems likely that sooner or later they will have to come to terms in some manner with a variety of roads to socialism. In other words, the straghtforward Lenin-Stalinist position has gone, possibly for ever. In the U.S.S.R., the de-Stalinisation campaign includes the cautious posthumous rehabilitation of some of the condemned bourgeois-nationalist leaders, including the Ukrainian Skrypnyk (though not, so far, Sultan Galiev). Ideological differences with China consist to some extent of disagreement on the correct attitude to the new states. Both these facts suggest a certain re-assessment concerning this range of problems, a re-assessment which has not yet been fully thought out. Experience at home has severe drawbacks because the tiresome political problems inherent in multi-national states or in confederal structures were swept aside in the name of the overriding needs of socialism in one country. In many cases restitution for past crimes has not yet been made. When in Pasternak's phrase, ' the roof was torn off the whole of Russia ',[1] (by the October revolution) all sorts of nationalist, separatist, egalitarian and anarchist desires were revealed under that roof, and permeating these, the confident hope among non-Russians that the provisional government and later the bolsheviks would be the first ' decolonisers '. But from the suppression of the Kokand national government in 1918 to Stalin's 1936 constitution, one autonomous and de-centralist position was lost after another, with an ever mounting loss of lives. The central government did not have to bother with interim franchises and practice legislatures because communalism in the Soviet Union was overcome quite bluntly by a combination of the Red Army with the centrally-directed and closely knit communist party, which not only gave sole political direction (as eventually written into the constitution in 1936), but also provided the key administrators. Throughout the decades when Britain and her Asian dependencies were experimenting with ways of handing over power while preserving the basic freedoms of the groups within the prospective states, Stalin's government did not have to experiment with anything except methods of tightening or shifting administrative pressures,

---

[1] Pasternak, B., *Doctor Zhivago*, Milan, 1957, pt. V, 7.

and on the contrary kept constant watch that no centres of power gathered in either national or professional groups.

It was not until Stalin's death and more specifically until the Twentieth Congress that some de-centralisation and the restoration of certain national minorities to their original territories took place, and even then this was done by the back door of administrative decree. But doctrinally there is more to consider. Lenin had always seen (what Stalin, though himself a Georgian, had not) how very carefully national aspirations and foibles had to be handled if they were to support rather than postpone and hinder the revolution. The secession clause, which had appeared in every soviet constitution, was due to his personal insistence. In the de-Stalinisation process it was therefore possible to advance cautiously on the nationalities' question under Lenin's name, to give the constituent republics of the Union rather more elbow room and to rehabilitate certain national leaders. Besides these limited steps at home, articles have begun to appear in professional journals discussing not only the constitutional arrangements and party political programmes of the new states, but also books by American and British writers on their political and social structure and the relevance of western models to their needs.[1] The fact that Almond and Coleman or Chester Bowles are criticised for trying to separate ' the anti-feudal democratic revolution from the imperial one ' is less important than the fact that these writers are discussed at all. Dr. Yudin may accuse the British government of foisting bogus constitutions onto Central Africa or Kenya, but it is nevertheless significant that discussion of the merits of federal as compared with unitary states or whether or not written constitutions are meaningless have re-appeared in print in Russian after an interval of nearly thirty years. In its programme published in the summer of 1961, the Communist party launched its own category of ' national democracies ' into the spectrum of state typologies. The relevant paragraph reads:

' Establishing and developing national democracies opens vast prospects for the peoples of underdeveloped countries. The political basis of a national democracy is a bloc of all the progressive

[1] Almond, G. A., and Coleman, J. S., *The Politics of the Developing Areas*, Princeton, 1960, Plamentatz, J., *On Alien Rule and Self-Government*, L., 1960, Lipset, S. M., *Political Man*, L., 1960, Bowles, Chester, *Africa's Challenge to America*, Berkeley, 1956, Park, R. L., and Tinker, H., *Leadership and Political Institutions in India*, Princeton, 1959.

patriotic forces fighting to win complete national independence and broad democracy and to consummate the anti-imperialist, anti-feudal democracy revolution '.[1]

An article in *Kommunist* defines national democracies as states which are politically and economically independent, which oppose imperialism and its blocs and refuse to have military bases on their territory, which oppose new forms of colonialism and of capitalist penetration, as well as all forms of dictatorship.[2] To an outside eye the main characteristics of the new category seem to be those pertaining to alignment or non-alignment with western power alliances and only incidentally those pertaining to internal political and social structure, but there is at least a possibility of development as a ' different road to socialism '.

The party programme has also something to say concerning nationalities within the Soviet Union itself. The programme intimates that the time has come for the gradual confluence of national forms into the new all-embracing form of communism —that mature soviet culture expressing the new soviet man. The Armenian commentator on this in *Kommunist* warns readers that one must expect national characteristics and prejudices to be the last and most tenacious survivals of capitalism, and that one must meet with patience their continued manifestations in the new era. Since these will not be class antagonisms, they need not be overcome by force. He adds that it is a matter of individual opinion where and for how long these characteristics and frictions will survive. This comment is important because it is one of the few attempts in soviet writings on nationality probems to relate what happens inside the U.S.S.R. to what goes on in the world outside. It tries to mitigate in advance the impact of Asian and African experience on opinion in the Soviet Union now that it is opening its doors to ever wider contacts with this new world and particularly with its students.[3]

If one now looks at what African leaders and intellectuals might expect to find of interest in the U.S.S.R. itself and in the

[1] *C.P. Programme*, 1961, English translation in *The New York Times International edition*, 1961, Aug. 2.

[2] Ponomarev, B., *O gosudarstve natsional'noy demokratii*, in *Kommunist*, 1961, 8. (On national democracies as state forms).

[3] Azizyan, A., *Stroitel'stvo kommunisma i razvitiye natsional'nykh otnosheniy* in *Kommunist*, 1961, 15 (The building of communism and developments in national relationships). Gardanov, V. K., et al. *Osnovnye napravleniya etnicheskikh protsessov u narodov S.S.S.R.*, in Sov. Etnogr., 1961, 4 (Basic tendencies in the ethnographic processes of the U.S.S.R.).

considerable soviet literature devoted to the new states, one might make up a longish list but always of matters on the periphery of nation-building, never of its essence. One might start with economic planning to build up industrial potential, and the creation of a regional organisation which, through many vicissitudes and false trials, is nevertheless working towards economic coherence and cooperation. To this one could legitimately add basic education on a large scale as a very early priority, energetic literacy campaigns and the provision of cheap printed matter for the newly literate to read. The Soviet Union has also been energetic in building up a numerous and competent technical intelligentsia in the non-Russian minorities, which can stand comparison with first generation technical elites elsewhere. In language, a clear policy of primary education in the mother tongue is an asset as is, too, an educational structure which ultimately produces a bilingual educated stratum among those whose mother tongue is not Russian. To this policy are added attention to folk cultures and opportunities for their display, as well as the material (though not spiritual) conditions for the encouragement of a modern literature. Active social engineering, which pays very little attention to seemingly immutable stratification, can be added with reservation to the list. The results of these governmental skills can usefully be looked at in the Soviet Union particularly in its national peripheries; moreover since many of these things have been built up largely in a life-time (not wholly, though few soviet sociologists or economists will admit this) from small beginnings, they do not carry that weight of wealth and long experience which may well be an inhibiting factor for leaders of new states contemplating the institutions and industries of the old, stable countries of the west.

But all these things are not the essentials. And it is in dealing with the essentials that one comes to the clear division in political thinking. The division is between governments who remain faithful to the sanctity of basic human freedoms in the process of carrying out what they and their citizen conceive as the legitimate ends of rule, and those governments which conceive their mission as the achievement of an all-justifying end in relation to which the basic freedoms are only contingent.[1] Since the political philosophy

---

[1] Cf. Carter, G. M., and Herz, J. H., *Government and Politics in the Twentieth Century*, L., 1961, ch. 1.

of communism belongs to the latter category, the soviet theory of nationalities and its practice belongs to this category too, and soviet discussions of state building in Africa have stemmed from it. It has not been part of Russia's political genius to produce institutions and laws which establish and safeguard basic personal freedoms, although her greatest writers have been preoccupied with them with agonised intensity. It *has* been the political genius of England and France to crystallize these freedoms both in a political philosophy and in legal systems and institutions of government. The rule of law and the mechanisms for changing governments by consent are positive acquisitions for the service of all humanity. They do not constitute the all-solving formula for human society, as the socialist thinkers of the 19th century and indeed Marx discovered, but they are too precious a part of it to lose or to overlay for too long when looking for the other elements. The peoples from the colonial empires of France and Britain who form the new independent states of to-day have had prolonged contact with these concepts. If the overtones of antagonism to the entire western heritage, which all but very few of the soviet writers on Africa introduce into their work, succeed in eradicatng these ideas from the political ideologies and institutions of the new states, it would be a tragedy of a different order altogether from that of an unaligned position in the mid-century power conflict between west and east.

These, then, are some of the features of the Soviet-African encounter, which comes at a crucial time, though in different respects, for both parties. The encounter, in a sense, is marginal to the main activities of each. African states can choose the collaborators who will best suit their purposes. Russians have yet to prove their value in the day-to-day-tests of practical usefulness. For soviet students and political commentators the discovery of Africa may well become an important experience, both because it follows a period utterly barren in intellectual enquiry and because the break up of imperialism is moving quickly into reality in forms very different from those that were prophesied. There are possibilities of political dialogue which may have wide repercussions, but a dialogue is not a monologue accompanied by echoes, nor are Africa's leaders likely to cast themselves in the latter role .

JOHN PLAMENATZ

SELF GOVERNMENT RECONSIDERED

Those who dislike colonialism and are eager to see it come to an end often mistake the intentions of whoever seems to them luke-warm on what to them is the burning issue. They denounce what they take to be marks of western arrogance or liberal timidity. They deny that freedom and democracy are European or western ideas, or they resent the assumption that the ' backward ' peoples of Asia and Africa are trying to catch up with or imitate the West. The very word *westernization* is suspect to them, and they wish to put another in its place. Or they deny that western institutions are needed to achieve freedom and democracy. Why, they ask, should it be assumed that because western democracies mostly have two or more political parties, an African country which has only one is not democratic? Or they insist that it is absurd to apply the criteria of the western liberal in estimating the political systems of newly independent and poverty-stricken countries. Why should it be taken for granted that what the West values is either possible or desirable in them?

I

Freedom and democracy are today everywhere well spoken of; and it is everywhere taken for granted (as it used not to be) that freedom and democracy go together. People never did say, *We care for democracy but not for freedom*, and now they scarcely ever say, *We care for freedom but not democracy*. In Russia and China, as much as in the West, to call a country *democratic* is to praise it, and to say that its citizens are *free* is to imply that they have something worth having. Therefore the claim that freedom and democracy are *European* or *western* ideas is apt to be resented by non-Europeans. Why should the Europeans of the Old World and the New assume that what all peoples now find desirable is somehow peculiarly their own, their gift to the world, their grace imparted to lesser nations thus redeemed from barbarism?

Yet those who make this claim are often misunderstood. Perhaps it is their fault that they are so; perhaps they do not explain their meaning sufficiently, or do not qualify the claim as they should; or, if they do qualify it, do not do so insistently enough. Men listen more carelessly than they speak, read more carelessly than they write. The writer who repeatedly assumes that freedom and democracy are European ideas and warns his readers in only one or two places that he has in mind particular notions of freedom and democracy is likely to be misunderstood.

Freedom is a word of several meanings of which only some are European; and these meanings are European only because the situations in which it became possible and important to make certain claims for the individual first arose in Europe, and arose elsewhere after the Europeans had begun to intrude upon other continents. It may be that, even if there had been no European intrusions, other peoples would have come eventually to make these claims. Certainly, there is no reason to believe that they come 'more naturally' to peoples of European stock than to the others; any more than that English comes 'more naturally' to Americans of British descent than to others. Yet no one refuses to call the language of Shakespeare and Milton *English* merely because the ancestors of most persons whose language it now is once learned it as an alien tongue. So it is with freedom in some important senses of that word; it is something (or a family of things) which has come to Asia and Africa from Europe. It is an idea having many implications, and is difficult to realize in conditions very unlike those in which it was born. It takes time to assimilate it and to learn how to realize it; indeed, the assimilation and the learning are parts of the same process.

To say this about it is not to set it apart from other moral ideas, as being higher or more sophisticated or more refined than they are. The assimilation and realization of Asian and African ideas in Europe would be just as difficult. The trouble with European intrusion in Asia and Africa is that it has set off changes, social, cultural and political, on a scale and at a speed unknown before.

In societies where there is a considerable apparatus of government, where a distinct public or political authority has arisen over and above the domestic or tribal, where there is a state, there is usually a sphere in which the state is held not to have the right to intrude. There is a private sphere. But, until quite recent times in Europe, this sphere has been less a personal than a family or communal sphere. It was held that the authority of the supreme ruler was limited; and if he exceeded it, he was condemned as a tyrant. The defence of the autonomy of the family or other small ' face-to-face community ' (to use Mr. Laslett's expressive phrase) was often put forward as a defence of freedom. About freedom thus understood there is nothing specifically western.

And this idea of freedom is connected with the western idea. The family or other community with an autonomy to protect against the state had someone to speak for it in its dealings with the remote public power or its local agents; and this spokesman —elder, chief, lord or merely father—came to be looked upon as the bearer of definite rights which the public power ought to respect. This conception of a bearer of definite rights, applied to begin with to those having a circle of dependents, came later to be applied to all adult males or to all adults. And as the conception was applied more widely, the rights changed in character. They came to be looked upon as rights of the mere individual against the public power. Therefore, since it was in the West that the family and other close communities first lost ground or changed character in ways which brought the individual much more directly into contact with the public power, and which also made that power much greater, it is only to be expected that it should be in the West that the rights of the mere individual, the rights of man, should be first asserted. The fast growing public power was felt to be dangerous and yet also potentially beneficent, a creator of opportunities for those subject to it. The doctrine of the rights of man expresses the European's fear of the state and also his hopes of it.

Again, in societies where morality has ceased to be entirely conventional, where philosophy and dogmatic religion flourish, where men construct cosmologies whose function is to give them a sense of place and direction or, as the saying is, ' to give purpose to their lives,' there arises an idea of freedom which is no more European than Indian, Islamic or Chinese.

Where morality has ceased to be entirely conventional, where there is some conception of a good life which consists of more than just following custom and doing what is required by authority or by one's neighbours, where there is an ideal to be lived up to, there is the idea of a chosen way of life. There is the idea of commitment and self-discipline. There are held to be standards higher than those which all men are required to conform to; and whoever adopts them chooses to live as most men do not live. Where such choices are widely approved, or at least tolerated, there exists a kind of freedom which to those who make use of it is precious. The chosen life may require withdrawal from ' the world ', from forms of intercourse allowed to other men; and the withdrawal may be either into solitude or into a community whose rules differ greatly from those of society at large. Or it may require no such conspicuous seclusion but merely the observance of a moral discipline over and above the discipline imposed by society on its members generally. The idea that it is right for men to make such choices has long been widely accepted in Europe, and not less widely outside Europe by peoples as yet untouched by European influences.

The Stoics aspired to a higher than conventional morality without seeking to withdraw from ' the world '. They also asserted the equality of all men without challenging existing social inequalities. Any man, they said, can live ' according to reason ' and can attain freedom thereby; no man is debarred by his position in society from doing so. The slave can do it as well as his master. But the Stoics, though they thought the life of reason within the reach of all men, no matter what their social position, did not think it an easy life and believed that most men would not choose it. In practice their philosophy was for the few.

Withdrawal from ' the world ' has attracted Christians much more than Stoics, though Christianity has never made it a condition of salvation. And Christians have also preached the equality of all men without denouncing the inequalities of ' the world '. They held the slave or the serf as likely to receive grace and to deserve heaven as the master or the lord; they did not confine the ability to choose and to live the good life to any part of society. Yet they believed that only a few would choose to live it.

This idea of the freely chosen moral or ' other-worldly ' life, of self-commitment, is not peculiar to the Stoics and Christians; it is also to be found among the Hindus and the Buddhists. It comes with systematic philosophy, with the emergence of more or less coherent theories about the world and man's place in it. Such theories, whatever their social origins, and whether or not they assert the existence of a personal God, weaken the hold of habit and convention on the individual. They are a challenge to

SELF GOVERNMENT RECONSIDERED

him to live ' rationally ', or at least as God (and not mere custom) requires. They are a challenge, not to this or that group or to the community at large, but to the individual. They appeal to his reason or to the voice of God in him; they appeal to him, if not against society, then in some sense apart from it. They present him with a spiritual problem which *he* must solve.

This challenge may mean little or nothing to the great majority, and yet the minority to whom it matters greatly and whose lives are changed when they meet it may be not merely tolerated but revered. This toleration and this reverence are a kind of respect for freedom, for the right of whoever has the strength and the courage to live a strenuous and exacting life to commit himself to it.

Yet this right is not freedom as the western liberal conceives of it. It is the right of those capable of it to live *the* good life; it is not the right of any man to live what seems to him a good or worthwhile life. The good, or the better-than-conventional, life is defined by a philosophy or a religion which is respected or tolerated, either generally or by those in authority. Most men are not expected, still less required, to live this life, and those who aspire to live it are allowed to do so. They are free to choose what is widely accepted as a better-than-ordinary life but not to choose any kind of life which seems good to them. They are not free to make their own standards provided that they allow others to do the same and carry out the obligations which society must impose if its members are to have the security and the opportunities they expect.

In all societies, no matter how liberal, men's right to choose how they shall live is severely limited. Everywhere the values men live by are largely conventional and are accepted by them without much thought given to the matter. And yet it is an important difference between liberal and other societies that only in the first is it admitted that all values may be criticized and that men should be free to choose how they shall live provided they do not choose to live in ways which diminish the security and restrict the opportunities upon which this freedom depends. It is above all in this sense of freedom that freedom is a western idea.

Where men and women are free to choose how they shall live, they are free also to choose their occupations and whom they shall marry. Their obligations to the family they are born into, the family they have not chosen, are smaller than in societies where they lack this freedom, but their obligations to the family they have created by choosing to marry and to have children are as great, though different in kind. In all societies there are obligations which do not arise out of freely-taken decisions, but in liberal societies obligations which do so arise acquire a special importance. Often, no doubt, they are deemed to have arisen in this way when in fact they have not; but even this is evidence of the value placed on a certain kind of freedom. In liberal societies the individual may be less free than he thinks, but he is freer than he would be if he did not aspire to freedom.

Two conditions favour the emergence and widespread acceptance of this idea of freedom: the consciousness that values are diverse and changing, and great social mobility. Where it is recognized that all men do not share the same values and that the values of one age are not those of the next, there gradually arises a new attitude to values. Men ask themselves how values come to differ and to change. Yet they cannot do without values, for it is in terms of them that they construct their ideas of a worth-while or a happy life. They need them to give a sense of purpose to their lives and also to hold together the communities they belong to. And so, when they come to recognize that values differ and change, and that efforts to prevent their doing so are unavailing, they first reconcile themselves to the inevitable and later come to think it good. But the need for values persists. Men must live and work together, and if life is not to be empty and without savour, must have goals not wholly out of reach. To live and to work together, they must, despite the divergence of their values, accept some common rules, conform to some common standards; and if, in an unusually permissive society, they are to be autonomous (and not just morally at sea), they must be so educated as to be able to choose goals within their reach. And so there arises a new attitude to social discipline and to education, characteristic of liberal societies, an attitude which first arose in the West.

Where social mobility is great, where men move readily away from their families in order to make a living, it soon comes to be widely accepted that it is for every man to choose his occupation and his wife. And it is for him and his wife to make their home, to create their own circle of privacy.

The assertion that democracy is western also needs to be

qualified. Outside the West, in many small communities, primitive and not so primitive, there has been popular government. Decisions affecting the community have been taken by acclamation or in other ways enabling the people to give effective expression to their will. Just how effective is often difficult to estimate, and no doubt also often exaggerated, now that democracy is everywhere well spoken of. Tribal or village communities having popular assemblies where only the chiefs or elders speak and there is no counting of heads are not so much democracies as oligarchies tempered by democracy. If they are to be called democratic, they must be allowed to be so in a different sense from the western democracies of our time. For in the West votes are counted, and there are elaborate rules to ensure that voters cast their votes freely and that divergent interests find expression, both in elected assemblies and outside them. It is in the West that democracy on a large scale was first attempted; and this kind of democracy requires the assertion of well-defined personal and group rights, and an elaborate structure of law and government.

So, for that matter, does every vast and intricate community in which there is great social mobility. If men and women are to move readily from region to region, they must be able to secure their rights and to prove their competence wherever they go; there must be courts administering a uniform system of carefully defined rules and professional bodies issuing certificates of competence recognized over a vast community. Therefore, if there is to be democracy at all, it must be adjusted to a structure of law and government suited to the needs of an immense and highly integrated community.

There have been great empires outside the West and unaffected by it, but they were not, by the standards of our day, highly integrated. They consisted of many small and almost self-sufficing communities with a light structure of imperial government superimposed upon them. Such traces as there may have been of democracy were confined to the small communities; to communities where the idea of the individual as the chooser of his own way of life and the bearer of rights protected by professional and impartial courts barely existed.

No doubt, we could use some other word than *westernization* to refer to the spread to Asia and Africa of these and other ideas (and of the practices needed to implement them). But what would

Q

be the point of our doing so? The word is widely used and is convenient. The process to which it refers is complex and calls for careful analysis; its various aspects have still to be distinguished from one another and named. But *westernization* serves well enough when what we want to refer to is the process as a whole. The important changes now taking place in Asia and Africa are by no means all parts of the process. Some are not effects of the impact of the West; and others, which are reactions against it, do not involve the use of western methods and ideas. And they are not the less important or desirable on that account. But the process called *westernization* is important, and is suitably named.

Asians and Africans who, whether they admit it or not, have acquired values first widely accepted in the West, need to put two questions to themselves: *To what extent do we desire (and are we able) to accommodate these values to others which still survive among us or could be revived?* and, *To what extent do we need to draw on western experience to achieve what we desire?* To be able even to begin answering these questions, they must look at their countries as their ancestors used not to do, and as Europeans did not do until quite recently. They must use ideas which the systematic study of the past and of social structure and social change have made familiar. But these studies first emerged in the West. There is a sense of history which is not mere respect for tradition, and there is also a kind of social self-consciousness which must be theirs if they are to be able to decide what goals to strive for and what to do to attain them. If they are not to be bewildered and frustrated by events, by the impact of the West upon their countries, if they are to be able to think and act to much purpose, they must learn to think in western ways.

This is not to say that they must not think for themselves nor strive for other goals than western peoples have striven for; true though it is that whoever assimilates a set of ideas, a way of looking at the world, acquires some of the values of the peoples among whom those ideas first arose.

Westernization is not a process of becoming exactly like the West (which, in any case, differs greatly from part to part), still less of consciously imitating the West, but of learning to use western ideas and methods. Long before the intrusion of the West upon Asia and Africa, there were peoples learning to use ideas and methods not invented by themselves nor inherited from their ancestors but coming to them from abroad. The peculiarity of westernization is that it involves the quick learning of an exceptionally large number of ideas and methods and the acquisition of a new type of social philosophy—the type which does not reconcile man to his social environment but moves him to transform it. Those who have learnt to use new methods and ideas may improve upon them or modify them and use them to move in directions peculiar to themselves. Westernization is not imitation of the West, though it involves, in its early stages, a good deal of imitation, conscious and unconscious.

II

Just as the claim that freedom and democracy are western ideas gives offence, so too does the assumption that the West supplies the model of how peoples who aspire to be ' modern ' and ' progressive ' should be governed. Those who reject this assumption do so on various grounds. Some argue that poor and illiterate peoples, if they are to make material and cultural progress quickly, have to mobilise their resources in ways which make it impossible for them to practise democracy as it is understood in the West.

Others dismiss the western model as largely irrelevant in the very different circumstances of Asia and Africa. They do not deny the need to adopt some western institutions and practices, but they insist that a political system can be democratic and liberal even though it does not incorporate everything that westerners believe to be essential to genuine democracy. They deny, for example, that a country is necessarily undemocratic and illiberal if it has only one political party. They argue that, just as the western democracies differ considerably from one another without ceasing to be democratic, so the political systems of Asia and Africa may come to differ considerably from the democracies of the West and yet be as truly democratic.

Indeed they may. But we must take care what conclusions we draw from this admission. Because western democracies differ considerably from one another, and other democracies may come to differ greatly from them, it does not follow that western experience has not taught us that some institutions and practices are necessary to democracy on a large scale and that others are incompatible with it. No one western system is *the* model of liberal democracy; and it may be that the ideal models constructed by western political scientists to include the ' minimal apparatus ' of democracy are all misleading. Yet, since there are institutions necessary to democracy, it is in principle possible to construct such a model, and if we want to construct it, we have to look mostly at western experience. Fifty years from now there may be a wealth of relevant experience outside the West, but at the moment there is not.

There are now about a dozen countries in the West which have been liberal democracies for a considerable time. If we take only these countries, without considering others whose experience of democracy is shorter, we already have a wide variety of systems of government. And all these countries, if we compare them with what Aristotle or Rousseau had in mind when they spoke of democracy, are large.

Some of them have two parties, some have more, and of one (Switzerland) it is often said that it has *virtually* none. That is to say, in some sense of *party* in which parties are important in most of these countries, Switzerland has no party or none that is important. And just as the political systems vary greatly, so too do the parties. Britain and the United States have each two parties that are important, and yet the British parties differ greatly from the American ones, both in their internal structures and their functions. In France, under the third and fourth republics, there were not only many more parties than in Britain and the United States, but they differed considerably from the British and American parties and from one another. If we accept what some writers say about the nature and functions of parties, we have to conclude that many of the groups called parties in France were not so. If we construct a definition of *party* enabling us to treat as parties all groups called so in all these democracies, we may find ourselves with a concept of *party* so broad as to be useless; and if we construct a useful definition, we may find ourselves obliged to conclude that a democracy can function effectively without parties. For though, even in the narrower and more useful sense of *party*, we may find in all our twelve democracies some groups which are parties, we may not find in all of them that the groups are important.

It has been said that there cannot be democracy unless there are at least two parties competing effectively for power. This assertion, thus unqualified, is not true. A country may have no parties competing for power, in the sense in which they compete for it in Britain or the United States, and yet be a democracy; or it may have, at one election after another, only one party with a chance of getting power. Those who make this unqualified assertion—and I have myself made it in the past—take too simple a view; they construct a false model of what is essential to democracy on a large scale. But those who reject this false assertion often do so only to make another, equally false. For example, having denied that a country, to be a democracy, must have at least two parties competing effectively for power, they go on to say that the Soviet Union, which has only one party, is democratic. They do not roundly declare that, since two parties are not necessary to democracy, the Soviet Union, which has only one, is democratic; for the argument, put in this way, is clearly absurd. Yet they do expect those who reject the false model of ' essential democracy ' to agree that the Soviet Union (or some other country accused of being undemocratic) is a genuine democracy.

The doctrine that there can be democracy only where there are at least two parties competing effectively for power has been even better received in the English-speaking countries than on the European Continent. Since two of the English-speaking peoples are world Powers, and all have unusually stable political systems, a view of democracy which finds favour with them is indeed impressive. If they are agreed that at least two parties are essential to democracy, are they not likely to be right?

In the English-speaking democracies parties are for the most part tightly-organized bodies seeking to control legislatures and governments, and they often appeal much more strongly to some classes and groups than to others. The effects of a party's winning the American Presidency or a majority in Congress are, of course, very different from the effects of a party's winning a majority in the British House of Commons, but in each case they are important. That the competition of parties for seats and offices enables different groups to bring pressure to bear on legislatures and governments without subjecting the groups to any party is evident in both Britain and the United States. It also weakens the hold of any one group on a party, for the party will take care not to sacrifice to that group the interests of others and so move them to transfer their allegiance. No doubt, not all sections of the people have organised groups to promote their interests, and such groups vary greatly in their influence on those who make the important political decisions; so that it never happens that all needs are taken into account and groups exert pressure according to their size. Some persons and groups are always highly privileged in comparison with others. Nevertheless, wherever there are solid parties competing for power, and a wide variety of groups looking for political favours, the competition helps to ensure that the elaborate system of persuasion and negotiation on which effective government depends in the modern state remains relatively *free*: that is to say, not controlled by any group or coalition of groups active inside it.

If we take the countries in which competition for office and power between large and well-organized groups helps to maintain democracy, and if we define the term *party* so that it covers any group having certain characteristics shared by these groups, we can perhaps say that no country which has one party can long *remain* democratic unless it acquires at least two, and that no country can *be* democratic if it *allows* only one. If we can say this, we can then readily admit that a country may be democratic even though it has no parties competing for office and power, and still deny that the Soviet Union (or, say, Ghana), is democratic. And we can also admit that, if we take some other sense of *party*, a country might have only one party for a long time and yet remain democratic.

Where there is only one party putting up candidates for all public offices, it might be a party hospitable to groups promoting a wide variety of interests and points of view, and might be so run that no group inside it gained control of the organization. This, though perhaps unlikely, is not impossible. Or there might be one party so much more popular than its rivals that, over a period covering many elections, nearly all the successful candidates were put up by it. To retain for long this overwhelming popularity it would need to be hospitable to a wide variety of interests and points of view, even though it first became popular owing to some great service done to the country. This is a more likely situation, and a good example of it is provided by India and the Congress Party. If the Congress Party were more tightly organized and less hospitable to diverse interests and points of view, it could not win such sweeping victories at the polls without resorting to methods incompatible with democracy. And its having rivals, even though for the moment they are weak, helps to keep it diverse and hospitable. If the Congress Party became more exclusive and India remained democratic, its rivals would gain in importance.

In a country like the United States, which has been for generations a democracy with a tradition of respect for minority views and interests, there might be one only mass party for a long time and democracy still survive. Functions now performed by the two competing parties between them might come to be performed by the one surviving party. In that case, the structure of that party would change considerably; it would cease to be the kind of party of which it could be said that, if a country has one, it must have at least two to remain democratic. Already, in some states of the Union, one party is so much stronger than the other that the states are one-party states, and the one party does what the two parties between them do in the Union. It provides electors with alternative choices in such a way that persons elected to office have strong motives for taking account of the wishes of a wide variety of independent groups. Even in the states where the Negro is deprived of his rights, there are free elections for the whites and there are diverse groups among them not controlled by the party and able to bring pressure on the government. Though the whites are intolerant of the Negroes, they care for their own liberties enough to preserve them. Indeed, it has been argued that the existence of only one party makes it easier for the whites to deprive the Negroes of their rights while maintaining their own. Certainly, a state is not authoritarian merely because it has only one party and there are many adults without effective political rights. Whether or not it is authoritarian depends on the structure and functions of the one party; and whether or not it is undemocratic depends on the proportion of adults without political rights.

Where the function of the one party is to preserve the political rights of a large privileged section of the people long accustomed to enjoying these rights and denying them to the rest of the people, a state having only one party may long continue to be undemocratic without becoming authoritarian. The privileged may accept the values of liberal democracy, making only one large and usually tacit reservation. They may speak of their state as if it were a democracy, and their claim for it is not entirely mistaken; for it does secure to a large part of the people rights which in a liberal democracy are secured to all. The privileged, when they give vent to their liberal and democratic sentiments, turn a blind eye on the unprivileged. They do not think of themselves as rich or aristocratic or highly educated, and for the most part are not so; they are, in their own eyes, *ordinary folk*. The idea that they are better than ordinary, that they are privileged and exclusive, as the rich and aristocratic used to be before *ordinary folk* got the vote, is repulsive to them. They are *ordinary folk*, and therefore the excluded are somehow not *folk* at all; they are best forgotten on those occasions when it is fitting that freedom and democracy should be praised or the rights they imply asserted.

No doubt, freedom and democracy are praised in countries where nobody enjoys these rights. But the point about these self-consciously democratic *ordinary folk*, who are privileged without admitting that they are, is that they do enjoy these rights and have long done so. If the excluded were removed from their midst, their state would then be what they claim that it is, a democracy; but their political and social attitudes would remain much what they are, except that they would no longer need to make the one large and tacit reservation. They would not, like the self-consciously privileged groups of old Europe, have to acquire new habits of thought and feeling in order to adapt themselves to an equalitarian and democratic society.

But if the unprivileged are much more numerous than the privileged and are acquiring aspirations and abilities which make them dissatisfied with their condition and impatient to end it, the task of keeping them down while preserving the liberties of the privileged becomes much more difficult. If the privileged refuse concessions, the tension between them and the unprivileged may be so great, and their need for solidarity so urgent, that they sacrifice many of their privileges to retain others: that they give up their liberties in order to preserve their estates or their right to all the easier and better paid jobs or merely their exclusiveness.

The structure and functions of parties in liberal democracies vary so much that we cannot say that such democracies must have at least two parties competing effectively for power. But we can make other assertions instead. We can say that a country is not democratic where only one party is allowed to put up candidates for office, or where the party whose candidates are nearly always elected prevents the emergence of rival parties or their success otherwise than by gaining the confidence of the voters who are free to vote as they please. We can say also that, where in one election after another the candidates of only one party are successful in a country without a liberal and democratic tradition, this is strong evidence that the country is not democratic. Those who deny that there can be democracy where there are not two parties competing effectively for power would probably accept both these assertions. They are less concerned to stand by their denial than to establish a criterion enabling them to distinguish between what is democratic and what is not, and to refute those who say that a country like the Soviet Union is democratic.

When we speak of western democracy, we have in mind highly industrialized countries with large populations; countries such as Britain, France, West Germany and the United States. They are either unitary states or their central governments are fast gaining in power. We think of countries large in area or in population (or in both), and we notice that they all have mass parties competing for power. And even if we turn to look at the smaller democracies, at Belgium and Holland, at the Scandinavian countries, we notice that they too have rival parties, well organized and appealing to a mass electorate. Only in Switzerland is the rôle of mass parties conspicuously less important than elsewhere, and Switzerland is ' a special case '.

No doubt, Switzerland is a special case; but then so, too, in one respect or another, is every western democracy. Because all the western democracies except one are alike in a particular respect, we cannot assume that countries outside the West, if they are to be democratic, must be like them in that respect. Besides, as we have seen already, the western democracies are less alike, even in that respect, than they seem to be; for the word *party* is used to refer to organizations differing greatly from one another.

Some of the newly independent peoples are less numerous even than the Swiss, and are much less industrial and urbanized. And yet it is unlikely that they can do without organized mass parties. Their situation differs from that of the Swiss: they have to to set up new institutions and to learn to work them, they have get rid of old habits and to acquire new ones. They are out, as the Swiss are not, to transform themselves, to create a state and a nation. To achieve their aims, they may need at least one mass party, which will not be incompatible with democracy provided it is hospitable to a wide variety of interests and points of view. Of course, this party, since its function is to maintain a sense of national unity and national purpose, must discourage some kinds of activity. But it may be able to control the state without preventing rival parties from challenging its supremacy; it may tolerate criticism and opposition within wide limits and yet retain its hold on the people by sharing their aspirations. The Indian Congress Party comes perhaps closer than any other to being a party of this type. There may be reasons making the emergence of such a party more likely in India than in other parts of Asia or in Africa; but it is not impossible elsewhere. One-party supremacy serves a quite different purpose in India from what it does in some parts of the United States, and in neither case can we say that it has led to authoritarian government. Is India more or less democratic than the states of the solid South? It is more democratic in the sense that it treats no section of its people as beyond the pale; it is less democratic in the sense that a smaller proportion of Indians understand what rights individuals and groups must have in a democracy or know what to do to maintain them.

III

It is often said that dependent people who achieve independence and ' backward ' peoples in the first stages of their endeavours to catch up with the ' advanced ' ones need *authoritarian* government. Or it is said that they need, if not *authoritarian* government, then something which stands between it and *democracy*.

These two assertions may seem so much alike as to be virtually the same. One man uses the word *democracy* narrowly and precisely, calling every state *authoritarian* which is not democratic in his sense of the word; while another uses the word *democracy* more broadly, and will call a state democratic even though it does not secure to its citizens all the rights secured to them in the older and more stable democracies of the West. One man may speak of a need for *authoritarian* government where another speaks of a need for a government which is incompletely democratic, or chooses some other way of conveying his meaning. Yet they may both have in mind much the same type of government.

I admit this to guard against misunderstanding. Nevertheless, there are two very different attitudes which call for comment. Two men may agree that in a ' backward ' country democracy, as the West knows it, is impossible, and yet may disagree profoundly about the type of government it ought to have. One of them may believe that the country needs the kind of government which the Russians have known since 1917, and yet he may be no Communist. He may believe that there are to be accomplished urgent tasks, requiring severe discipline, and that a small minority with the vision and courage to drive the people to accomplish them have the right to do so. He may say that the minority are acting for the common good; he may welcome every mark of their popularity and defend them from criticism, and yet be willing to have them use the most ruthless methods. His argument is not that the country, in its present condition, cannot be democratic; it is rather that it needs to be ruled by a minority able and willing to use drastic methods involving great suffering.

The man who says all this may be a native or he may be a foreigner. If he is a native, he will be more careful how he speaks, especially if the minority whose cause he espouses already have power or are expected soon to get it. He will speak of the minority as they wish to be spoken of, and will call them democrats if they aspire to the name. But if he is a foreigner and a westerner to boot, he may speak more freely; he may be ready to admit that they are not democrats. He may also admit other things about them, which he would condemn in the rulers of his own country, but which in their case he excuses as necessary evils.

The other man, though he too admits that the country is incapable of democracy, and even that there are urgent tasks which require a discipline more severe than democracy allows of, is anxious that government should be as mild as possible. He is not easily persuaded that urgent tasks do require a very severe discipline or that tasks which require it are urgent. Both his values and his priorities are different: he has different ideas about the relative values of things, and also about the order in which things should be done. And, of course, his values and his priorities are closely connected. Because he cares so much about some things he looks critically at the arguments of those who say

that other things must come first as means to them. He is afraid
that the methods used to attain the things which ' come first ' will
prevent the attainment of others, which to him seem to matter as
much or more.

We have here two attitudes which differ greatly, though the
difference is masked by the language used to express them. Both
men readily agree that a ' backward ' people may be incapable of
democracy as the West knows it, and may need to do urgently
things requiring a discipline incompatible with democacry. It
is not until they come to look at a particular country and to pass
judgements on it, that it is borne in upon them how greatly they
differ.

Perhaps I am too suspicious of persons who are quick to
accuse others of lacking *realism*. I find the world a complicated
place; and their conclusions about what cannot be prevented or
what ought to be done seem to me based on too simple arguments.
Human beings, these *realists* tell us, must be adequately fed,
clothed and housed if the rights precious to the liberal are to mean
anything to them, and therefore they must *first* be provided with
food, clothing and houses and *then* have these rights secured to
them. But we can ask, of both the premise and the conclusion of
this argument, *How is it to be interpreted*? How adequately must
people be fed, clothed and housed to be able to appreciate these
rights? Are the methods which increase material welfare the most
quickly also the most likely to bring this appreciation?

Among the poorest of the poor in Europe are the Balkan
peasants, and whoever knew them before the war will admit that
freedom did not mean to them what it meant to the Englishman.
He will admit also that they were more concerned about food,
clothes and houses than about free elections or the right to
criticise their rulers or the right to an education giving them a
wider choice of occupations. But he will bear witness that they
cared very much for their dignity and for not being bullied. They
did not think of themselves as citizens, as the English or the
Americans do, but they did want their customs respected and also
their needs: not the needs ascribed to them by others with aspirations which they did not share but what they themselves recognized
for such. They were keener to get more food and better clothes
and houses than to acquire the rights and opportunities of Englishmen, but they were not keener to get them than to preserve their

self-respect. They wished to be treated as men with wills of their own. They already had food, clothing and houses; their desire to have more and better was not so desperate that they were willing to suffer anything that their rulers might require of them if only it brought these material things more quickly.

Even the poorest peasants have moral as well as material needs. Therefore, though there may be rights and opportunities which they cannot appreciate until they are better off materially, there are also moral values which they already appreciate, no matter how poor they are. And if these values are seriously impaired, an increase in wealth will not have the desired effect. Men may need to be wealthier than most Balkan or Indian or Chinese peasants are, if they are to care for freedom and democracy, but this greater wealth is only a *necessary* and not a *sufficient* condition of their caring. If we grant that the poorer peoples must become wealthier if they are to appreciate rights and opportunities hitherto denied to them, we need not allow that they will appreciate them no matter what is done to make them wealthier.

I agree that the poor should become richer and the illiterate should go to school. But I suspect that the better-to-do and the educated, even when they are benevolent, have some gross illusions about the poor and the illiterate. It comes easily to them to speak as if it did not much matter what is done to the poor by improvers of their lot provided they are cured as quickly as possible of poverty and illiteracy. It was the son of a well-to-do father, an intellectual, a student of philosophy, who, speaking of the urban poor, the proletariat, said of them that they had *nothing to lose but their chains*. They had nothing to lose that he could see, that he could appreciate, that he could imagine their caring for. But then he was not one of them, just as he was not one of the peasants, whom he despised. He spoke of them as if, in order to get self-respect, in order to live as becomes human beings, they had to cease being what they were, the poorest class in society. That they already had as much self-respect as other classes, and even a culture of their own, seems not to have occurred to him. He spoke of progress as if it were a kind of war, and was willing that men should suffer greatly that the evils denounced by him might quickly end. He was the most famous doctrinaire revolutionary of them all, and his doctrine has long been attractive to those who have felt as he did. I do not find it surprising that

revolutionaries should care so little for the misery and the indignities they bring upon the very people whose misery has moved
them to eloquence and whose spokesmen they claim to be.

It may be that in most ' backward ' countries, as they move
towards independence or (if they never lost it) as they strive to
catch up with the ' advanced ' countries, there will be established
nationalist and authoritarian régimes making larger demands on
the unconsenting people than used to be made by the imperial
Power or the old native rulers. Some writers say that it is *inevitable*,
others that it is *likely*; and if I agree with the second rather than the
first, it is because I mistrust the word *inevitable* used in this context.
I have often been told that it was *inevitable* that Yugoslavia should
have an authoritarian and nationalist régime after the war, and I
admit that she now has one; but I still believe that if a number of
leaders, Yugoslav and foreign, had made different decisions,
which they could have made without losing the support of their
followers or otherwise sacrificing their interests, Yugoslavia,
which is indeed a backward country, might to-day be as liberal
and democratic as India. And what is true of Yugoslavia may be
true also of other ' backward ' countries. Who knows just how
' backward ' a country must be to be incapable of democracy and
to need a firm authoritarian government if it is to make ' progress'?

Nevertheless, it is likely that most ' backward ' countries
will have nationalist and authoritarian régimes. Such régimes
can do much good to the peoples subject to them, deepening their
loyalties to the community, setting up an efficient administration
and impartial courts, building up trade and industry, providing
education. And where such a régime is firmly established,
it is not much use insisting that, if different decisions had been
taken a decade or a generation ago, the country might have had
a more democratic form of government no less capable of bestowing
these benefits upon it.

But if we reconcile ourselves to the spread of nationalist
and authoritarian régimes, we must take care not to condone
brutal methods. We must condemn the simple-minded, tough,
first-things-first, draconian school, who do not mind how much the
poor and the ignorant are made to suffer ' for their own good '
who believe that the ' masses ' must make the sort of ' progress '
which they themselves have made before they can know what is
good for them and acquire the right to be treated as if they did

know. We must condemn their arrogance and their stupidity. For, except when their real object is to get power and importance for themselves by exploiting the grievances of others, they are stupid; they advocate or use methods which are grossly inappropriate to their ends.

KENNETH ROBINSON

AUTOCHTHONY AND THE TRANSFER OF POWER

I

Autochthony Reconsidered

To those familiar words in the Commonwealth vocabulary, *autonomy* and *equality*, Dr. Wheare has recently added[1] a new and unfamiliar one: *autochthony*. That it should be unfamiliar, not to say pedantic, is not inappropriate for it is intended to refer to one aspect of a way of thinking about constitutional matters which is fundamentaly strange to the older approach to the British embryology[2] of political and legal systems within the Commonwealth. This way of thinking about constitutional matters mainly stems from the ideas of those communities incorporated in what was the British Empire whose cultural tradition is radically distinct from that of the United Kingdom. The older British approach still conditions nonetheless the form and manner in which power is normally transferred to the new states established in what were once British dependencies. The argument of this essay is that even if this is not a bad thing it is at any rate not a particularly good one.

Dr. Wheare introduced his discussion of autochthony in these words: ' For some members of the Commonwealth it is not enough to be able to say that they enjoy a system of government which is in no way subordinate to that of the United Kingdom. They wish to be able to say that their constitution has force of law and if necessary of supreme law within their territory through its own native authority and not because it was enacted or authorised by the parliament of the United Kingdom; that it is, so to speak, ' home grown ', sprung from their own soil, and not imported from the United Kingdom. They assert not the principle of autonomy only: they assert also a principle of something stronger, of self sufficiency, of constitutional autochthony, of being constitutionally rooted in their own soil '.[3] Although

[1] See *The Constitutional Structure of the Commonwealth* (Oxford, 1960) Ch. IV.
[2] Professor Hart's phrase, see *The Concept of Law* (Oxford, 1961), p. 116.
[3] Wheare, *op. cit.*, p. 88.

R

at one point in this passage Dr. Wheare writes in deceptively broad terms, the rest of his discussion makes it plain that, in his usage, autochthony is a characteristic of the origin, not the content, of constitutions. A constitution might originally have been ' made in Britain ' in the sense that it was given the force of law by an Act of the British parliament, it might indeed be an exact replica of the British constitution, but it would nonetheless be autochthonous if subsequently embodied in a document which owed its validity and authority to no country or institution outside that to which it applied. On the other hand a constitution which bore no resemblance in the political arrangements it prescribed to anything ever known in Britain (or anywhere else, if that be conceivable) would fail to achieve autochthony if ' enacted ' by a Commonwealth country by any method whatsoever authorised by a law passed by a legislature whose authority might be argued to be ' derived ' from a United Kingdom statute. On this test, as Dr. Wheare shows, the 1956 Constitution of Pakistan evidently fails, that of the Indian Union probably passes but only the Irish Constitution of 1937 indubitably succeeds. The Constitution of Pakistan of 1956 was ' in fact and in law enacted by the Constituent Assembly with the assent of the Governor-General and it derived its forces of law from the Indian Independence Act of 1947 ';[1] the constitution of India did not receive the Governor-General's assent and accordingly if such assent was under the Indian Independence Act requisite for the completion of the process of enacting constitutional measures, as the Federal Court of Pakistan later held, the Constitution of India does not owe force of law to the Indian Independence Act and India achieved constitutional autochthony with its ' enactment '; the Irish Constitution of 1937 was merely approved by Dail Eireann and thereafter submitted to the people in a referendum but the Act which provided for this plebiscite was studiously silent about what effect an affirmative vote might have. The constitution was an act of the people as declared in its preamble and its ' enactment ' constituted a revolution in law.[2] I have discussed elsewhere[3] the 1960 Constitution of Ghana and shewn that, although submitted to the people in draft in a

[1] *Ibid.*, p. 103.
[2] *Ibid*, p. 94.
[3] ' Constitutional Autochthony in Ghana ' (*Journal of Commonwealth Political Studies* I (1961), pp. 41–55).

plebiscite, it was in fact and in law enacted by a Constituent Assembly which derived its authority from an Act of the Ghana Parliament which received the Governor-General's assent in the usual way. It fails, therefore, to achieve autochthony as Dr. Wheare uses that term.

There is, however, as Dr. Wheare recognises, a certain artificiality about so austere a usage. It may be maintained, he concedes, that ' there is no need to make a break in continuity on the Indian or the Irish model; the break was made ', so far as the older Commonwealth countries are concerned, in 1931 by the Statute of Westminster and, so far as the newer Commonwealth countries are concerned, by the appropriate Independence Acts, the effect of which is ' to renounce for ever the power of the parliament of the United Kingdom to make laws ' for those countries. Since Dr. Wheare's book was published, this view of the position has been most clearly restated by Professor Hart;[1]

'At the beginning of a period we may have a colony with a local legislature, judiciary, and executive. This constitutional structure has been set up by a statute of the United Kingdom Parliament which retains full legal competence to legislate for the colony; this includes power to amend or repeal both the local laws and any of its own statutes, including those referring to the constitution of the colony. At this stage, the legal system of the colony is plainly a subordinate part of a wider system characterised by the ultimate rule of recognition that what the Queen in Parliament enacts is law for (*inter alia*) the colony. At the end of the period of development we find that the ultimate rule of recognition has shifted, for the legal competence of the Westminster Parliament to legislate for the former colony is no longer recognised in its courts. It is still true that much of the constitutional structure of the former colony is to be found in the original statute of the Westminster Parliament: but this is now an historical fact, for it no longer owes its contemporary legal status in the territory to the authority of the Westminster Parliament. The legal system in the former colony has now a ' local root ' in that the rule of recognition specifying the ultimate criteria of legal validity no longer refers to enactments of the legislature of another territory. The new rule rests simply on the fact that it is accepted and used as such a rule in the judicial and other official operations of a

[1] Hart, *op. cit.*, pp. 116–7.

local system whose rules are generally obeyed. Hence, though the composition, mode of enactment, and structure of the local legislature may still be that prescribed in the original constitution, its enactments are valid now not because they are the exercise of powers granted by a valid statute of the Westminster Parliament. They are valid because under the rule of recognition locally accepted, enactment by the local legislature is an ultimate criterion of validity.' Such a development, Professor Hart observes, may be achieved in various ways: the parent legislature may finally renounce legislative power over the former colony or the break may be achieved by violence. But, he continues, 'in either case we have at the end of this development two independent legal systems. This is a factual statement and not the less factual because it is one concerning the existence of legal systems.' In *Parliamentary Sovereignty and the Commonwealth*, Dr. Geoffrey Marshall had earlier expressed a similar view: 'All that is necessary for the phrase ' totally distinct *grundnorm* ' or ' local and national root for municipal law ' correctly to describe the legal situation is that the way a Commonwealth court applies the law should be consistent with the regarding of the rules laid down in a local instrument as being the basic rules of a legal system. If memories of the ' source ' of a constitution in a historical sense offend nationalist sentiment, it may none the less be a matter of some moment to secure specific proclamations of independence and adopt a more congenial enacting formula than that of the Queen-in-Parliament.'[1]

On this view, the essential requirement for it to be true to say that a Commonwealth country enjoys an independent legal system is that the local courts recognise that full powers of legislation (including powers to amend the constitution) exist in the country and that no such powers exist anywhere else. Unless there has been a revolution (whether ' in law ' or the more usual sense) it is, no doubt, necessary if the local courts are to take such a view, that there should have been a full and complete transfer of power from the United Kingdom in the course of which the British Parliament has made what the local courts regard as a valid and irrevocable renunciation of authority and given, once for all, to the legislature of the former colony as ample status and powers in respect to that country as the British Parliament,

[1] *Op. cit.*, pp. 101–2.

subject only to the constitution defining it, which it may amend as therein provided. Of course, on the view that there can be no such irrevocable redefinition of its powers by the British parliament there can be, as Dr. Marshall put it ' simply no escape from the strait-jacket of imperial sovereignty '[1]—at any rate in English law. But if, on the other hand, it is accepted that a renunciation of authority by the British parliament would be regarded as final by the courts of the Commonwealth country concerned, such a view could as well be taken of Sections 2 and 4 of the Statute of Westminster (and the similar provisions of the Ceylon and Ghana Independence Acts) as of Section 6(4) of the Indian Independence Act or, even, the corresponding sections of the more recent Independence Acts in respect of Nigeria, Sierra Leone, Tanganyika, Trindad and Jamaica (which include no provision whereby future Acts of the United Kingdom parliament ' shall extend or be deemed to extend ' to any of those countries if they contain an express declaration that that country has ' requested and consented ' to their enactment.)

In my discussion of Constitutional Autochthony in Ghana, I sought to express a similar view in terms of the notion of autochthony. It was there suggested that although a break in legal continuity, whether achieved by a ' revolution in law' or by a revolution in the ordinary sense was evidently a sufficient condition of autochthony, it might not be a necessary one. ' From a legal, though not perhaps from a political point of view, it is hard to see how the achievement of autochthony could be questioned if the separateness of the *grundnorm* had first been explicitly recognised by the Courts and thereafter a constitution (whether identical with its predecessor or not seems from this point of view immaterial) was enacted by what the courts had recognised as the new source of ultimate authority. There would be a wholly separate legal order and its *grundnorm* would be entirely of its own making.'[2] This was written before the publication of *The Concept of Law* and was based on the assumption that if it was accepted that the Statute of Westminster and the later Independence Acts had effected a valid and irrevocable redefinition of the power of the British parliament so far as concerned the making of laws for the countries to which those acts respectively applied, the link

[1] *Ibid.*
[2] Robinson, *op. cit.*, pp. 48–51.

with the United Kingdom legal system was thereby severed and separate *grundnorms* came into existence. The test of this would be ' the view taken by the courts in deciding constitutional issues ' in the respective countries. By ' explicit recognition ' I had in mind some such declaration as that of the Chief Justice of South Africa in *Harris's case:* ' The only legislature which is competent to pass laws binding in the Union is the Union legislature. There is no other legislature that can pass laws which are enforceable by Courts of Law in the Union '.[1] If after explicit statements of this kind a constitution were enacted by a legislature so recognised, what I called a ' wholly separate legal order ' would manifestly exist with a constitution evidently of its own making (whatever the historical origin of the authority of that legislature or of some features that might be incorporated in the new constitution). Such a state of affairs, could clearly be distinguished from ' autochthony ' as Dr. Wheare seemed to use the term but also from the separate legal order whose existence could be deduced so to speak from an examination of the way in which the courts in practice behaved, the ' independent legal system ' to use Professor Hart's terminology, which is evidenced by the fact that the new rule of recognition is accepted and used in the judicial and other official operations of the system, though it may not have been expressly formulated in so many words by the local courts.[2]

Professor Hart's account of these matters enables us to see clearly what is *not* needed for it nonetheless to be true that an independent legal system exists. This includes any explicit declaration by the courts of the new source of ultimate authority (or, in his terminology, any statement of the rule of recognition specifying the ultimate criteria of legal validity); any local enactment of a new, or reenactment of an old constitution; and *a fortiori* any ' break of legal continuity '. From this point of view countries whose constitutions are, in the restricted sense in which Dr. Wheare generally uses that term, autochthonous simply form a special class of those with independent legal systems. But another special class within that larger group may also be distinguished, a class which in ' Constitutional Autochthony in Ghana ' I sought to distinguish from merely ' separate legal

[1] Harris v Dönges (1952), 2 SALR (AD) 418 per Centlivres C. J.
[2] ' For the most part, the rule of recognition is not stated but its existence is *shown* in the way in which particular rules are identified, either by courts or other officials or private persons or their advisers ' (Hart, *op. cit.*, p. 98).

orders ' on the one hand and those in which a fully autochthonous constitution in Dr. Wheare's sense had been established, on the other. This class includes, for example, Pakistan and Ghana, and would possibly have included South Africa had she not left the Commonwealth with the coming into force of the republican constitution, enacted in Act No. 32 of 1961. It might conveniently be described as one made up of countries in which there exist ' nationally defined' legal systems. Legal systems which are merely independent are no less so than those which are nationally defined or those which are autochthonous though the fact of their independence is made more evident by national definition or autochthony. Like autochthony, national definition is, in relation to the legal system, a characteristic of origins not content. It may, nevertheless, be, in Dr. Marshall's words, ' a matter of some moment' to transform an independent legal system into one which is also nationally defined or even autochthonous. The reason why this may be so, as Dr. Wheare more than once implies, is not because such changes render the legal system ' more ' independent. It is because, in their absence, the origins of the system, in a historical sense, are considered seriously to weaken its claim to legitimacy.

In practice, however, considerations of this kind have seldom, if ever, been alone in determining the procedure actually adopted. It would no doubt be absurd to minimise the extent to which the republican tradition of popular sovereignty found expression in Irish nationalism but Mr. de Valera himself drew the Dail's attention to the legal uncertainties which were avoided by the procedure adopted in making the 1937 Constitution.[1] Similarly, although the historical origins of the procedure actually adopted in India are no doubt to be found in Congress's insistence that ' the recognition of India's independence and the right of her people to frame their constitution through a Constituent Assembly is essential to remove the taint of imperialism from Britain's policy ' and that ' a Constituent Assembly is the only democratic method of determining the constitution of a free country ',[2] their advocacy of a Constituent Assembly elected on the basis of adult suffrage

---

[1] Robinson, *op. cit.*, p. 47 and Mr. de Valera's comment cited in note 32 (*Ibid.* p. 55).
[2] Resolution of the Working Committee, Indian National Congress, *Indian Annual Register* (1939) ii p. 238 (In the event, of course, this was not the basis on which the Constituent Assembly was elected).

had, as was well understood by all their critics, practical political advantages in being the method most likely to ensure that Congress ideas prevailed in the constitution such an Assembly might be expected to draft. Again, it would appear that the constitution-making procedure adopted in Ghana in 1960 was influenced in part by doubts of the powers of constitutional amendment vested in the Parliament of Ghana under existing law as well as by the desire to give expression in the new constitution to the conception of popular sovereignty.[1] Whatever views on autochthony may have been held by the South African Government in 1961 (and there is no indication in the relevant Parliamentary Debates that any member so much as considered the matter), it would evidently have been politically and legally unwise to have reopened the constitutional debates by attempting to bring about a republican régime on the basis of a ' break in legal continuity' .

Can any similar analysis be made of the notion of autochthony in the much wider sense in which it is thought of as a characteristic of the content, as opposed to the origin, of a constitution, the desire to frame a constitution in keeping with the conditions or traditions of the country, one which will be ' home-made ' in substance or as a matter of historical fact, no matter how it may be given force of law? The implications of this question cannot be appreciated apart from the incidents of the transformation of the British Empire into a group of sovereign independent states freely associated in the Commonwealth. The peculiarity of the method of creating new independent states which has developed in this process is a consequence of the fact that the earlier instances began and were completed within the assumptions appropriate to a devolution of power within a single monarchy. Even in their later stages they were not conceived as transfers of power completing a process whereby independent legal and political systems came into existence which would thereafter be linked to the parent system only because the same person was Head of State in both. In the bringing into existence of Canada, Australia, and South Africa, the advantages of a 'home made' constitution were of course recognised in the sense that it was accepted that the local political leaders would be best qualified to work out together constitutional proposals appropriate to their needs and circumstances. But the arrangements envisaged were alike in presupposing (inevitably in

[1] F. A. R. Bennion, *Constitutional Law of Ghana* (London, 1962), pp. 74.

the climate of ideas then prevailing) that the country would remain part of the dominions of the Crown, with a parliamentary government similar in many essentials to that of Britain. In time, the implications of these very large devolutions of power were seen in practice to have involved the emergence of fully self-governing countries ' in no way subordinate to ' the parent country and each enjoying full control of its external relations. It was to describe the resulting independent states which yet remained ' united by a common allegiance to the Crown and freely associated as members of the British Commonwealth of Nations' that the phrase ' Dominion Status ' came into use between the two world wars.

Dominion Status had its characteristic ambiguities which time has resolved. All of them were associated with that ' common allegiance to the Crown ' which united the members of the Commonwealth. Although the fact that the Dominions were gradually coming to control their own external relations was eventually recognised (and arrangements made to make this fact evident in the formalities of diplomatic relations) it remained a subject of debate whether a Dominion could be neutral in a war in which Britain was engaged: could the King be at war in respect of some parts of his dominions but not of all of them? This was answered in practice, if not finally resolved, by the undoubted neutrality of Eire during the second world war. Secondly, was a Dominion free to secede? This in turn was settled by the terms of the War Cabinet proposals for Sir Stafford Cripps's discussions with the Indian leaders in 1942. It was clearly stated that no restriction would be imposed on the new Indian Dominion which it was hoped might be created after the war ' to decide in the future its relationship to the other Member States of the British Commonwealth '.[1] The point has been driven home by the actual circumstances of the withdrawal of Ireland and, more emphatically, South Africa. Lastly, although nothing in Dominion Status, of course, restricted a Dominion from adopting whatever constitutional arrangements it pleased, these had to be consistent with maintaining allegiance to the Crown;[2] the example of Eire in 1937 showed how far a member

---

[1] Cmd. 6350, reproduced in P.N.S. Mansergh, *Speeches and Documents on British Commonwealth Affairs* 1931–51 (London, 1953), ii, p. 616.

[2] ' Dominion Status has nothing to do with the form or type of internal constitution in a Dominion. It is only concerned with the external position. It is a matter, so to speak, of the ' international' relations between the members of

might go without being regarded by the other members as having thereby made 'a fundamental alteration' in its position as a member.[1] Not only had it adopted an autochthonous constitution but also one in which the Crown was nowhere mentioned and the Governor General was replaced by a President elected by universal popular suffrage. Since the Declaration of 1949 consequent upon the decision that India, on becoming a Republic, should yet remain a member, it is, of course, no longer necessary to maintain allegiance to the Crown and a member of the Commonwealth may provide for a republican form of government, as India, Pakistan and Ghana have done, or indeed, for a distinct local monarchy of its own, as in the Federation of Malaya.[2] Finally, events have made it clear that 'membership of the Commonwealth', the contemporary successor of 'Dominion Status', does not, any more than its predecessor, require a member's internal constitution to be parliamentary: a country in which parliamentary government has been suspended, as in Pakistan, or in which a form of executive Presidency has substantially qualified the 'Westminster model' as in Ghana, does not, by that fact, find its membership of the Commonwealth called in question.

Like the question whether or not a legal system is independent,

the Commonwealth. It fixes that relationship as one of equality. It may be hard to imagine the Commonwealth as anything but an association of states under parliamentary government; but Dominion Status does not require a Dominion's internal constitution to be parliamentary. A Dominion might enjoy Dominion status under any domestic régime provided (1) that it maintained allegiance to the Crown; (2) that it contained no element of subordination to any other member of the Commonwealth; and (3) that it accepted free association with the other members' R. Coupland, *The Times*, 20 Feb., 1935, reprinted in *The Empire in These Days* (London, 1935), pp. 275–6.

---

[1] Mansergh, *op. cit.*, i pp. 366–7.

[2] So far as membership of the Commonwealth is concerned a vestige of inequality arises in that if a member which is one of the Queen's realms (i.e. part of the dominions of the Crown) changes its constitution so that this ceases to be so, its remaining a member requires the consent of the other members. Although this has so far arisen in consequence of the adoption of a republican form of government, such consent would equally it is submitted be requisite if, in one of the Queen's realms, it were desired to replace the present monarchy by a new local one, no doubt an unlikely but not an inconceivable contingency. Similarly, it does not appear that if the Federation of Malaya were to become a Republic, its remaining a member would require such consent. From the international point of view, however, all this in no way qualifies the independence of a country possessing 'fully responsible status within the Commonwealth' (i.e. one of the Queen's realms). So long as it is prepared, if necessary, to cease to be a member, such a country is entirely free to change its constitution in whatever way it pleases.

the question whether or not a state is independent is a question of fact, depending on the answer to the question ' does its governmental powers extend to the conduct of its external relations? ' or, more broadly ' who controls its external relations? '[1] The significance of the developments discussed in the preceding paragraph is that they have clearly established that countries which enjoy what is now called, in the relevant Independence Acts[2] of the British parliament, ' fully responsible status within the Commonwealth ' are, in this sense, every bit as independent as India, Pakistan, Ghana, Tanganyika, each of which has become, in the words of the relevant Consequential Provision Acts ' a Republic while remaining a member of the Commonwealth ' or Cyprus, which at independence became 'an independent sovereign Republic' and only subsequently decided to seek membership, or indeed as Ireland, Burma or South Africa which after being part of the dominions of the Crown (and, in the case of Ireland and South Africa, members of the Commonwealth) have ceased to be so and become republics outside the Commonwealth. The fact that members of the Commonwealth are all fully independent states has, at last, come to be generally recognised, not least by political leaders in the new states that are members of the Commonwealth who make it abundantly clear that they are in no doubt about the independence of their countries even if their constitutions may still be those set out in a Statute of the British parliament or a British Order in Council and their Head of State the Queen, represented in the new state by a Governor General.

The class of countries with independent political systems, like that of countries with independent legal systems, thus evidently includes all members of the Commonwealth, whatever the form of their constitutions. Each provides for the control of its own external relations (and in fact controls them) just as it is free to amend its own constitution. But if, in the eyes of some nationalists, an independent legal system is not enough, neither is an independent political system: it must be reshaped so that it can claim to be in keeping with the circumstances and traditions of the country. One aspect of this desire, which might be described as the desire to give a constitution a ' national form ', was very clearly expressed

---

[1] See J. L. Brierly *The Law of Nations* (5th Ed., Oxford, 1955), pp. 121-2.
[2] *I.e.* Ceylon, Nigeria, Sierra Leone, Trinidad and Jamaica. It is also the status of Canada, Australia and New Zealand.

by Mr. Costello, then Taoiseach (Prime Minister) of Eire in 1948:[1]

' With the passage of the Statute of Westminster, the sovereignty of Ireland and the other members of the Commonwealth was beyond all question complete and absolute . . . any possibility of doubt as to our sovereignty had been removed; the question had become *not* whether our association with the Commonwealth and the constitutional provisions in which it was expressed represented a limitation of our freedom or sovereignty but whether our Constitutional arrangements relating to these matters were in a form which the people as a whole could accept as being compatible with our national sentiment and historical tradition.

' Nothing that has been done since the passing of the Statute of Westminster has added to, or increased the stature or strength of the constitutional structure or the measure of our national freedom. What has been done since then has been rather in the direction of using the legislative omnipotence of our Parliament to bring our constitutional and political institutions into accord with the traditional political concepts of our own people.'

The most obvious expressions of the desire to give a Commonwealth political system a national form are perhaps to be seen in the elimination of those aspects of the system which, in Mr. Costello's phrase, suggest ' the dependent status of the early colonial period instead of proclaiming the reality of the freedom ' which now exists. ' These forms to anyone save those who, having grown up with them understood their significance in practice, inevitably implied dependence.' The examples he went on to quote are indeed typical in the sense that they can easily be paralleled in other Commonwealth countries:[2]

' The abolition of the Oath of Allegiance in 1932; the provision in the Irish Nationality and Citizenship Act, 1935, under which Irish citizens were declared to be Irish citizens for all purposes, national and international, and by which both the British Nationality and Status of Aliens Act 1914 and the British Common Law relating to British subjects were declared no longer to have the force of law in Ireland; and finally the provisions of the Constitution of 1937 under which the office of Governor General was abolished in favour of an elected President and the British Crown

[1] Mansergh, *op. cit.*, p. 800.
[2] *Ibid.*, pp. 800–1.

denuded of all powers and prerogatives so far as this government of Ireland was concerned—all may be explained as steps in this process of bringing our political institutions into closer harmony with national tradition and sentiment.'

Whether any change in a constitution can be wholly ' formal ', related exclusively to what Bagehot called its ' dignified ' parts, those parts which ' excite and preserve the reverence of the population ' may perhaps be doubted. But many changes evidently have only minor consequences in respect of its ' efficient ' parts, ' those by which it in fact works and rules '. Consider, for example, the substitution of a President, elected by a unicameral legislature, for the Crown, represented by a Governor-General appointed ' on the advice ' of a government composed of members of the party with a majority in the legislature. Such changes are made, not because of any practical consequences they are expected to have on the way in which a political system works but because of the symbolic significance which is attached to them, the effect they are expected to have on the way in which the constitution, and the political system as a whole ' excites and preserves the reverence of the population '. Their object is to evoke or strengthen a feeling of national identity and when national identity is the object of considerable uncertainty these aspects of a constitution assume a special importance. Such uncertainty may be the result of a period of foreign rule over an ' historic nation '[1] or over an area which had no previous existence as a national unity and may be made up of many units previously separate, or even of the influence of a more advanced technology on a society hitherto isolated from such contacts.

The extent to which a particular constitution has achieved a ' national form ', in this wider sense, can obviously never be the subject of a precise criterion comparable with that which, Dr. Wheare allows, may in the last resort achieve certainty in the quest for autochthony. On the other hand, much of the urge to achieve a ' national form ' is closely related to the particular way in which, for historical reasons, the transfer of power has generally been brought about in what were formerly parts of the British Empire. Mr. Costello's discussion of the Irish position is only one (though perhaps the clearest) of many expositions of the

---

[1] To use the term made familiar in the debates over Central European nationalisms in Austria-Hungary.

desire to give a *Commonwealth* political system a ' national form '
which suggest that for many people nothing more recondite is
required than the replacement of any features of the system
which recall former colonial status by suitable alternatives which
do not. Some examples of this process which occasioned much
controversy in the inter-war years (such as the use of a national
flag or national anthem instead of the Union flag or the British
national anthem, or the creation of separate nationalities in place
of the common status of a British subject) have since the second
world war become generally accepted even in respect of those
Commonwealth countries which remain part of Her Majesty's
dominions. Others, including the monarchy itself (in spite of the
admission of Republics), continue, as will be seen, to be a source
of nationalist uneasiness while such hitherto acceptable relics of
imperialism as the Speaker's wig and the mace have in some new
states recently become targets for nationalist arrows. But it should
be remarked that, if features of a constitution or of the political
system as a whole, which were, as a matter of historical fact,
innovations received from the former ruling power or other
foreign countries, are considered ' neutral ' from the point of view
of national sentiment, they must be regarded as having been
assimilated or adopted by the new state. The test is whether they
are in fact attacked on national grounds or accepted; in this
context, the actual historical origins of particular features of the
system (e.g. modes of election) are no more relevant than is the
fact that the composition and mode of enactment of the legislature
may still be those originally prescribed in a British statute when
one is considering a legal system whose independence is shown by
the behaviour of the courts. There may be some convenience in
describing the process of replacement of what are considered
specifically colonial features of a Commonwealth political system
by the phrase ' national restatement '. From this point of view
what we have called the ' national definition ' of a constitution is
simply one part of that process, one concerned with replacing the
legal form in which a constitution has been prescribed, as, for
example, an Order in Council, redolent of colonialism, by one
free of any such taint.

The argument of this section may now be summarised. First
the problem of ' autochthony ', whether in the restricted legal
sense discussed by Dr. Wheare or in the wider political sense so

well explained by Mr. Costello, arises solely because of the historical circumstances and the legal forms of the transfer of power by which the British Empire has been transformed into a Commonwealth of Nations. Second, ' autochthony ' in its restricted legal sense is not a necessary condition for the existence of an independent legal system nor in a broader political sense is it a necessary condition for the existence of an independent state. Thirdly, ' autochthony ' in its restricted legal sense involves a ' revolution ' however achieved, and, in a broader political sense, the achievement of a ' national form ' of political system for which no comparable criterion, in the nature of the case, can be proposed. Finally, it is possible to discern a stage in which the desire for ' autochthony ' is satisfied by the elimination of surviving 'colonial' forms: for this process it may be convenient to employ the phrase ' national restatement '. In the restricted legal sphere an independent legal system may make its independence manifest by a local enactment of the constitution without a ' break in legal continuity ' and this special aspect of a process of ' national restatement ' may conveniently be described as one of ' national definition '.

II

The Search for Autochthony: Some Commonwealth Debates

Englishmen, who have made much of their practical commonsense in political matters, readily brush aside the issues we have been discussing; the countries concerned, they assert a little testily, are unquestionably independent and if they attach importance to fine theoretical points in legal nationalism, quite free to make whatever constitutional changes they wish. But most of these problems arise from the English obsession with their own political symbols, their inordinate conservatism in legal forms, and their continued employment of procedures which still reflect more of the ambiguities of the earlier developments culminating in ' Dominion Status ' than of the admitted realities of the contemporary transfer of power. Nor can it plausibly be maintained that such difficulties arise only in the early days of heady nationalism immediately after independence or in African countries. It is true that debate on these issues has recently resulted in the creation of a republic in Tanganyika, proposals for which were brought before the National Assembly at the fourth sitting of its first meeting, only two months after it had been opened by the Duke of Edinburgh. But a similar debate has been almost continuous in South Africa in the half century of the Union's existence and another has been intermittent in Ceylon since independence. It is now proposed briefly to review these debates.

Tanganyika

Tanganyika became independent on 9 December, 1961. The Constitution of the new state was contained in the Tanganyika (Constitution) Order in Council 1961,[1] made ' in the exercise of the powers conferred on Her Majesty by the Foreign Jurisdiction Act, 1890, and of all other powers enabling Her Majesty in that behalf '. The Constitution itself was set out in the Second Schedule to that Order and included a short preamble stating that ' recognition of the inherent dignity and of the equal and inalienable rights of all members of the human family is the foundation of freedom, justice and peace ', specifying certain of these rights which ' are best maintained and protected in a democratic society where the government is responsible to a freely-elected Parliament representative of the people and where the courts of law are independent and impartial '. This Constitution, it continued, ' makes provision for the government of Tanganyika as such a democratic society '. It provided that Parliament (i.e. the Tanganyika Parliament) might ' alter any of the provisions of this Constitution or (in so far as it forms part of the law of Tanganyika) any of the provisions of the Tanganyika Independence Act ', but that such an amending Act should not be passed unless it was supported by the votes of not less than two-thirds of the members of the National Assembly. The Order was to come into operation immediately before 9 December, 1961. The Tanganyika Independence Act 1961,[2] of the British parliament provided that on 9 December, 1961, Tanganyika (which had previously been a Trust Territory) should become part of Her Majesty's dominions and the United Kingdom government should have no responsibility for the government of Tanganyika. No Act of the British parliament passed on or after 9 December, 1961, should ' extend or be deemed to extend to Tanganyika as part of the law thereof '. Full

[1] U.K. Statutory Instrument, No. 2274 (1961).
[2] 10 Eliz. 2 Ch. 1.

powers of legislation were conferred on the Tanganyika parliament including power to amend the Constitution as therein provided.

These arrangements were the outcome of a Constitutional Conference held in Dar-es-Salaam in March 1961 attended by a British delegation, consisting of the Secretary of State for the Colonies (Mr. Macleod) and four officials, the Governor of Tanganyika, and a Tanganyika delegation consisting of the Chief Minister (Mr. Julius Nyerere), nine other Ministers and five other members of the legislature. The Conference was followed by further discussions between Tanganyikan ministers and the British government held in London later in the year. Mr. Nyerere had assumed office as Chief Minister in 1960 after an election at which 70 of the 71 seats in the legislature were won by candidates of his party, the Tanganyika African National Union, 58 of whom were returned unopposed. The franchise was a qualified one and 21 of the 71 seats were reserved for non-Africans. In the contested elections, T.A.N.U. candidates secured just over 100,000 votes, independents just over 20,000 and African National Congress candidates 337. The Report of the Constitutional Conference, while fixing a date for independence and recording that the Tanganyika government reaffirmed its intention to apply for membership of the Commonwealth made no reference to the form of government to be adopted by Tanganyika on attaining independence.[1]

In opening the Thirty-sixth (and, as it proved, last) session of the Legislative Council in Tanganyika on 11 October, 1960, the Governor announced that a Constitutional Conference would be held in March 1961 ' to advise the Secretary of State on the arrangements which need to be made for the attainment of self-government; and to consider the steps that will have to be taken to prepare the way for independence and the termination of the Trusteeship Agreement '. He added, ' The way ahead is comparatively clear and uncontroversial '. So much was this apparently considered to be the case that neither the Legislative Council nor the National Assembly, as it was renamed, was so much as called upon to consider the arrangements agreed upon at the

---

[1] *Report* of the Tanganyika Constitutional Conference 1961 (Cmnd. 1360). By contrast, the *Report* of the Uganda Independence Conference 1962 (Cmnd 1778) recorded that 'All the Uganda representatives . . . were united in desiring that after independence Uganda should be under the sovereignty of Her Majesty the Queen as Queen of Uganda '.

S

Conference or those later settled for the final transfer of power. In an ' unsolicited article ' (published in the London *Observer* on 12 March, 1961), however, Mr. Nyerere, then Chief Minister of Tanganyika, discussed the problem of ' South Africa's application for readmission (to the Commonwealth) as a Republic ' and observed that ' we are forced to say that to vote South Africa in is to vote us out '.[1] South Africa's decision to withdraw made it possible for Mr. Nyerere to assure the Secretary of State at the opening of the Conference a fortnight later that ' the people of this country look forward to their early independence within the Commonwealth of Nations which has just given such convincing proof of its attachment to the ideals of liberty and brotherhood amongst men.'[2] The only time the independence arrangements appear to have been even formally considered by the National Assembly was on 5 June, 1961, when Mr. Nyerere moved a resolution asking the British government to introduce as soon as practicable ' legislation . . . for the establishment of Tanganyika . . . as an independent sovereign state ' and to seek the support of other members of the Commonwealth for Tanganyika's admission.[3] The motion was seconded by the Minister of Justice and agreed to without a division or even a debate.

In such circumstances, some members were able to show, or at least to affect, a surprising ignorance of the constitutional arrangements which were about to become those of the new state when, hardly a week before independence, the National Assembly debated the Citizenship Bill, on 1 December, 1961. Earlier debates on these proposals had shewn that some members wished to restrict citizenship to Africans and had also resulted in the inclusion of provision to enable citizens of any African state whose government agreed to make suitable reciprocal arrangements to apply for citizenship of Tanganyika on terms comparable to those laid down for Commonwealth citizens. During the debate on the Citizenship Bill, several members took exception to the oath of allegiance; the Prime Minister's brother, Mr. Joseph Nyerere, asked ' when we are going to have an Oath of Allegiance bearing

[1] Text reprinted in the *Journal of Commonwealth Political Studies*, Vol. I (1961), pp. 72–74. Strictly speaking, South Africa sought the consent of the other Members to *remain* within the Commonwealth on becoming a Republic, and the word ' readmission ' is incorrect.

[2] Cmnd. 1360, p. 13.

[3] Tanganyika National Assembly *Debates*, 5 June, 1961, c. 975.

relation to the people of Tanganyika; ' while Mr. Mtaki enquired whether it was necessary ' that the oath of allegiance must be followed like this to prove that the Queen is Head of State of Tanganyika ' and whether it could not be amended ' to say to the Prime Minister or to the Government of Tanganyika '. He also objected to a provision empowering the Governor General to make regulations for the registration of aliens and thought ' we must have some advisers who should co-operate with the Governor '. The shape of things to come was already casting its shadow when the Minister for Home Affairs, after explaining the constitutional position of a Governor General, went on to observe ' It is possible to change the Constitution in the future and then not to have the Queen as head of state but as at present constituted the Constitution of Tanganyika does make the Queen head of state and it is normal for an oath of allegiance to be sworn to the Head of State and at the moment the Queen is, and I am afraid whether the Member likes it or not, that is his own constitution '.[1]

In January, 1962, Mr. Nyerere resigned and was succeeded as Prime Minister by Mr. Rashidi Kawawa. The reasons for this change are not wholly clear, though it was officially explained as enabling Mr. Nyerere to devote his whole time to reorganising T.A.N.U. and both Mr. Nyerere and Mr. Kawawa emphasised that there was no disagreement between Mr. Nyerere and his Cabinet colleagues and there would be no change in government policy. Some observers nonetheless contended that Mr. Nyerere's resignation was the result of pressures from the more radical African nationalists in T.A.N.U. Very soon afterwards, on 13 February, the new Prime Minister moved a resolution in the National Assembly inviting the government to provide for Tanganyika to be a Republic. He said that this was ' a subject on which ' they ' were likely to be generally agreed '. The institution of the monarchy was no doubt ' admirably suited to the traditions and needs of Britain and those other Commonwealth countries whose peoples originate from the British isles. But here we have quite different traditions. Some of our people have their own traditions of chieftainship, others have been almost republics without a formal head at all. In neither case does the institution of a monarchy in the form that has developed in Britain really assist the transition to a national democracy '. The monarchical

[1] Tanganyika National Assembly *Debates*, 1 Dec., 1961, c. 51; 91–2.

system was, moreover, difficult for Tanganyikans to understand. Although it did not ' detract in the slightest way from the absolute sovereignty of this National Assembly ' it might nonetheless appear to do so to ' those who were not sophisticated in constitutional forms '.

The ensuing debate clearly reflected some desire for a constitution which would seem less foreign and more national in form. Arguments of this kind were bound up with suspicions of the reality of Tanganyikan independence and the alleged incompatibility of membership of the Commonwealth with non-alignment or African unity, though such suspicions which were also voiced owed perhaps as much to neo-Marxist propaganda as to straightforward nationalism. One member, after enquiring whether Tanganyikans were ' really independent to do what we wish to do ', went on not merely to the thought that ' one day we must . . . be absolutely independent ' but also to urge that no experts ' to lay down the constitution ' should be invited from outside: ' it must be the people of Tanganyika '.[1] Another, on the contrary, was prepared to consider suggestions from outside but ' when drafting the Constitution of Tanganyika Republic it should be based on our African tradition '. To have a President who was one person and a Prime Minister who was another was, he thought, ' a foreign constitution . . . the African tradition is mainly having one person as the President and Prime Minister '. ' Things like the Crown etc.' were ' causing much embarrassment to a lot of people '.[2] A third member thought they were ' entitled to be asked what our freedom means if we still have a foreign Head of State. . . . This is a black state and it is only wise to have a black Head and a black body not a white Head and a black body . . . We must get away with this foreign model of constitution under which we are now.'[3] The Prime Minister, whose reply included a vigorous defence of the Commonwealth, was equally firm on independence. The suggestion that Tanganyika was ' now moving towards full independence ' was ' a very unfortunate remark to make because Tanganyika became a sovereign state on the 9th of December last year '.[4]

[1] Tanganyika *Parliamentary Debates* First Session Fourth Meeting, 15 Feb., 1962, c. 167.
[2] *Ibid*, cc. 170–171.
[3] *Ibid*, c. 182.
[4] *Ibid*, c. 185.

The Government's proposals for a Republic, published later in pursuit of the motion, emphasised that before independence Tanganyika had not been part of Her Majesty's dominions and its relationship with the Crown depended on ' the position of the Monarch as Head of State in the country charged with the duty of administering the territory .' For Tanganyika, therefore the British Monarchy had ' always been a foreign institution '. It claimed that ' the attainment of independence has greatly increased the sense of alienation from the Crown '. It was essential ' to devise a new constitutional form more appropriate for an independent African State and more capable of inspiring a sense of loyalty in the people '. The White Paper went on to argue that the division between formal authority and real authority to be found in republics ' where the Head of State occupies the same constitutional position as that occupied by a Constitutional Monarch ' was ' entirely foreign to our tradition ' in which the honour and respect accorded to a Chief, or a King or to a President was ' indistinguishable from the power he wields '. It accordingly proposed an executive President whose election would (substantially on the Ghana model) be directly linked with that of the National Assembly. The proposals recommended the abolition of appeals to the Judicial Committee as inappropriate once the connection with the monarchy was severed, and the replacement of the provisions for the appointment of High Court judges by a Judicial Service Commission by appointment by the President. ' In independent countries, with the exception of some former colonial territories, the appointment of judges is normally a matter for the executive.' Finally, ' whatever the merits ' of the arrangement whereby civil service appointments were made by the appropriate commission acting in an executive capacity in a country with an established civil service of its own, they were inappropriate in a country like Tanganyika where such appointments should be vested in the President, the existing commissions acting in an advisory capacity.[1]

In the debate on the Government's proposals, the same arguments were used. The ' Westminster Model ' was more foreign than an executive presidency; the oath of allegiance was undesirable, the ' last stage against colonialism ' was signified

[1] *Proposals of the Tanganyika Government for a Republic* (Govt. Paper No. 1), Dar-es-Salaam, 1962.

by the republic; of the arguments in favour of a republic the one most emphasised was that the position of the Governor General was incomprehensible to the people and would be equally so ' if the Governor General was a Mr. Maganga from somewhere in Sukumaland '. What made the British system logical, said Mr. Nyerere, was ' history not reasoning; . . . we lack these historical circumstances which can give that sense here; and therefore, Sir, let us frame something that makes sense and an Executive President makes sense in our own circumstances.'[1]

The new Constitution was, in the event, ' enacted by the Constituent Assembly of Tanganyika ', in accordance with the Constituent Assembly Act of 1962,[2] which was passed by the National Assembly and received the Governor General's assent in the usual way. This Act, following the model of the Constituent Assembly and Plebiscite Act in Ghana,[3] authorised the National Assembly to ' resolve itself into and constitute ' a Constituent Assembly and provided that any Bill passed by that Assembly ' in accordance with the provisions of this Act shall become law notwithstanding that the Governor General has not assented thereto '. Unlike the Ghana Act, however, no provision was made for submitting the Constitution to the people in a plebiscite. The Constituent Assembly Act was introduced and passed through all its stages on 25 September. There was no discussion and no division, the Speaker recording the number of members present and declaring that the second and third readings had obtained a two-thirds majority as required by the Constitution.[4]

Ceylon

The Independence Constitution of Ceylon was contained in the Ceylon (Constitution) Order in Council 1946, as amended by three further Orders in Council in 1947 and the Ceylon (Independence) Order in Council 1947.[5] The Ceylon Independence Act 1947 of the British parliament was described as an

---

[1] Tanganyika *Parliamentary Debates* First Session Second Meeting, 28 June, 1962, cc. 1083–1116.
[2] Act No. 66 of 1962.
[3] No. 1 of 1960.
[4] Tanganyika *Parliamentary Debates*, First Session Third Meeting, 25 Sept., 1962, c. 17.
[5] For the texts of the Orders in Council, the Independence Act and the Agreements see Sir Ivor Jennings, *The Constitution of Ceylon*, 2nd ed. (Bombay, 1951).

Act ' to make provision for, and in connection with, the attainment by Ceylon of fully responsible status within the British Commonwealth of Nations '. It was the first time that the phrase ' fully responsible status ' had been used in such an Act. (The Statute of Westminster refers to ' Dominions ' and the Indian Independence Act made ' provision for the setting up in India of two independent Dominions '.) The Ceylon Act provided that on independence ' His Majesty's Government in the United Kingdom shall have no responsibility for the government of Ceylon ' but unlike the Indian Independence Act, it included the ' request and consent ' formula of section 4 of the Statute of Westminster. In addition, the arrangements for the transfer of power included three Agreements between the British government and the Ceylon government, relating respectively to Defence, External Affairs and Public Officers.

The Independence Constitution was not the result of a constituent assembly or of a formal constitutional conference between the British government and the Ceylon government or Ceylon political leaders (including members of the opposition parties) such as those which have been held in connection with more recent constitutional developments in Africa and elsewhere in the British colonial Empire in the period preceding the final transfer of power. The way in which the arrangements for the transfer of power in Ceylon came about is somewhat complex but it must be briefly recounted since it is essential to a correct appreciation of some of the points raised in the debates on constitutional matters subsequently. In 1943 the British government made a Declaration that their examination of constitutional reform in Ceylon after the war would be ' directed to the grant of fully responsible government in all matters of internal civil administration ' but that control of defence and external matters and some minor points of detail would remain in the hands of the British government. They undertook to examine ' by a Commission or Conference ' after the war such detailed proposals on this basis as Ceylon Ministers might meanwhile prepare but stated that no proposals would be acceptable which had not secured the approval of threequarters of the members of the State Council, a proviso dictated by the wish to ensure constitutional arrangements that took account of the problem of minority communities in Ceylon. Ceylon Ministers produced a scheme early in 1944 and eventually the British government appointed a Commission with Lord Soulbury as Chairman and two other (British) members. The Commission was instructed to provide full opportunity for consultation with local interests including the minority communities. Ceylon Ministers took exception to this point on the ground that such consultation had not been envisaged in the 1943 Declaration. They thereupon withdrew their scheme which was not, officially, before the Commission, to which neither ministers nor leaders of the left wing parties gave evidence. As a result of the Commission's report,[1] the British government refused immediate Dominion Status but expressed the hope that a constitution on the lines recommended (which were substantially the same as the Minister's scheme, with the addition of a Senate) would be so worked that it would in a comparatively short time evolve to Dominion Status. These proposals were accepted after a two day debate in the State Council, by 51 votes to 3, and brought into effect in the Ceylon (Constitution) Order in Council of 1946.[2] In 1947 the Leader of the State Council (Mr. D. S. Senanayake) again pressed for Dominion Status. A general election was meanwhile held at which Mr. Senanayake's United National Party received just under 41 per cent of the votes and won 42 of the 95 seats. When he had taken office as Prime Minister under the 1946 Constitution, negotiations between the new government and the British government resulted in the signature of three Agreements relating to Defence, External Affairs and Public Officers, the removal by the Ceylon (Independence) Order in Council of the limitations on full self-government in the 1946 Order in Council, and the enactment by the British parliament of the Ceylon Independence Act. In December 1947, the action of the Ceylon cabinet in the negotiations was approved after debate by 59 votes to 11 (with 29 abstentions) in the House of Representatives and by 21 votes to 5 in the Senate and the Independence Constitution came into effect on 4 February, 1948.[3]

In the debate on the independence proposals, Mr. Senanayake, the first Prime Minister, who more than anyone else deserved to be regarded as their architect, made a forthright claim that they constituted a final renunciation of power by Britain. 'This Bill ',

[1] *Report* of the Commission on Constitutional Reform (Cmd. 6677).
[2] Ceylon State Council *Debates*, 8–9 Nov., 1945.
[3] Ceylon *Parliamentary Debates* (House of Representatives), Vol. I, 1 Dec., 1947, c. 739. Ceylon *Parliamentary Debates* (Senate) Vol. I, 3–4 Dec., 1947.

he said, ' gives us all the powers that the United Kingdom parliament is capable of giving us. It hands Ceylon over to the people of Ceylon. It deprives the British parliament and the British government of their power over us.' And, again, ' Sir, what are the requisites of a sovereign independent state? Legislative autonomy? We have it. Freedom to order our external relations as we wish? We have it. Freedom to take such measures as we want to ensure our defence and security? We have it.'

The Ceylon Independence Act was criticised on many grounds. The independence it offered fell short not merely of ' independence in the fullest sense of the word ' but even of ' Dominion Status '. The Act did not so much as refer to the concept of a Dominion, it contained no provision for its own amendment by the legislature of Ceylon (and so ruled out secession since a Ceylonese Secession Act would be repugnant to the Independence Act itself), it contained the 'request and consent ' clause on the lines of Section 4 of the Statute of Westminster instead of the ' complete disallowance of the British parliament to legislate at all for the Indian Governments' which had been incorporated in the Indian Independence Act. Moreover, unlike that Act, it did not contemplate the establishment of a Constituent Assembly ' an essential ingredient in the modern concept of independence, even Dominion Status within the British Empire '.[1] There was to be only a Constitution ' imposed upon us by an award from outside '[2] and accepted by a fraction of the people, by a State Council which was then eleven years old and not representative of the people '.[3] Most of the debate was in fact concerned with the obligations accepted under the Defence and External Affairs Agreements and it was contended that if they were repudiated, Ceylon might find its ' fully responsible status ', whatever in fact that novel phrase meant, withdrawn by another United Kingdom Act. Commonwealth membership was opposed because it was simply a cover for a shady alliance between British imperialism and Ceylon capitalism, because it involved, through the Defence Agreement in particular, the association of Ceylon with a ' power bloc ',

[1] *Ibid*, c. 610. The omission of the word Dominion was at least originally at the request of Ceylon Ministers.

[2] *Ibid*, c. 466.

[3] *Ibid*, c. 575. The Constitution was a modification of that provided by the Ceylon (Constitution) Order in Council 1946, accepted by the former State Council in 1945.

and because it impeded the proper development of a South Asian association. Dominion Status, in any event, was inappropriate to an Asian country: 'I should like to see, Mr. Speaker, one Sinhalese gentleman in our country who could give England the assurance that he proposes to treat England as his mother country.'[1] Why, another member asked, ' a Governor General for Ceylon? Why not a President of the Republic, elected by the people? Why should we be attracted and allured by this kind of thing? '

Much of this belonged to an era of uncertainty about the independence of the Dominions, an era which was already almost past, and of which only the faintest of echoes could be detected in the Tanganyika debates. Much of it was eloquent testimony to Marxist theory and reproduced many of the classic divisions among Marxists themselves. Much of it would be made wholly obsolete by the march of events, the revocation of the Defence Agreement, Ceylon's belated admission to the United Nations. But something would persist: the feeling that a Republic was the proper form for a country like Ceylon and the hostility to an ' imposed ' Constitution, the product of secret intergovernmental negotiation, a Constitution which must lack the legitimacy conferred by a Constituent Assembly.

When, in the General Election of 1956, some of the much splintered ' Leftist ' opposition parties in Ceylon formed an electoral alliance, the Mahajana Eksath Peramuna, their Manifesto declared that the Constitution needed amendments ' to bring it into line with the needs of a free country '. These included the establishment of a democratic republic, the abolition of Appointed Members, and a reconsideration of the position of the Senate. It called for the withdrawal of all ' foreign ' troops and abandonment of bases.[2] The Communist Party for its part thought that Ceylon had only a ' so-called ' Independence: it retained its loyalty to the Queen and was not ' completely free '. The new Government secured the agreement of the other members to Ceylon's remaining in the Commonwealth when it became a republic,[3] at the Commonwealth Prime Ministers' Meeting in London in July 1956. In April 1957 the Government proposed the appointment of a Joint Select Committee of both Houses

[1] *Ibid*, c. 505.
[2] See I. D. S. Weerawardana, *The Ceylon General Election 1956* (Colombo, 1960), pp. 66–7 and p. 78.
[3] *Commonwealth Survey* (Vol. 2) (1956), p. 531.

' to consider the revision of the Ceylon (Constitution and Independence) Order in Council 1946 and 1947 and other written law and to make recommendations with reference to the following among such other matters as the Committee may consider necessary: (1) the establishment of a Republic, (2) the guaranteeing of fundamental rights, (3) the position of the Senate and Appointed Members of the House of Representatives, (4) the Public Service Commission and the Judicial Service Commission.

It was interesting to see, in the debates on this proposal, how most of the purely legal arguments of earlier years had disappeared. The emphasis was decidedly on the need for a ' national restatement ' of the Constitution. Ceylon, it was claimed, was ' one of the few free countries in the world which are functioning under a Constitution which is embodied in an Order-in-Council and which is reminiscent of the colonial days '.[1] Why, asked another member, was Ceylon ' content to suffer from a Constitution that has been brought about by two Orders in Council '.[2] But it was not a mere matter of form . The Constitution was the result of ' certain-hush-hush negotiations between the late Mr. D. S. Senanayake and the British government ', ' hatched in the backrooms of colonial officers or cabinet rooms '.[3] It had not even been accepted by Parliament. It was, in short, an imposed constitution, imposed by the British government, and consequently inspired no loyalty or veneration. Why? ' Because,' said Senator Kanaganayagam, ' it is like something imported from elsewhere. We did not fashion it. It is not our child. We do not feel proud of it.'[4] This situation could be remedied only by a constituent assembly, so that an attempt could be made ' to frame our own Constitution in the light of our own requirements '.[5] The Prime Minister (Mr. Bandaranaike), however, thought that Ceylon was ' functioning under a free constitution, at least a Constitution that confers what is understood as ' Dominion Status ' on this country though it is defective in many respects' and therefore a Constituent Assembly, which was usually ' appointed when a country is thinking of a constitution for the first time, as it were, for a free

---

[1] Ceylon, *Parliamentary Debates*, Senate, Vol. 10, c. 1482.
[2] Ceylon, *Parliamentary Debates*, House of Representatives, Vol. 30, Part I, C. 1430.
[3] *Loc. cit.*, Vol. 27, cc. 2793–4.
[4] Ceylon, *Parliamentary Debates*, Senate, Vol. 10, cc. 1491–2.
[5] *Ibid*, c. 1482.

country ', was hardly desirable.[1] There was, perhaps, an echo of the old argument about secession in Dr. Perera's doubt whether ' by merely changing the constitution ' the source of power, which was at present Her Majesty, could be replaced by a new source of power ' The People '. It was, he thought, ' a very moot legal point, whether in point of fact we can transform ourselves into a republican form of government without going to the people and getting the source of power from the people.'[2] Another member (Mr. Suntharalingan) thought that ' any Bill which abrogates the right of the Queen might not have her assent '. He went on to point out the Lanka (Ceylon) had been for over 2,000 years the home of one or more kingdoms and asked, pertinently enough, ' whether it is part of the Sinhala culture whether it is part of the Buddhist culture to have presidents selected as heads of government.'[3]

Reappointed from time to time, the Joint Select Committee issued a questionnaire[4] and reported on certain matters connected with delimitation, but although at the General Elections of March and July 1960 both the major parties, the Sri Lanka Freedom Party, which had been the major component of the Mahajana Eskath Peramuna coalition, and the United National Party stated their intention to establish a republican form of government in Ceylon,[5] at the time of writing Ceylon remains one of the Queen's realms and a Governor General still lives in Queen's House.

South Africa

The Union of South Africa was created and its Constitution prescribed by the South Africa Act 1909, an Act of the British parliament. But that constitution was drawn up by a National Convention in which the four constituent colonies were represented on a basis agreed upon at an intercolonial conference. The draft Act, writes the historian of the Unification of South Africa, ' having been signed by every delegate in the Convention, was endorsed to an overwhelming extent by the white electorates

---

[1] Ceylon, *Parliamentary Debates*, House of Representatives, Vol. 27, cc. 2808–9.

[2] *Loc. cit.*, Vol. 30, 3.

[3] *Ibid*, c. 1191.

[4] See especially Ceylon *Parliamentary Series* (Third Parliament Second Session, 1957–8), No. 12.

[5] For the Election manifestos, see Ceylon Daily News, *Parliaments of Ceylon, 1960* (Colombo, n.d.).

or their parliamentary representatives, in each of the four colonies. The Transvaal and Orange River Colony parliaments, whose assemblies were elected by all the white male adults, approved it without dissentient vote. The two Houses of the Cape Parliament, whose members were returned by an 85 per cent white electorate approved it with only two dissentients. And the Natal electorate, which was 99 per cent white approved it by a three-quarters majority of the votes cast in a referendum.'[1] Such changes as were subsequently made by the British government before the Bill was submitted to parliament were agreed by South African delegates at a conference in London with the Secretary of State. ' The result was ', says Dr. Thompson, 'that the South Africa Bill which was introduced into the British parliament was in every detail accepted in advance by the South African delegation. Furthermore it was essentially the same as the draft South Africa Act which had been approved by the South African parliament '.[2] The Bill was not amended by the British parliament.

In spite of the high degree of consensus which such a record suggests, many of the Afrikaans-speaking people in South Africa were far from reconciled by what Smuts once called ' a miracle of trust and magnanimity '. To them South Africa was a conquered country on which the national symbols of conquest and of the conqueror had been imposed. It could only become free when this had been undone: ' The symbols so dear to Afrikanerdom had to be restored and recognised as the only symbols to be cherished by all true South Africans '.[3] To the Afrikaner nationalist in South Africa, the political history of the Union can be regarded simply as the gradual step by step realisation of this process of ' national restatement '. In the debates on the Referendum Bill, for example, the Minister of Finance (Dr. Donges) claimed that national unity was impossible ' so long as we have a monarchy '. They had ' gone step by step in that direction ' and ' had made great progress ': ' to-day we have our own flag and our own national anthem and in 1949 we brought about this tremendous change; we obtained our own citizenship but the final and greatest step still remains to be taken. This is not simply a change in nomenclature. It is a step that will convert a monarchy into a

[1] L. M. Thompson, *The Unification of South Africa* (Oxford, 1960), p. 369.
[2] *Ibid*, p. 414.
[3] P. N. S. Mansergh, *South Africa*, 1906–1961: *The Price of Magnanimity* (London, 1962), p. 55.

republic and that will make every son and daughter of South Africa a republican '.[1] Similarly, the Minister of Defence (Mr. J. J. Fouché), replying to opposition criticism that the electorate would not know what kind of a republic they were voting for, asserted that besides being one ' in which the basic principles of apartheid will be maintained ' it would also be one in which there would be only a single citizenship, in which only one flag would fly, and one which would have ' its own legal system, something this Government ensured when it abolished the right of appeal to the Privy Council '.[2] Professor Fourie, an independent Afrikaans-speaking member, after a forthright recognition that the major problems of South Africa would not be affected by whether or not a republican form of government was adopted, nevertheless explained that the Afrikaner regarded the Republic as ' the climax to a national struggle which comes from the very soul of the people '. He regretted that English-speaking South Africans did not realise that ' that act of restitution on the part of Campbell-Bannerman should be rounded off in South Africa so that the deep wound which was inflicted on the soul of the Afrikaner would heal and heal completely '.[3]

But although speaker after speaker on the Government side of the House returned to these themes[4] some speakers, all of them Afrikaans-speaking and not all of them from the opposition, emphasised the reality of South Africa's independence. Mr. D. J. du P. Basson set this fact in the historical context of that ' national restatement ' of the Constitution to which Nationalist spokesmen, as has been shown, constantly returned. Not so long ago, he remarked, a whole series of political matters had been ' tied up with the case for the republic: the divisibility of the Crown; membership of the Commonwealth and the right to secede; the right to remain neutral; the right to appeal to the Privy Council; a South African as Governor General; a single South African citizenship; and a national flag and anthem—emotional issues which for years divided political opinion in the country. To-day not one of these questions trouble our political scene any longer. Our independence is complete and the symbols which

[1] House of Assembly *Debates*, Vol. 105, 22 April, 1960, c. 5908.
[2] *Ibid*, 25 April, 1960, c. 5946.
[3] *Ibid*, c. 6039.
[4] *E.g.* Mr. Van Den Heever (*ibid*, c. 5962), Mr. Luttig (c. 5974), Mr. Leroux (Vol. 106, c. 799).

express it are universally accepted. Neither a monarchy nor a republic can detract from, or add one iota to, the freedom we possess internally and externally.'[1] Some, who claimed fully to accept this, felt, all the same, that ' the constitutional position of the South African queen, who is at the same time also the British queen ' was a ' confusing and misleading position ' which ' to some extent ' limited their freedom and could only be ended by a republic.[2]

The difficulties of this ' duality of the monarchy ' were discussed by several speakers, sometimes in language remarkably reminiscent of the debates in Tanganyika and Ceylon, to say nothing of those in Ghana, whose adoption of republican status was noted with approval by the member for Namaqualand, enlarging its lesson to parts of Africa nearer home: there could, said Mr. Scholtz, ' be no love and goodwill between a Black man living in South Africa, thousands of miles away from the monarch and the monarch with whom he has absolutely nothing in common and whose history, traditions, language and everything else are strange to him '.[3] Loyalty moreover was inevitably divided in such circumstances: ' in spirit half the population[4] of this country have a divided heart . . . the one heart is attached to this country and the other is attached to the monarchy and Crown 6,000 miles away.'

The monarchy was ' associated with humiliation and injustice ' and had been forced upon the people of South Africa. ' The Union,' said Mr. F. S. Steyn, ' has never yet had a choice. . . . In 1909, at the National Convention, which was held shortly after the Anglo-Boer war, at a time when the Colonial Laws Validity Act was still valid, when Britain was still, in fact, an imperial power, there was at no stage any reasonable or serious doubt as to whether the Union of South Africa would be a monarchy.'[5] In spite of the evidence of the acceptance of the South Africa Act by the white electorate or their representatives, summarised earlier, it can hardly be denied that the fundamental assumption in 1909 was that what was being offered to South Africa was a position within

---

[1] *Ibid*, 25 April, 1960, cc. 5998–9.
[2] *Ibid*, 26 April, 1960, c. 6018.
[3] *Ibid*, c. 6051.
[4] *Ibid*, c. 6035 (It seems that for Mr. M. J. Van den Borg, the member for Krugersdorp, only white men are people.)
[5] *Ibid*, 2 May, 1960, cc. 6437–8.

the British Empire analogous to that of Canada, Australia and New Zealand. On another aspect of what may be regarded as virtually the final stage in the effective ' transfer of power ' in South Africa, the Nationalist government reversed the usual nationalist contention that the ' independence ' terms may be regarded as ' imposed ' to the extent that they were accepted by something less than ' the people '—a government not a legislature, or an ' unrepresentative ' legislature because elected on a franchise short of universal suffrage, or finally a legislature not a constituent assembly or referendum. In South Africa they in effect contended[1] the wishes of the true ' people ', the whites, had been thwarted ' in the interests of imperial objectives ' by the non-white vote. Hence in so vital a matter as the republic, however much coloured voters might have a voice in the final decision (since they were still represented in the House of Assembly) the decision of principle must be taken in a referendum of white voters only, otherwise it would be tainted with illegitimacy. (That the coloured electorate might be expected to vote against the republic was not, of course, admitted).

Unlike many peoples within the Commonwealth, Afrikaners could plausibly maintain that their political tradition was one of representative democracy (so long as non-white people are considered not to be political animals). But their Presidents were far from the powerless cyphers Governors General had become and their constitutions (at least in the Free State) were entrenched and subject to the ' testing ' right. The Nationalist government did not propose to ' restore ' an executive Presidency still less an entrenched constitution and most of its followers were in fact wedded to the utmost extreme of the doctrine of unfettered parliamentary sovereignty. They were able, however, to avoid relying entirely on the argument that the British form of parliamentary government (so long as it was republican) best met the contemporary needs of South Africa by claiming that the acceptance of some features of the British political system represented concessions to the national tradition of English-speaking South Africans. They were thus able to produce a *rationale* for the maintenance, in the new ' nationally restated ' political system, of features which could not plausibly be claimed

---

[1] See the debates *passim*, and especially Dr. Verwoerd's speech on 11 March, 1960 (loc. cit. Vol 104, cc. 3208–9).

to have been part of Afrikaner political tradition. Such a *rationale* will not readily find a counterpart in the newer states of the Commonwealth who may wish to claim some form of representative government (which as a matter of historical fact was an innovation received from outside) as not incompatible with ' national ' tradition.

That the adoption of a republican form of government in South Africa, even if the Republic had remained within the Commonwealth, was regarded by many Afrikaner nationalists as the final stage in a long process of what we have called ' national restatement ' of the political system is evident. That the reenactment of the South African constitution in a republican form by means of an ordinary Act of the Union legislature which received the Governor General's assent in the usual way was also considered satisfactorily to effect what we have called a ' national definition ' of the legal system was made equally evident by the Prime Minister, Dr. Verwoerd, in moving the Second Reading of the Constitution Bill; at the same time he made it clear that he at least felt no need for autochthony (in Dr. Wheare's sense). The Prime Minister said:

' With all due respect for what we have viz the Constitution we have had for fifty years and recognising the fact that we ourselves could amend the constitution and have often done so, the basis of it, the South Africa Act, was given to us by the Parliament of another country. This time we are giving our own Constitution to our own fatherland. In that sense it will have a deeper meaning for us because its existence is due to our own free will and our own deliberations alone. In saying that I am not belittling the fact that the Act containing the Constitution which was given to us in 1910 by the British Parliament was the fruit of a National Convention which sat here in South Africa. I am not belittling that in the least. Nevertheless, whilst I appreciate what we had and how it came about that cannot derogate from my gratitude and joy because of the fact that our Union Parliament is now itself able to give a Constitution to the Republic of South Africa.

' In addition, the Republican Constitution, which will be adopted by our own Parliament, . . . is based . . . in fact on the traditions of both elements of our population. . . It is now our joint creation and it is born out of our common history.'

T

That so classic a statement of the case for a ' national form ' of political system expressed in a nationally restated and defined constitution should be made by the leader of a tiny minority of the total population of South Africa is a fitting example of the irony seldom absent from the tragic history of that country.

III

Autochthony and the Transfer of Power

How should a transfer of power be judged? This of course depends on the point of view from which an assessment is being attempted. From that of the student of politics, it is submitted, the new state should start its independent existence with a political system that is both efficient and stable: efficient in terms of satisfying a sufficient majority of those without whose participation or acquiescence its survival may be seriously threatened and stable in the sense of being accepted as legitimate by a sufficient majority of those whose loyalty is essential to its operation. The ' efficient parts ' of the constitution (to return to Bagehot) must provide a system of government appropriate to the needs and circumstances of the country; the ' dignified parts ' must so far ' excite and preserve the reverence of the population ' that they serve to promote and enhance a feeling of national identity and to associate with that feeling the institutions of government. But, it may be objected, are not the maintenance of friendly relations with the former colonial power and, in the British case, accession to membership of the Commonwealth also important objects of the transfer of power? Important as in practice they have been, these objects are surely subordinate to the larger aim of political stability: that this is so (at least in the last resort) may be seen in the admission that dependencies have a right to independence outside the Commonwealth (as in the case of Burma) or to join with neighbouring foreign states (as in the case of Somaliland or the South Cameroons), for consent is rightly held to be a necessary condition of political stability. And if political efficiency is not enough, neither is a ' national form ' of constitution. (The whole history of ' indirect rule ', in its widest sense, is a commentary on this theme.)

Can any conclusions legitimately be drawn from cases so widely separated in time and place as those of South Africa,

Ceylon and Tanganyika, three very different countries brought together only by their common experience of British rule, in each of which the ' transfer of power ' took place in historical contexts very different from one another?

' They gave us back,' said Smuts, ' in everything but name— our country ' and it is obvious that in the context of 1906–1910 it would have been unthinkable to restore the ' name ' as well.[1] Colonial self-government represented the limit of the possible in 1906; the South Africa Act's major defect had its origin in Article 8 of the Treaty of Vereeniging rather than in the manner in which the Union was created; under the South Africa Act, for forty years all governments were coalitions of English-speaking and Afrikaans-speaking and it took half a century before the Cape coloured franchise was finally removed. To recognise all this does not preclude one from drawing any conclusions relevant to *later* transfers of power. Similarly, when Ceylon became independent, membership of the Commonwealth still required the maintenance of allegiance to the Crown and ' Dominion Status ' had by no means been entirely freed from the ambiguities which had attended its birth. If a procedure much more in accordance with the notion of popular sovereignty was contemporaneously adopted for the transfer of power in Burma, Ceylon's independence was nonetheless brought about by peaceful negotiation, not merely without bloodshed but without violence,[2] and notwithstanding ' leftist ' Ceylonese criticism, the constitution that then came into force has survived, to all intents and purposes unchanged, for fifteen years. When considering the criticism of its ' colonial ' form and origins, it is proper to point the contrast with Indochina or Indonesia no less than with Burma or the Philippines. Once again, however, all this does not mean that none of the criticisms have any relevance to the arrangements by which power is being transferred, in very different circumstances, to-day.

By contrast, the transfer of power in Tanganyika took place more than a decade after the transformation of the Common-wealth which began in 1949 as a result of the agreement that

[1] As it was, the grant of responsible self-government to the Transvaal and Orange River Colonies in 1906 and 1907 respectively (which was of course the decisive move) was effected by Letters Patent to avoid, in Professor Mansergh's words, ' certain repudiation by the Lords ' (*op. cit.*, p. 18).

[2] Though some members of the Marxist parties were detained or imprisoned owing to their opposition to Ceylon's participation in the war.

India should remain a member after she became a republic. An aspect of that transformation somewhat less remarked at the time was the fact that Indian membership entailed no provision in the Constitution adopted in 1949 but rested solely on a Resolution of the Constituent Assembly, ' an agreement by free will to be terminated by free will '.[1] However much the other members might, for greater comfort, assert that the basis of their own membership was not thereby changed, it is not mere hindsight which sees that the Indian precedents were bound to be followed by others, sooner or later. And in considering the arrangements made in Tanganyika, it is assuredly relevant that they had indeed been followed, in different ways, by Pakistan, Ghana, and South Africa, while Ceylon had long since announced her intention of doing so. Moreover, there was another precedent. However unique the case of Cyprus may be, it may be wondered whether it may not remain so mainly because there are few British dependencies left to notice that it offered an example of a colony becoming, on the transfer of power, ' an independent sovereign Republic ' over which ' Her Majesty shall have no sovereignty or jurisdiction ' and, after an interval of some months and after debate in its new House of Representatives seeking membership of the Commonwealth for a trial period of five years.[2]

In short, to allow that subsequent criticism of the South Africa Act or the independence arrangements in Ceylon may deserve weight in relation to our contemporary transfers of power does not necessarily involve accepting them as wholly valid, still less decisive, criticisms of what was done in 1909 or 1947. Equally what can properly be argued in defence of the forms then adopted has no necessary application in the wholly different circumstances of 1962. What, then, are we to conclude from the debates in South Africa, Ceylon and Tanganyika?

The strength of the British method has always been in its readiness to admit the peculiarities of each territory and to try to provide appropriately for them. Although, as the pace of independence has quickened, a certain standardisation of the procedure in the later stages of the transfer of power has been perceptible, it is quite unlikely that any single formula would be adopted even in the relatively small number of instances where the

---

[1] Nehru's speech of 16 May, 1949, Mansergh, *Documents*, ii, pp. 847–857.
[2] *Commonwealth Survey* 7 (1961), p. 257.

final transfer of power has not yet occurred. Nor would it be desirable to attempt to prescribe such a formula: here we are emphatically in the world of *ceteris paribus*. (The ' imposition ' of Dominion status, for example, made the independence of India and Pakistan possible.) But, granting this, it is surely evident that the arrangements for the transfer of power (and especially the independence constitution) should not merely be acceptable to the political leaders of the new state but should be *seen to be* acceptable not only to them but also to the representatives of the people (and here the franchise is important) and, indeed, preferably to the people themselves. This principle may be variously applied: it may be that the best course is for an existing colonial government to be made ' independent ' by the minimum constitutional changes and left to work out for itself the constitutional arrangements in the new state (which might be described as the ' India model '); alternatively, there might be a short agreed interim period during which the independence constitution might be prepared by a constituent assembly; or by the local government or legislature followed by submission to the people in a referendum, a procedure which is perhaps more practicable than the hazards of a constituent assembly. This might be described as the ' Burma model '. The dangers of either of these methods are illustrated by the example of Pakistan; its possibilities by that of Burma. At the least, if a new constitution is agreed by negotiation between local political leaders and the British government, it should be submitted to the local legislature for approval.

Secondly, it is hard to see what possible advantage there can be in pressing upon the new state the residual forms of colonialism which are inescapable from the modified ' Dominion model ' in use today. If the leaders of new states insist on their becoming one of the Queen's realms, must they be compelled to have a ' Governor General ', appeal to the Privy Council, a Constitution promulgated in an Order in Council? Surely it would be possible to find a suitable ' national restatement ' of the title for the Queen's representative, to reconstitute the Judicial Committee as something more than a committee to advise the Crown in the exercise of prerogative powers[1] and to arrange for a constitution, even one

[1] In view of the extent to which the appeal has already been abolished, one would hardly have thought this worth while but the recent belated decision to reinforce the Committee by the appointment of some Commonwealth judges suggests that in some quarters at any rate ' its importance as a Commonwealth link ' is rated more highly. (*Commonwealth Survey* 8 (1962), p. 781.)

negotiated in the kind of intergovernmental conference now usual, to be 'adopted' by the legislature, or even by 'the people' in a referendum, so that it could at least be 'brought into effect' on the appointed day without being enshrined in an Order in Council.

Thirdly, it seems questionable whether the elaborate provisions for the appointment of judges and civil servants by commissions rendered constitutionally independent of the executive which has been a feature of recent Commonwealth 'independence' constitutions are worth much. Such provision does not correspond particularly closely to the legal (or indeed the practical) position in Britain itself and as both the Ceylon and Tanganyika examples show, is resented as implying a remnant of colonialist distrust. Both Ghana and Tanganyika have lost no time in vesting legal responsibility for such appointments in the executive. The statutory independence of these commissions was no doubt intended to promote confidence in the new régimes but the practical effect may actually be to cause excessive alarm when they are rapidly reduced to an advisory rôle.

Finally, though we may agree with Dr. Wheare that 'it must be expected ... that Members of the Commonwealth will as a rule take steps quite soon after they achieve independence through a constitution made in Britian'[1] to bring about what we have called a 'national restatement' of that constitution, it may be doubted whether they will attach as much importance to 'autochthony' in its restricted sense as he suggested. This seems the more likely since the examples of Ghana, Tanganyika and South Africa have, in different ways shown how a country in which (to use Dr. Perera's words in the Ceylon debates) 'the source of power' is the Crown can adopt a new constitution in which the Crown is replaced by a new source of power 'the people'. The 1960 Constitution of Ghana was in fact enacted by a Constituent Assembly empowered thereto by an Act of the Ghana parliament which received the Governor General's assent; and the Constitution Act of South Africa passed in 1961 by which a republican form of government was adopted in that country (and the Status of the Union Act and all except the two entrenched clauses of the South Africa Act repealed) was an ordinary Act of the South African parliament which also received the Royal Assent in the

[1] Wheare, *op. cit.*, p. 113.

usual way through the Governor General. Though the South Africans were at pains to provide a fitting preamble for a republican constitution they apparently saw no difficulty in doing this in an Act which thereafter continues with the usual enacting formula ' Be it enacted by the Queen's most excellent Majesty ' etc., or indeed in continuing with a provision which substitutes the President for the Governor General in existing legislation, something which surely would have been more appropriately tucked away in traditional provisions. Had they thought it important that their Constitution should be, as it were, ' self-contained ', they could quite simply have set it out in a separate schedule to the Act, excluding from that schedule all transitional provisions, and in due course this would no doubt have come to be used as ' The Constitution '. With examples such as these before them, member states are perhaps unlikely to attach so much importance to effecting a break in ' legal continuity ', except indeed where this may provide a way of circumventing such limitations of their amending powers as may have been imposed in the ' independence ' constitutions. Both in Ceylon and Tanganyika a two-thirds majority is necessary for all constitutional amendments. The requirement has often been referred to in the Ceylonese debates but there has never been any suggestion that it need not be complied with; while Tanganyika, as in other African countries in their present stage of political development, such a requirement is unlikely to present any practical political difficulties.[1] It may not always be so and in other parts of the Commonwealth it may not be so now: in such cases perhaps the attraction of ' autochthony ' may be as much in providing a method of amendment which can at least be justified in terms of a political myth as in giving substance to the myth itself.

[1] The requirement has been retained in the new Constitution (C.A. Act No. 1. Tanganyika *Gazette* vol. XLIII No. 65).

BIBLIOGRAPHY OF WORKS BY MARGERY PERHAM,
1925—63

[1925] *Major Dane's Garden*, London, pp. 318.

1927 *Josie Vine*, London, pp. 304.

1930 'White Rule in Samoa,' *The Times*, 10 and 11 April.
'Tribal Rule in Africa. Tanganyika,' *The Times*, 26 and 27 December.

1931 'The System of Native Administration in Tanganyika,' *Africa*, July, pp. 302–12.
'The Future of East Africa,' *The Times*, 13, 14 and 15 August.

1932 'Nigeria To-day,' *The Times*, 28, 29 and 30 December.

1933 'France in the Cameroons,' *The Times*, 17 and 18 May.
'The New Africa. Protectorates in Transition,' *The Times*, 28 September.
'The Census of Nigeria 1931,' *Africa*, October, pp. 415–30.

1934 'Teaching the Native African to Govern himself,' *The Listener*, 28 February.
'Some Problems of Indirect Rule,' *J. Royal Society of Arts*, 18 May, pp. 689–701.
'A Re-statement of Indirect Rule,' *Africa*, July, pp. 321–34.
'A British Trust. The South African Protectorates,' *The Times*, 5 and 6 July.

1935 With Lionel Curtis, *The Protectorates of South Africa*, London, pp. 119.

1936 Editor, *Ten Africans*, London, pp. 356.

1937 *Native Administration in Nigeria*, London, pp. 404. Reprinted 1962. British Native Administration in Africa: I. Policy. II. Application.
Summaries of Lectures, pp. 99–103, *Oxford University Summer School on Colonial Administration*, Oxford.
'Kenya Revisited. European and African,' *The Times*, 17 February.
'Tanganyika Now,' *The Times*, 5 August.

1938 British Native Administration: I. Problems. II. Prospects. Lectures pp. 48–51; 102–6, *Oxford University Summer School on Colonial Administration*, Oxford.

'Tribal Advance in Africa. The Model Baganda,' *The Times*, 25 August.

1939 'The Sudan,' *The Times*, 6 and 7 June.

1940 'Educating the Colonies,' *The Times*, 2 March.
'The Somaliland Campaign,' *The Times*, 10 August.
'Free France in Africa,' *The Times*, 14 September.

1941 *Africans and British Rule*, London, pp. 98.
'The Ethiopian Background,' *The Times*, 26 and 27 November.

1942 *The Colonies*, Reprinted from *The Times*, London, pp. 24.
'Oxford and the Colonial Empire,' *Oxford*, Summer, pp. 51–60.
'The Colonial Empire,' *The Times*, 13 and 14 March.
'America and the Empire,' *The Times*, 20 and 21 November.

1943 'From Power to Service,' *The Listener*, 22 April.

1944 With Huxley, E., *Race and Politics in Kenya*. A Correspondence between Elspeth Huxley and Margery Perham, London, pp. 247, rev. ed. 1956, pp. 302.
'African Facts and American Criticisms,' *Foreign Affairs*, April, pp. 444–57.

1945 'Lord Lugard: a general appreciation,' *Africa*, July, pp. 114–22.
'Education for Self-government,' *Foreign Affairs*, October, pp. 130–42.

1946 *Colonial Administration*, Reading List, Oxford, duplicated.
Edited with Introduction, Wight, M., *The Development of the Legislative Council* 1660–1945, London, Studies in Colonial Legislatures I.
Edited with Preface, Forde, D. and Scott, R., *The Native Economies of Nigeria*, London. The Economics of a Tropical Dependency I.
Edited, Bower, P. A., *Colonial Economics*, Select Reading List, duplicated.
With Simmons, J., *African Discovery*. An Anthology of Exploration, London, pp. 280. 2nd ed. 1957. Penguin Edition, abridged, 1948.

1947 Edited, Comhaire, J:, *Urban Conditions in Africa*, Select Reading List, duplicated, rev. ed. 1952.
Edited with Preface, Wight, M., *The Gold Coast Legislative Council*, London. Studies in Colonial Legislatures II.

Edited, Mayer, P., *Reading List on Rural Conditions and Betterment in the British Colonies.*

Foreword to: Awolowo, O., *Path to Nigerian Freedom.*

1948 *The Government of Ethiopia*, London, pp. 481.

Edited with Preface, Davidson, J. W., *The Northern Rhodesian Legislative Council*, London. Studies in Colonial Legislatures III.

Edited with Introduction, Bower, P. A., Brown, A. J., Leubuscher, C., Mars, J., Pim, Sir Alan, *Mining, Commerce and Finance in Nigeria*, London. The Economics of a Tropical Dependency II.

Edited, Meek, C. K., *Colonial Law*, a Bibliography.

'Destiny of the Sudan,' *The Times*, 3 May.

1949 'Creating a New Nation. Parliamentary Government in the Sudan ', *The Times*, 20 June.

'The Sudan Emerges to Nationhood,' *Foreign Affairs*, July, pp. 665–77.

'The Colonial Dilemma,' *The Listener*, 14 July.

1950 *Colonial Government.* Annotated Reading List on British Colonial Government with some General and Comparative Material upon Foreign Empires, etc., London, pp. 80.

Edited with Introduction, Wheare, J., *The Nigerian Legislative Council*, London. Studies in Colonial Legislatures IV.

'Lord Lugard: a Preliminary Evaluation,' *Africa*, July, pp. 228–39.

1951 Edited with Preface, Namasivayam, S., *The Legislatures of Ceylon*, London. Studies in Colonial Legislatures V.

Edited with Preface, Stahl, K., *The Metropolitan Organization of British Colonial Trade.* Four Regional Studies. Colonial and Comparative Studies.

'The British Problem in Africa,' *Foreign Affairs*, July, pp. 637–50.

1952 Edited with Preface, Craig, H., *The Legislative Council of Trinidad and Tobago*, London. Studies in Colonial Legislatures VI.

Edited with Preface, Abbas, M., *The Sudan Question.* The Dispute over the Anglo-Egyptian Condominium 1884–1951, London. Colonial and Comparative Studies.

Foreword to, *East African Future*. A Report to the Fabian Colonial Bureau.

'A Changing Continent. Conflicts and Ambitions in Africa,' *The Times*, 28 October.

1953 Edited with Introduction, Henderson, K. D., *The Making of the Modern Sudan*. The Life and Letters of Sir Douglas Newbold, London. Colonial and Comparative Studies.

' Struggle against Mau Mau,' *The Times*, 22 and 23 April.

1954 Edited with Preface, Proudfoot, M., *Britain and the United States in the Caribbean*. A comparative Study in Methods of Development, London. Colonial and Comparative Studies.

' Delicate Transfer of Rule in the Sudan,' *The Times*, 16 June.

' Britain's Response to the End of Colonialism,' *The Listener*, 30 December.

1955 ' Nigeria Prepares for Independence,' *The Times*, 17 and 19 March.

'African Pro-Consul,' *The Listener*, 2 June.

' The Royal Commission on East Africa,' *The Listener*, 18 September.

1956 *Lugard: The Years of Adventure* 1858–1898. The First Part of the Life of Frederick Dealtry Lugard, later Lord Lugard of Abinger, London, pp. 750.

Foreword to, Mboya, T., *The Kenya Question*. An African Answer.

1957 ' Kenya after Mau Mau,' *The Times*, 18 March.

' Out of the Fellowship,' *Africa South*, July-Sept., pp. 35–9.

1959 With Bull, M., Editors, *The Diaries of Lord Lugard*, Vols. 1–3 East Africa 1889–1892, London, pp. 432; 481; 454.

Edited with Preface, Gaitskell, A., *Gezira*, A Story of Development in the Sudan, London. Colonial and Comparative Studies.

' White Minorities in Africa,' *Foreign Affairs*, July, pp. 637–48.

1960 *Lugard: The Years of Authority* 1898–1945. The Second Part of the Life of Frederick Dealtry Lugard, later Lord Lugard of Abinger, London, pp. 748.

' The Psychology of African Nationalism,' *Optima*, March, pp. 27–36.

' Kenya: the Decisive Years,' *The Listener*, 12 May.

' Federation in Africa on the Defensive,' *The Listener*, 9 June.

'A Prospect of Nigeria,' *The Listener*, 20 October.

1961   *The Colonial Reckoning* (An Expanded Version of the Reith Lectures), London, pp. 160.

' The Colonial Reckoning, the Reith Lectures,' *The Listener*, 16 November–21 December.

1962   ' Political Aspects of Tensions in Development,' *Restless Nations: A Study of World Tensions and Development*, London, pp. 13–34.

1963   With Bull, M., Editors, *The Diaries of Lord Lugard*, Vol. 4.

Foreword to: Kariuki, J. M., *Mau Mau Prisoner*, the Account by a Kenya African of his Experience in Detention Camps, 1953–1960.

Introduction to: Heussler, R., *Yesterday's Rulers*, the making of the British colonial service.

' What place now for the Kenya settlers? ' *The Times*, 20 February.

(There were many letters published in *The Times* between 1933 and the present day of which some sixty concern Africa. Others were on rural matters, animal welfare, and capital punishment.)

CONTRIBUTORS

F. Madden	Fellow of Nuffield College, Reader in Commonwealth Government and Director, Institute of Commonwealth Studies, Oxford.
D. Fieldhouse	Beit Lecturer in the History of the British Commonwealth, Oxford. Sometime Student of Nuffield College.
Mary Bull	Henry Charles Chapman Junior Research Fellow, Institute of Commonwealth Studies, London, formerly of the research staff, Nuffield College.
Elizabeth Chilver	Senior Research Fellow, Institute of Commonwealth Studies, London. Sometime Director, Institute of Commonwealth Studies, Oxford.
G. Bennett	Senior Lecturer in Commonwealth History, Oxford.
M. McWilliam	Sometime Student of Nuffield College.
B. Keith Lucas	Fellow of Nuffield College and Senior Lecturer in Local Government, Oxford.
Mary Holdsworth	Principal of St. Mary's College, Durham. Sometime Scholar of St. Hugh's College and Senior Research Officer, Institute of Commonwealth Studies, Oxford.
J. Plamenatz,	Fellow of Nuffield College and Lecturer in Social and Political Theory, Oxford.
K. Robinson	Director, Institute of Commonwealth Studies and Professor of Commonwealth Affairs, London. Sometime Fellow of Nuffield College, Oxford.